CENSUS OF INDIA 1911

Owing to the antiquity and rarity of this book, certain pages are regrettably absent, and readability is compromised due to the blurring of the original text. If you possess any insights regarding the availability of these missing sections, kindly inform us. Your assistance is crucial in ensuring the completion of this significant work for the benefit of future generations.

CENSUS OF INDIA, 1911

VOLUME - XV

UNITED PROVINCES OF AGRA AND OUDH

PART III - PROVINCIAL TABLES AND APPENDICES

E. A. H. BLUNT

GYAN

Published by

Gyan Publishing House
5, Ansari Road
Daryaganj, New Delhi-110002
Phone: 011-47034999, 9811692060
E-mail: books@gyanbooks.com

Distribution Network
gyanbooks.com
India, USA, Canada, UK, Australia

ISBN: 978-81-212-7127-1 (Set) 23 Vols. In 41 Bindings

ISBN: 978-81-212-7445-6 (PB) Vol. XV, Pt. III

First Published, 1915

2nd Impression 2024

Printed at: Gyan Press, Delhi.

CENSUS OF INDIA 1911

CENSUS OF INDIA, 1911.

VOLUME XV

UNITED PROVINCES

OF

AGRA AND OUDH.

PART III.

PROVINCIAL TABLES AND APPENDICES.

(N.B.—Provincial Tables I and II have been printed with the Imperial Tables in Volume XV, Part II.)

BY

E. A. H. BLUNT, I.C.S.,

SUPERINTENDENT, CENSUS OPERATIONS.

ALLAHABAD:

PRINTED BY F. LUKER, SUPERINTENDENT, GOVERNMENT PRESS.

1915.

PROVINCIAL TABLE III.

Population of Police Circles by religion.

NOTE.—In the hill portions of the Kumaun division each patti has been treated as a police circle in this table.

There are certain enclaves in various districts (Allahabad, Partabgarh, Sultanpur, &c.,) which belong for criminal purposes to a thana in one district, but for revenue and general purposes to a neighbouring district. This explains the entry of certain thanas which are situated in one district under another. These cases are all explained in footnotes.

Population of the Police Circles Distributed by Religion.

Name of district.	Serial number of thana.	Name of thana.	Population.			Hindus.			Muhammadans.			Others.		
			Total.	Males.	Females.	Total	Males.	Females.	Total	Males.	Females.	Total.	Males.	Females.
1	2	3	4	5	6	7	8	9	10	11	12	13	14	15
		British Territory	47,182,044	24,641,831	22,540,213	40,122,238	20,949,641	19,172,597	6,658,375	3,466,287	3,192,088	401,433	225,905	175,528
		Agra Province	34,624,040	18,157,131	16,466,909	29,289,754	15,349,789	13,939,965	4,957,686	2,596,958	2,360,728	376,600	210,384	166,216
		Meerut Division	5,808,630	3,150,957	2,657,673	4,369,481	2,371,188	1,998,293	1,285,330	693,995	591,335	153,819	85,774	68,045
		Dehra Dun	205,075	120,908	84,167	169,614	99,241	70,373	27,794	17,108	10,686	7,667	4,559	3,108
Dehra Dun.	1	Chakrata	54,812	30,518	24,294	53,474	29,573	23,901	899	669	230	439	276	163
	2	Dehra	85,886	51,078	34,808	65,830	38,929	26,901	15,957	9,542	6,415	4,099	2,607	1,492
	3	Mussooree	11,820	8,159	3,661	7,782	5,585	2,197	1,916	1,575	341	1,822	999	823
	4	Rajpur	11,912	7,082	4,830	10,358	6,170	4,188	1,337	808	529	217	104	113
	5	Rani Pokhri	13,583	9,771	3,812	13,845	8,598	5,247	1,333	961	372	405	212	193
	6	Sahaspur	25,362	14,300	11,062	18,323	10,386	7,937	6,357	3,558	2,799	685	361	324
		Saharanpur	986,359	541,091	445,268	638,354	350,151	288,203	329,094	179,846	149,248	18,911	11,094	7,817
Saharanpur.	1	Behat	80,748	42,890	37,858	46,014	24,417	21,597	34,063	18,111	15,952	671	362	309
	2	Bhagwanpur	29,854	16,077	13,777	17,007	9,169	7,838	12,376	6,625	5,751	471	283	188
	3	Badgaon	57,651	32,142	25,509	47,990	26,797	21,193	8,208	4,539	3,669	1,453	806	647
	4	Chilkana	32,229	17,295	14,934	16,426	8,748	7,678	15,704	8,487	7,217	99	60	39
	5	Dauseni	21,667	11,874	9,793	14,377	7,937	6,440	6,507	3,486	3,021	783	451	332
	6	Deoband	81,677	45,003	36,674	54,889	30,336	24,553	25,285	13,867	11,418	1,403	800	603
	7	Fatehpur	44,119	23,351	20,768	33,823	15,153	18,670	15,094	8,084	7,010	202	114	88
	8	Gangoh	53,358	29,496	23,862	35,256	19,116	16,140	18,614	10,070	8,544	488	310	178
	9	Jwalapur	55,708	29,864	25,844	37,182	19,916	17,266	17,945	9,587	8,358	581	361	220
	10	Muzaffarabad	39,563	20,908	18,655	26,410	13,986	12,424	13,032	6,864	6,168	121	58	63
	11	Manglaur	63,658	34,627	29,031	42,466	23,161	19,305	19,441	10,451	8,990	1,751	1,015	736
	12	Mohand	13,576	7,388	6,188	10,718	5,790	4,928	2,111	1,197	914	747	401	346
	13	Nakur	52,508	28,933	23,575	39,022	21,785	17,237	12,787	6,789	5,998	699	359	340
	14	Nagal	53,864	29,413	24,451	39,500	21,602	17,898	13,358	7,226	6,132	1,006	585	421
	15	Rurki	73,543	43,066	30,477	37,971	21,289	16,682	33,017	20,010	13,007	2,555	1,767	788
	16	Rampur	54,079	29,536	24,543	41,739	22,740	18,999	11,069	6,097	4,972	1,271	699	572
	17	Saharanpur	109,787	60,525	49,262	52,631	29,352	23,279	53,540	29,048	24,492	3,616	2,125	1,491
	18	Sarsawa	31,286	17,077	14,209	20,353	11,148	9,205	10,254	5,567	4,687	679	362	317
	19	Sultanpur	19,420	10,549	8,871	14,958	8,173	6,785	4,307	2,291	2,016	155	85	70
	20	Mayapur	12,313	7,926	4,387	11,259	7,161	4,098	901	677	224	153	88	65
		Muzaffarnagar	808,360	444,862	363,498	558,793	308,607	250,186	231,873	126,338	105,535	17,694	9,917	7,777
Muzaffarnagar.	1	Bhopa	60,593	33,271	27,322	42,416	23,329	19,087	17,575	9,595	7,980	602	347	255
	2	Budhana	94,377	52,264	42,113	65,716	36,551	29,165	26,425	14,475	11,950	2,236	1,238	998
	3	Bidauli	22,460	12,269	10,191	15,032	8,244	6,788	7,312	3,962	3,350	116	63	53
	4	Jansath	76,042	40,893	35,149	50,421	27,226	23,195	25,068	13,346	11,722	553	321	232
	5	Kairana	56,979	31,440	25,539	31,491	17,674	13,817	24,210	13,091	11,119	1,278	675	603
	6	Kandhla	73,064	40,147	32,917	53,300	29,491	23,809	17,030	9,188	7,842	2,734	1,468	1,266
	7	Khatauli	72,754	39,880	32,874	51,745	28,334	23,411	18,447	10,125	8,322	2,562	1,421	1,141
	8	Muzaffarnagar	77,001	43,163	33,838	47,359	26,558	20,801	27,687	15,461	12,226	1,955	1,144	811

Population of the Police Circles Distributed by Religion.

Name of district.	Serial number of thana.	Name of thana.	Population.			Hindus.			Muhammadans.			Others.		
			Total.	Males.	Females.	Total.	Males	Females.	Total.	Males.	Females.	Total.	Males.	Females.
1	2	3	4	5	6	7	8	9	10	11	12	13	14	15
Muzaffar-nagar—(concluded).	9	Purqazi	53,210	29,335	23,875	37,968	21,011	16,957	13,555	7,379	6,176	1,687	945	742
	10	Shamli	61,716	34,417	27,299	49,295	27,437	21,858	11,066	6,212	4,854	1,355	768	587
	11	Thana Bhawan	63,791	34,944	28,847	43,892	24,299	19,593	18,516	9,845	8,671	1,383	800	583
	12	Titawi	96,373	52,839	43,534	70,158	38,453	31,705	24,982	13,659	11,323	1,233	727	506
		Meerut ..	*1,519,364*	*822,305*	*697,059*	*1,124,867*	*609,606*	*515,261*	*344,888*	*184,472*	*160,416*	*49,609*	*28,227*	*21,382*
Meerut.	1	Baghpat	69,472	37,904	31,568	55,433	30,210	25,223	10,668	5,826	4,842	3,371	1,868	1,503
	2	Baraut	81,543	44,512	37,031	64,426	35,167	29,259	11,721	6,351	5,370	5,396	2,994	2,402
	3	Begamabad	80,666	42,680	37,986	63,936	34,006	29,930	15,873	8,213	7,660	857	461	396
	4	Binauli	76,538	42,322	34,216	59,780	33,176	26,604	10,949	5,965	4,984	5,809	3,181	2,628
	5	Baisuma	21,645	11,935	9,710	18,333	10,117	8,216	2,693	1,458	1,235	619	360	259
	6	Chhaprauli	73,154	39,557	33,597	57,178	30,815	26,363	12,359	6,729	5,630	3,617	2,013	1,604
	7	Daurala	48,956	26,689	22,267	38,156	20,751	17,405	9,979	5,499	4,480	821	439	382
	8	Garhmuktesar	85,631	45,595	40,036	62,026	33,114	28,912	22,931	12,099	10,832	674	382	292
	9	Ghaziabad	76,202	41,010	35,192	55,098	29,750	25,348	17,989	9,592	8,397	3,115	1,668	1,447
	10	Hapur	103,695	55,163	48,532	77,006	41,104	35,902	25,007	13,181	11,826	1,682	878	804
	11	Jani	80,250	42,833	37,417	63,772	34,211	29,561	15,745	8,246	7,499	733	376	357
	12	Kharkhauda	54,208	28,644	25,564	39,984	21,350	18,634	13,419	6,889	6,530	805	405	400
	13	Khekrah	70,114	37,783	32,331	59,281	32,081	27,200	8,929	4,708	4,221	1,904	994	910
	14	Kithor	48,666	25,778	22,888	29,975	16,142	13,833	17,941	9,225	8,716	750	411	339
	15	Lalkurti	30,915	16,497	14,418	22,131	11,827	10,304	8,754	4,656	4,098	30	14	16
	16	Mawana	74,902	40,545	34,357	56,676	30,557	26,119	16,247	8,914	7,333	1,979	1,074	905
	17	Meerut	160,421	90,509	69,912	92,777	52,086	40,691	59,561	32,861	26,700	8,083	5,562	2,521
	18	Parichhatgarh	60,455	32,335	28,120	44,332	23,781	20,551	13,755	7,302	6,453	2,368	1,252	1,116
	19	Pilkhua	74,212	39,524	34,688	54,294	29,106	25,188	18,446	9,619	8,827	1,472	799	673
	20	Sadr Bazar	13,924	7,635	6,289	10,782	5,811	4,971	2,884	1,684	1,200	258	140	118
	21	Sardhana	86,127	46,997	39,130	59,757	32,793	26,964	21,896	11,676	10,220	4,474	2,528	1,946
	22	Shahdara	47,668	25,858	21,810	39,734	21,651	18,083	7,142	3,779	3,363	792	428	364
		Bulandshahr ..	*1,123,792*	*592,267*	*531,525*	*886,219*	*467,937*	*418,282*	*208,367*	*108,724*	*99,643*	*29,206*	*15,606*	*13,600*
Bulandshahr.	1	Anupshahr	62,676	33,236	29,440	52,497	27,835	24,662	8,587	4,528	4,059	1,592	873	719
	2	Aurangabad	60,551	31,748	28,803	47,688	25,135	22,553	12,375	6,340	6,035	488	273	215
	3	Bulandshahr	97,564	51,384	46,180	65,513	34,630	30,883	29,713	15,521	14,192	2,338	1,233	1,105
	4	Dibai	92,803	49,025	43,778	78,795	41,773	37,022	12,069	6,238	5,831	1,939	1,014	925
	5	Dadri	65,139	34,483	30,656	55,111	29,240	25,871	8,080	4,226	3,854	1,948	1,017	931
	6	Dankaur	51,256	27,596	23,660	41,772	22,451	19,321	8,500	4,608	3,892	984	537	447
	7	Gulaothi	68,505	36,146	32,359	49,325	26,261	23,064	17,885	9,220	8,665	1,295	665	630
	8	Jahangirabad	67,428	35,134	32,294	51,981	27,100	24,881	11,991	6,190	5,801	3,456	1,844	1,612
	9	Jewar	49,238	25,877	23,361	41,890	21,969	19,921	6,687	3,544	3,143	661	364	297
	10	Jhajhar	52,418	27,430	24,988	44,951	23,466	21,485	5,734	3,025	2,709	1,733	939	794
	11	Khurja	96,902	51,260	45,642	70,079	37,104	32,975	23,671	12,420	11,251	3,152	1,736	1,416
	12	Pahasu	79,118	41,549	37,569	64,008	33,525	30,483	12,202	6,431	5,771	2,908	1,593	1,315
	13	Shikarpur	73,724	38,894	34,830	59,528	31,410	28,118	12,582	6,636	5,946	1,614	848	766
	14	Sikandrabad	83,039	43,729	39,310	62,422	33,045	29,377	17,300	8,952	8,348	3,317	1,732	1,585
	15	Surajpur	21,050	11,405	9,645	18,219	9,868	8,351	2,579	1,399	1,180	252	138	114
	16	Syana	102,381	53,371	49,010	82,440	43,125	39,315	18,412	9,446	8,966	1,529	800	729

	No.	Place												
		Aligarh	1,165,680	629,524	536,156	991,634	535,646	455,988	143,314	77,507	65,807	30,732	16,371	14,361
Aligarh.	1	Akrabad	79,495	42,952	36,543	66,123	35,764	30,359	9,651	5,172	4,479	3,721	2,016	1,705
	2	Atrauli	72,972	38,748	34,224	59,867	31,726	27,941	11,068	5,850	5,218	2,237	1,172	1,065
	3	Bhankri	75,012	40,035	34,977	66,256	35,294	30,962	6,828	3,714	3,114	1,928	1,027	901
	4	Barla	69,512	37,270	32,242	54,411	29,315	25,096	13,438	7,088	6,350	1,663	867	796
	5	Chandaus	64,169	34,026	30,143	58,081	30,794	27,287	5,225	2,770	2,455	863	462	401
	6	Dadon	61,383	33,404	28,979	54,153	29,530	24,623	6,058	3,255	2,803	1,172	619	553
	7	Gondah	56,953	30,858	26,095	52,770	28,601	24,169	3,286	1,783	1,503	897	474	423
	8	Harduaganj	76,091	40,258	35,833	63,431	33,581	29,850	9,522	5,006	4,516	3,138	1,671	1,467
	9	Hasayan	59,237	32,391	26,846	53,821	29,387	24,434	4,107	2,292	1,815	1,309	712	597
	10	Hathras	114,630	63,304	51,326	99,821	55 047	44,774	12,296	6,895	5,401	2,513	1,362	1,151
	11	Iglas	59,157	32,368	26,769	54,105	29,665	24,440	4,133	2,234	1,899	919	489	430
	12	Khair	56,859	30,083	26,776	50,856	26,900	23,956	5,287	2,797	2,4[illegible]0	716	386	330
	13	Koil	106,238	58,355	47,883	70,611	38,739	31,872	31,492	17,468	14,024	4,135	2,148	1,987
	14	Sasni	72,336	39,147	33,189	63,594	34,407	29,187	6,358	3,430	2,928	2,384	1,310	1,074
	15	Sikandra Rao	83,512	45,108	38 404	70,833	38,346	32,487	10,561	5,521	4,840	2,318	1,241	1,077
	16	Tappal	58,124	31,197	26,9[illegible]7	53,101	28,550	24,551	4,204	2,232	1,972	819	415	404
		Agra Division	5,007,921	2,742,988	2,264,933	4,467,781	2,452,456	2,015,325	462,111	247,231	214,880	78,029	43,301	34,728
		Muttra	656,310	361,507	294,803	584,647	322,049	262,598	61,759	33,917	27,842	9,904	5,541	4,363
Muttra.	1	Brindaban	28,683	15,673	13,010	26,820	14,591	12,229	1,437	864	573	426	218	208
	2	Baldeo	64,221	35,788	28,433	59,797	33,415	26,382	3,587	1,927	1,660	837	446	391
	3	Barsana	33,999	19,162	14,837	31,502	17,760	13,742	2,407	1,346	1,061	90	56	34
	4	Chhata	38,284	20,959	17,325	33,036	17,972	15,064	4,995	2,852	2,143	253	135	118
	5	Farrah	38,618	21,122	17,496	33,878	18,603	15,275	4,576	2,425	2,151	164	94	70
	6	Gobardhan	32,003	17,674	14,329	28,774	15,897	12,877	3,057	1,677	1,380	172	100	72
	7	Kosi	50,922	27,569	23,353	43,300	23,484	19,816	6,967	3,721	3,246	655	364	291
	8	Muttra	63,740	34,860	28,880	52,414	28,622	23,792	10,371	5,693	4,678	953	545	410
	9	Nohjhil	42,696	22,730	19,966	39,491	21,066	18,425	2,497	1,312	1,185	708	352	356
	10	Raya	58,335	32,185	26,150	53,185	29,333	23,852	3,543	1,997	1,546	1,607	855	752
	11	Shergarh	16,747	9,189	7,558	14,212	7,825	6,387	2,464	1,320	1,144	71	44	27
	12	Sadabad	62,568	34,959	27,609	57,061	31,995	25,066	4,748	2,558	2,190	759	406	353
	13	Sonkh	28,490	16,136	12,354	25,609	14,491	11,118	2,488	1,440	1,048	393	205	188
	14	Sahpau	39,263	21,621	17,642	35,553	19,632	15,921	2,799	1,509	1,290	911	480	431
	15	Surir	47,903	26,085	21,818	43,597	23,704	19,893	3,566	1,987	1,579	740	394	346
	16	Sadr Bazar	9,858	5,795	4,043	6,418	3,659	2,759	2,257	1,289	968	1,163	847	316
		Agra	1,021,847	557,320	464,527	885,841	483,777	402,064	114,555	61,360	53,195	21,451	12,183	9,268
Agra.	1	Achhnera	43,206	23,512	19,694	37,370	20,227	17,143	5,485	3,092	2,393	351	193	158
	2	Aharan	27,788	15,273	12,515	25,545	14,083	11,512	1,410	797	613	833	443	390
	3	Bah	44,150	23,746	20,404	42,186	22,677	19,509	1,562	864	698	402	205	197
	4	Chatta	24,233	13,399	10,844	17,564	9,803	7,758	5,720	3,031	2,689	999	562	437
	5	Dawki	25,167	13,820	11,347	23 819	13,074	10,745	1,143	668	510	205	113	92
	6	Etmaduddaula	18,870	10,486	8,384	17,369	9,582	7,7[illegible]7	1 249	748	501	252	156	96
	7	Firozabad	76,060	41,366	34,694	66,265	36,187	30,078	7,861	4,136	3,725	1,934	1,043	891
	8	Fatehabad	48,405	26,443	21,962	45,994	25,148	20,851	2,222	1,204	1,018	189	96	93
	9	Fatehpur Sikri	35,042	18,907	16,135	30,947	16,700	14,247	4,046	2,178	1,868	49	29	20
	10	Hariparbat	24,702	13,096	11,[illegible]03	19,081	10,098	8,983	4,810	2,511	2,299	811	487	324
	11	Itmadpur	75,672	41,849	33,823	69,039	38,327	30,712	4,676	2,462	2,214	1,957	1,060	897
	12	Iradatnagar	26,476	14,390	12,086	24,968	13,572	11,396	970	533	437	538	285	253
	13	Jaitpur	36,896	19,843	17,053	35,109	18,854	16,255	942	533	409	845	456	389
	14	Jagnair	37,744	20,671	17,073	35,428	19,392	16,036	2,285	1,257	1,028	31	22	9
	15	Kagaraul	33,441	18,386	15,055	30,681	16,88[illegible]	13,795	2,601	1,414	1,187	159	86	73
	16	Kotwali	35,165	18,723	16,442	19,873	[illegible],706	9,167	13,677	7,071	6,606	1,615	946	6[illegible]9
	17	Kakuba	24,124	13,070	11,054	22,585	12,268	10,817	1,454	750	704	85	52	33
	18	Khandauli	19,278	10,767	8,511	17,05[illegible]	9,513	7,538	1,932	1,089	843	295	165	130
	19	Khairagarh	20,854	11,100	9,754	12,275	10,245	9,030	1,575	852	728	4	3	1
	20	Lohamandi	36,996	19,678	17,3[illegible]5	25,466	13,633	11,833	10,744	5,613	5,131	788	427	361
	21	Lalkurti (Sadr Bazar)	21,514	12,392	9,122	13,677	7,517	6,150	4,957	2,770	2,187	2,890	2,105	785

PROVINCIAL TABLE III.

Population of the Police Circles Distributed by Religion.

Name of district.	Serial number of thana.	Name of thana.	Population. Total.	Population. Males.	Population. Females.	Hindus. Total.	Hindus. Males.	Hindus. Females.	Muhammadans. Total.	Muhammadans. Males.	Muhammadans. Females.	Others. Total.	Others. Males.	Others. Females.
1	2	3	4	5	6	7	8	9	10	11	12	13	14	15
Agra.	22	Malpura	33,277	18,038	15,239	31,065	16,872	14,193	2,000	1,059	941	212	107	105
	23	Narki	42,496	23,268	19,228	38,777	21,315	17,462	2,474	1,306	1,168	1,245	647	598
	24	Pinahat	44,756	24,377	20,379	43,244	23,549	19,695	1,195	650	545	317	178	139
	25	Bunkuta	17,797	9,775	8,022	16,179	8,894	7,285	1,409	767	642	209	114	95
	26	Bakabganj	39,692	22,520	17,172	22,211	13,115	9,096	15,265	8,322	6,943	2,216	1,083	1,133
	27	Shamshabad	42,365	23,200	19,165	39,128	21,414	17,714	2,592	1,400	1,192	645	386	259
	28	Saiyan	23,349	12,741	10,608	21,904	11,968	9,936	1,161	626	535	284	147	137
	29	Tundla	7,852	4,413	3,439	5,759	3,227	2,532	1,543	886	657	550	300	250
	30	Tajganj	34,428	18,076	16,362	28,292	14,988	13,309	5,595	2,806	2,789	541	287	254
		Farrukhabad	*900,022*	*494,017*	*406,005*	*788,623*	*435,300*	*353,323*	*104,293*	*54,804*	*49,489*	*7,106*	*3,913*	*3,193*
Farrukhabad.	1	Aligarh	73,269	40,775	32,494	68,659	38,258	30,401	3,796	2,064	1,732	814	453	361
	2	Chhibramau	69,471	37,939	31,532	65,252	35,745	29,507	3,833	1,990	1,843	386	204	182
	3	Farrukhabad	72,519	39,178	33,341	55,221	30,093	25,128	15,978	8,292	7,686	1,320	793	527
	4	Fatehgarh	32,325	18,738	13,587	26,007	15,185	10,822	5,135	2,955	2,180	1,183	598	585
	5	Gursahaiganj	80,288	44,210	36,078	69,166	38,139	31,027	10,664	5,811	4,853	458	260	198
	6	Kamalganj	58,301	31,763	26,538	49,402	27,105	22,297	8,628	4,512	4,116	271	146	125
	7	Kaimganj	67,578	36,368	31,210	54,778	30,099	24,679	12,535	6,123	6,412	265	146	119
	8	Kampil	35,650	19,483	16,167	32,083	17,632	14,451	3,219	1,666	1,553	348	185	163
	9	Muhammadabad	64,415	35,362	29,053	61,056	33,612	27,444	2,983	1,558	1,425	376	192	184
	10	Nawabganj	51,832	28,201	23,631	49,017	26,690	22,327	2,710	1,449	1,261	105	62	43
	11	Shamsabad	38,975	21,134	17,841	32,506	17,815	14,691	6,120	3,121	2,999	349	198	151
	12	Sarai Miran	93,207	50,491	42,716	74,577	40,668	33,909	17,951	9,458	8,493	679	365	314
	13	Saurikh	69,864	38,716	31,148	65,923	36,630	29,293	3,772	1,987	1,785	169	99	70
	14	Tirwa or Indargarh	61,339	34,249	27,090	57,709	32,276	25,433	3,605	1,960	1,645	25	13	12
	15	Thathia	30,989	17,410	13,579	27,267	15,353	11,914	3,364	1,858	1,506	358	199	159
		Mainpuri	*797,624*	*438,920*	*358,704*	*741,028*	*408,225*	*332,803*	*44,477*	*23,977*	*20,500*	*12,119*	*6,718*	*5,401*
Mainpuri.	1	Bewar	64,887	35,723	29,164	61,618	33,922	27,696	2,385	1,307	1,078	884	494	390
	2	Bhongaon	67,024	36,401	30,623	62,304	33,872	28,432	3,904	2,081	1,823	816	448	368
	3	Eka	64,134	35,732	28,402	59,277	33,101	26,170	3,216	1,745	1,471	1,647	886	761
	4	Ghiror	56,283	31,166	25,117	53,094	29,438	23,656	2,215	1,201	1,014	974	527	447
	5	Kishni	57,071	31,690	25,381	54,923	30,508	24,415	1,971	1,083	888	177	99	78
	6	Kuraoli	63,980	35,183	28,797	60,787	33,378	27,409	2,222	1,243	979	971	562	409
	7	Karhal	71,273	39,035	32,238	64,600	35,453	29,147	5,435	2,913	2,522	1,238	669	569
	8	Kurra	53,671	29,623	24,048	52,097	28,745	23,352	1,523	847	676	51	31	20
	9	Mainpuri	68,763	38,026	30,737	62,168	34,372	27,796	5,560	3,077	2,483	1,035	577	458
	10	Mustafabad	70,177	38,405	31,772	64,205	35,207	28,998	4,775	2,542	2,233	1,197	656	541
	11	Sirsaganj	76,329	41,887	34,442	71,079	39,039	32,040	3,393	1,799	1,594	1,857	1,049	808
	12	Shikohabad	84,032	46,019	37,983	74,882	41,190	33,692	7,878	4,139	3,739	1,272	720	552
		Etawah	*760,121*	*416,648*	*343,473*	*707,354*	*388,388*	*318,966*	*45,628*	*24,227*	*21,401*	*7,139*	*4,033*	*3,106*
	1	Auraiya	54,405	29,366	25,039	57,021	27,582	23,439	3,059	1,590	1,469	325	194	131
	2	Ajitmal	62,115	33,825	28,290	58,575	31,937	26,638	3,200	1,689	1,511	340	199	141

Etawah.	3	Barhpura ..	24,830	13,467	11,363	23,783	12,892	10,891	533	297	236	514	278	236
	4	Bakewar ..	79,121	42,967	36,154	76,290	41,412	34,878	2,424	1,329	1,095	407	226	181
	5	Bharthna ..	49,733	27,274	22,459	46,965	25,736	21,229	1,809	1,002	807	959	536	423
	6	Bidhuna ..	44,600	24,869	19,731	41,007	22,901	18,106	3,222	1,748	1,474	371	220	151
	7	Bela ..	45,830	25,632	20,198	43,535	24,368	19,167	2,220	1,221	999	75	43	32
	8	Chaubia ..	60,586	33,062	27,524	58,376	31,875	26,501	2,000	1,068	932	210	119	91
	9	Chhachhund	31,522	17,622	13,900	30,353	17,005	13,348	1,156	610	546	13	7	6
	10	Debiapur ..	48,050	26,732	21,318	46,141	25,624	20,517	1,783	1,029	754	126	79	47
	11	Etawah ..	79,420	42,739	36,681	61,278	33,214	28,064	15,375	7,936	7,409	2,767	1,559	1,208
	12	Jaswantnagar	59,642	32,568	27,074	56,465	30,854	25,611	2,750	1,473	1,277	427	241	186
	13	Phaphund ..	43,256	23,723	19,533	39,243	21,628	17,615	3,837	1,999	1,838	176	96	80
	14	Sahson ..	28,214	15,655	12,559	27,708	15,374	12,334	393	218	175	113	63	50
	15	Umrain ..	48,797	27,147	21,650	46,614	25,986	20,628	1,867	988	879	316	173	143
		Etah ..	*871,997*	*474,576*	*397,421*	*760,288*	*414,717*	*345,571*	*91,399*	*48,946*	*42,453*	20,310	*10,913*	*9,397*
Etah.	1	Aliganj ..	64,162	34,851	29,311	54,058	29,408	24,650	9,064	4,856	4,208	1,040	587	453
	2	Awah ..	51,926	28,562	23,364	45,194	24,926	20,268	4,352	2,327	2,025	2,380	1,309	1,071
	3	Etah ..	112,245	61,451	50,794	100,757	55,122	45,635	8,456	4,664	3,792	3,032	1,665	1,367
	4	Jaithra ..	54,112	29,595	24,517	51,487	28,149	23,338	2,221	1,226	995	404	220	184
	5	Jalesar ..	72,746	39,769	32,977	61,357	33,818	27,539	9,525	4,963	4,562	1,864	988	876
	6	Kadirganj ..	48,146	26,271	21,875	42,105	22,985	19,120	4,886	2,645	2,241	1,155	641	514
	7	Kasganj ..	87,476	47,574	39,902	70,947	38,660	32,287	14,190	7,644	6,546	2,339	1,270	1,069
	8	Marahra ..	73,348	39,794	33,554	64,243	34,991	29,252	7,181	3,815	3,366	1,924	988	936
	9	Patiali ..	59,881	32,388	27,493	48,005	26,172	21,833	11,212	5,873	5,339	664	343	321
	10	Sakit ..	61,237	33,558	27,679	57,247	31,446	25,801	2,942	1,577	1,365	1,048	535	513
	11	Soron ..	66,851	36,372	30,479	59,539	32,388	27,151	5,479	3,005	2,474	1,833	979	854
	12	Sahawar ..	58,824	31,513	27,311	48,458	26,013	22,445	8,563	4,550	4,013	1,803	950	853
	13	Sidhpura ..	61,043	32,878	28,165	56,891	30,639	26,252	3,328	1,801	1,527	824	438	386
		Rohilkhand Division ..	*5,650,518*	*3,050,265*	*2,600,253*	*4,153,593*	*2,260,282*	*1,893,311*	*1,411,809*	*742,713*	*669,036*	*85,116*	*47,210*	*37,906*
		Bareilly ..	*1,094,663*	*593,836*	*500,827*	*801,502*	*437,200*	*364,302*	*276,230*	*146,503*	*129,727*	*16,931*	*10,133*	*6,798*
Bareilly.	1	Aonla ..	66,798	36,590	30,208	52,531	28,952	23,579	13,080	6,995	6,085	1,187	643	544
	2	Bhutaha ..	38,365	20,978	17,387	34,235	18,750	15,485	3,911	2,114	1,797	219	114	105
	3	Baradari ..	70,210	37,257	32,953	43,545	23,579	19,966	26,283	13,481	12,802	382	197	185
	4	Bhojipura ..	50,229	27,145	23,084	33,711	18,369	15,342	15,408	8,178	7,230	1,110	598	512
	5	Bhamora ..	56,304	30,615	25,689	48,007	26,091	21,916	7,550	4,100	3,450	747	424	323
	6	Baheri ..	76,545	41,261	35,284	54,925	29,839	25,086	21,286	11,233	10,053	334	189	145
	7	Deorania ..	77,150	41,279	35,871	51,874	28,016	23,858	24,754	12,981	11,773	522	282	240
	8	Faridpur ..	58,684	31,875	26,809	46,921	25,545	21,376	11,295	6,069	5,226	468	261	207
	9	Fatehganj East	32,705	18,062	14,643	28,950	16,000	12,950	3,521	1,929	1,592	234	133	101
	10	Fatehganj West	33,336	17,917	15,419	26,866	14,407	12,459	5,969	3,220	2,749	501	290	211
	11	Gaini ..	36,993	20,355	16,638	29,179	16,081	13,098	7,127	3,889	3,238	687	385	302
	12	Hafizganj ..	63,711	34,694	29,017	50,538	27,558	22,980	12,407	6,718	5,689	766	418	348
	13	Killa ..	60,378	31,759	28,619	33,452	17,886	15,566	26,085	13,407	12,678	841	466	375
	14	Kotwali ..	70,012	39,155	30,857	39,488	22,884	16,604	28,044	15,007	13,037	2,480	1,264	1,216
	15	Mirganj ..	54,047	29,177	24,870	43,254	23,334	19,920	9,961	5,386	4,575	832	457	375
	16	Nawabganj..	64,769	34,945	29,824	51,390	27,847	23,543	12,732	6,742	5,990	647	356	291
	17	Sadr Bazar	34,488	20,617	13,871	20,566	11,890	8,676	10,882	6,101	4,781	3,040	2,626	414
	18	Sirauli ..	47,841	25,757	22,084	37,440	20,218	17,222	9,477	5,050	4,427	924	489	435
	19	Shahi ..	47,589	25,393	22,196	37,727	20,211	17,516	9,340	4,903	4,437	522	279	243
	20	Shishgarh ..	54,509	29,005	25,504	36,903	19,743	17,160	17,118	9,000	8,118	488	262	226
		Bijnor ..	*806,202*	*427,153*	*379,049*	*508,805*	*272,619*	*236,186*	*280,501*	*145,339*	*135,162*	*16,896*	*9,195*	*7,701*
Bijnor.	1	Amhera ..	64,246	34,443	29,803	44,820	24,184	20,636	18,411	9,693	8,718	1 015	566	449
	2	Afzalgarh ..	43,310	22,752	20,558	26,913	14,447	12,466	15,292	7,735	7,557	1,105	570	535
	3	Bijnor ..	62,969	33,937	29,032	39,528	21,623	17,905	22,711	11,944	10,767	730	370	360
	4	Barhapura ..	32,288	17,198	15,090	20,866	11,074	9,792	10,847	5,816	5,081	575	308	267
	5	Chandpur ..	81,910	43,310	38,609	57,048	30,583	26,465	23,057	11,781	11,276	1,805	946	859
	6	Dhampur ..	54,237	28,563	25,674	34,942	18,489	16,453	17,457	9,037	8,420	1,838	1,087	801

Population of the Police Circles Distributed by Religion.

Name of district.	Serial number of thana.	Name of thana.	Population. Total.	Population. Males.	Population. Females.	Hindus. Total.	Hindus. Males.	Hindus. Females.	Muhammadans. Total.	Muhammadans. Males.	Muhammadans. Females.	Others. Total.	Others. Males.	Others. Females.
1	2	3	4	5	6	7	8	9	10	11	12	13	14	15
Bijnor—(concld.)	7	Kiratpur	67,482	35,674	31,808	38,883	20,937	17,946	26,820	13,789	13,031	1,779	948	831
	8	Mandawar	39,317	20,808	18,509	29,250	15,591	13,659	8,905	4,629	4,276	1,162	588	574
	9	Nurpur	41,025	21,671	19,354	27,990	14,768	13,222	11,721	6,221	5,500	1,314	682	632
	10	Nihtaur	47,371	24,888	22,483	26,831	14,267	12,564	19,790	10,223	9,567	750	398	352
	11	Nagal	21,559	11,560	9,999	15,441	8,305	7,136	5,526	2,941	2,585	592	314	278
	12	Najibabad	63,871	33,856	30,015	35,451	19,090	16,361	27,345	14,167	13,178	1,075	599	476
	13	Nagina	75,179	39,382	35,797	42,865	22,762	20,103	31,107	15,971	15,136	1,207	649	558
	14	Rehar	15,220	8,203	7,017	10,959	5,909	5,050	4,103	2,206	1,897	158	88	70
	15	Shampur	6,091	3,780	2,311	4,357	2,538	1,819	1,233	810	423	501	432	69
	16	Sherkot	33,811	17,171	16,640	18,718	9,754	8,964	14,854	7,287	7,567	239	130	109
	17	Seohara	56,316	29,957	26,359	33,943	18,298	15,645	21,322	11,089	10,233	1,051	570	481
		Budaun	*1,053,328*	*577,561*	*475,767*	*859,688*	*473,457*	*386,231*	*176,376*	*94,727*	*81,649*	*17,264*	*9,377*	*7,887*
Budaun.	1	Budaun	69,039	36,772	32,267	37,667	20,747	16,920	29,422	15,014	14,408	1,950	1,011	939
	2	Benawar	55,185	30,455	24,730	42,865	23,761	19,104	10,980	5,968	5,012	1,340	726	614
	3	Bisauli	87,248	48,093	39,155	73,921	40,790	33,131	11,678	6,386	5,292	1,649	917	732
	4	Bilsi	91,956	50,961	40,995	78,886	43,688	35,198	11,579	6,434	5,145	1,491	839	652
	5	Dataganj	88,642	48,868	39,774	77,996	43,047	34,949	9,549	5,257	4,292	1,097	564	533
	6	Gunnaur	75,544	41,118	34,426	63,729	34,742	28,987	10,350	5,588	4,762	1,465	788	677
	7	Hazratpur	52,024	28,879	23,145	47,084	26,206	20,878	4,353	2,349	2,004	587	324	263
	8	Islamnagar	77,812	42,975	34,837	65,286	36,053	29,233	10,970	6,061	4,909	1,556	861	695
	9	Kakrala	58,132	31,249	26,883	40,816	22,145	18,671	16,677	8,758	7,919	639	346	293
	10	Qadirchauk	40,452	22,067	18,385	32,388	17,790	14,598	7,585	4,006	3,579	479	271	208
	11	Rajpura	61,958	33,914	28,044	54,705	29,955	24,750	5,486	2,992	2,494	1,767	967	800
	12	Sahaswan	75,346	40,981	34,365	53,069	29,188	23,881	21,437	11,354	10,083	840	439	401
	13	Usehat	55,585	30,431	25,154	50,272	27,502	22,770	5,052	2,775	2,277	261	154	107
	14	Ujhani	59,352	32,700	26,652	52,464	28,936	23,528	6,122	3,361	2,761	766	403	363
	15	Wazirganj	53,993	29,933	24,060	43,656	24,176	19,480	9,626	5,357	4,269	711	400	311
	16	Zarifnagar	51,060	28,165	22,895	44,884	24,731	20,153	5,510	3,067	2,443	666	367	299
		Moradabad	*1,262,933*	*676,151*	*586,782*	*784,550*	*424,397*	*360,153*	*453,269*	*238,140*	*215,129*	*25,114*	*13,614*	*11,500*
Moradabad.	1	Moradabad	125,104	66,747	58,357	59,498	32,517	26,981	61,421	32,031	29,390	4,185	2,199	1,986
	2	Mundha	55,402	30,347	25,055	33,103	18,376	14,727	20,698	11,079	9,619	1,601	892	709
	3	Manpur	65,999	35,302	30,697	33,449	17,985	15,464	31,583	16,788	14,795	967	529	438
	4	Bilari	77,884	42,385	35,499	52,047	28,446	23,601	23,943	12,921	11,022	1,894	1,018	876
	5	Chandausi	94,297	51,958	42,339	72,667	40,116	32,551	19,772	10,808	8,964	1,858	1,034	824
	6	Asmoli	64,749	34,407	30,342	43,522	23,124	20,398	20,010	10,623	9,387	1,217	660	557
	7	Bahjoi	70,295	38,453	31,842	58,755	32,080	26,675	9,628	5,323	4,305	1,912	1,050	862
	8	Mainather	72,106	38,889	33,217	42,133	22,911	19,222	28,346	15,117	13,229	1,627	861	766
	9	Sambhal	99,783	52,330	47,453	48,530	25,946	22,584	48,829	25,085	23,744	2,424	1,299	1,125
	10	Amroha	110,645	57,805	53,340	58,641	31,461	27,180	50,496	25,029	25,457	1,508	805	703
	11	Didauli	48,239	25,910	22,329	26,377	14,245	12,132	21,169	11,291	9,878	693	374	319
	12	Bachhraon	50,377	26,988	23,389	35,079	18,924	16,155	14,637	7,640	6,997	661	424	237
	13	Hasanpur	76,025	40,311	35,714	51,637	27,549	24,088	22,962	12,004	10,958	1,426	758	668
	14	Rehra	35,312	19,401	15,911	30,663	16,794	13,869	4,025	2,274	1,751	624	333	291
	15	Tigri	21,633	11,612	10,021	16,009	8,539	7,470	5,503	3,009	2,494	121	64	57

	16	Chhajlait	67,143	35,828	31,315	44,125	23,726	20,399	21,969	11,524	10,465	1,029	578	451
	17	Dilari	67,320	35,847	31,473	36,109	19,350	16,759	30,722	16,244	14,478	489	253	236
	18	Thakurdwara	60,620	32,131	28,489	42,206	22,308	19,898	17,536	9,340	8,196	878	483	395
		Shahjahanpur	*945,775*	*513,562*	*432,213*	*801,274*	*437,842*	*363,432*	*139,159*	*72,768*	*66 391*	*5,342*	*2,952*	*2,390*
Shahjahanpur.	1	Banda	71,336	38,488	32,848	65,488	35,368	30,120	5,589	2,977	2,612	259	143	116
	2	Dhakia	3,579	1,916	1,663	2,917	1,559	1,358	659	356	303	5	1	2
	3	Jaitipur	72,980	40,177	32,803	68,442	37,699	30,743	3,962	2,160	1,802	576	318	258
	4	Jalalabad	63,763	34,919	28,844	55,654	30,733	24,921	7,721	3,974	3,747	388	212	176
	5	Khudaganj	39,287	21,569	17,718	34,166	18,797	15,369	4,706	2,539	2,167	415	233	182
	6	Kant	70,966	38,541	32,425	64,191	34,915	29,276	6,445	3,436	3,009	330	190	140
	7	Khotar	30,097	16,199	13,898	26,195	14,119	12,076	3,852	2,052	1,800	50	28	22
	8	Kalan	75,129	41,651	33,478	69,555	38,607	30,948	5,093	2,782	2,311	481	262	219
	9	Kundaria	37,933	21,219	16,714	34,626	19,408	15,218	3,016	1,657	1,359	291	154	137
	10	Miranpur Katra	48,421	26,707	21,714	40,799	22,588	18,211	7,386	3,986	3,400	236	133	103
	11	Nigohi	44,014	24,034	19,980	38,496	20,981	17,515	5,441	3,006	2,435	77	47	30
	12	Pawayan	67,413	36,363	31,050	60,488	32,567	27,921	6,648	3,630	3,018	277	166	111
	13	Seramau South	54,610	29,655	24,955	48,384	26,323	22,061	6,118	3,271	2,847	108	61	47
	14	Seramau North	32,297	17,141	15,156	27,734	14,667	13,067	4,510	2,435	2,075	53	39	14
	15	Sindhauli	51,103	27,634	23,469	44,635	24,141	20,494	6,351	3,428	2,923	117	65	52
	16	Shahjahanpur	104,048	54,438	49,610	57,313	31,078	26,235	45,637	22,788	22,849	1,098	572	526
	17	Tilhar	78,799	42,911	35,888	62,191	34,292	27,899	16,025	8,291	7,734	583	328	255
		Pilibhit	*487,677*	*262,002*	*225,615*	*397,774*	*214,767*	*183,007*	*86,274*	*45,296*	*40,978*	*3,569*	*1,939*	*1,630*
Pilibhit.	1	Barkhera	63,161	33,874	29,287	57,003	30,578	26,425	5,786	3,100	2,686	372	196	176
	2	Bilsanda	67,753	36,769	30,984	62,312	33,824	28,488	5,246	2,838	2,408	195	107	88
	3	Bisalpur	78,094	42,555	35,539	65,100	35,542	29,558	12,073	6,517	5,556	921	496	425
	4	Jahanabad	52,130	28,204	23,926	38,641	21,028	17,613	12,925	6,872	6,053	564	304	260
	5	Neoria Hasanpur	32,155	17,086	15,069	23,223	12,444	10,779	8,728	4,523	4,205	204	119	85
	6	Madho Tanda	28,922	15,452	13,470	25,531	13,612	11,919	3,219	1,746	1,473	172	94	78
	7	Pilibhit	69,091	37,050	32,041	50,917	27,723	23,194	17,424	8,927	8,497	750	400	350
	8	Puranpur	64,058	33,763	30,295	55,473	29,435	26,038	8,292	4,167	4,125	293	161	132
	9	Amaria	32,253	17,249	15,004	19,574	10,581	8,993	12,581	6,606	5,975	98	62	36
		Allahabad Division	*5,494,284*	*2,844,746*	*2,649,538*	*4,947,366*	*2,561,208*	*2,386,158*	*509,030*	*261,380*	*247,650*	*37,888*	*22,158*	*15,730*
		Cawnpore	*1,142,286*	*623,437*	*518,849*	*1,029,563*	*561,249*	*468,314*	*104,001*	*56,828*	*47,173*	*8,722*	*5,360*	*3,362*
Cawnpore.	1	Anwarganj	32,198	18,890	13,308	25,372	14,980	10,392	6,452	3,703	2,749	374	207	167
	2	Akbarpur	50,751	27,722	23,029	46,425	25,400	21,025	4,136	2,212	1,924	190	110	80
	3	Bithur	45,247	24,362	20,885	42,219	22,734	19,485	2,670	1,450	1,220	358	178	180
	4	Bilhaur	65,012	35,396	29,616	57,765	31,659	26,106	7,038	3,629	3,409	209	108	101
	5	Bhognipur	64,441	34,190	30,251	56,883	30,287	26,596	7,425	3,817	3,608	133	86	47
	6	Bidhnu	35,388	19 001	16,387	33,889	18,212	15,677	1,386	731	655	113	58	55
	7	Cantonment	30,662	18,455	12,207	21,941	12,834	9,107	6,131	3,608	2,523	2,590	2,013	577
	8	Colonelganj	62,938	35,693	27,245	41,401	23,664	17,737	19,363	10,960	8,403	2,174	1,069	1,105
	9	Derapur	45,379	24,280	21,099	42,667	22,861	19,806	2,668	1,395	1,273	44	24	20
	10	Gajner	49,152	26,103	23,049	46,918	24,875	22,043	2,026	1,094	932	208	134	74
	11	Ghatampur	68,697	36,377	32,320	65,345	34,663	30,682	3,249	1,658	1,591	103	56	47
	12	Kalyanpur	23,836	13,249	10,587	22,655	12,553	10,102	1,083	639	444	98	57	41
	13	Kotwali	67,311	38,205	29,106	49,115	28,071	21,042	16,859	9,339	7,520	1,339	795	544
	14	Kakwan	43,741	24,300	19,441	41,363	22,995	18,368	2,366	1,300	1,066	12	5	7
	15	Mangalpur	61,556	33,537	28,019	58,498	31,908	26,590	3,022	1,602	1,420	36	27	9
	16	Musanagar	36,827	19,648	17,179	34,518	18,457	16,061	2,245	1,156	1,089	64	35	29
	17	Maharajpur	36,013	19,173	16,840	34,176	18,229	15,947	1,796	921	875	41	23	18
	18	Nawabganj	863	584	279	751	491	260	77	61	16	35	32	3
	19	Narwal	44 683	23,489	21,194	42,900	22,543	20,357	1,778	942	836	5	4	1
	20	Rasulabad	58,123	32,393	25,730	54,996	30,667	24,329	3,090	1,704	1,386	37	22	15
	21	Sheorajpur	47,954	26,120	21,834	46,035	25,060	20,975	1,879	1,037	842	40	23	17
	22	Sheoli	54,632	29,587	25,045	52,506	28,431	24,077	1,855	1,010	845	269	146	123

PROVINCIAL TABLE III.

Population of the Police Circles Distributed by Religion.

Name of district.	Serial number of thana.	Name of thana.	Population. Total.	Population. Males.	Population. Females.	Hindus. Total.	Hindus. Males.	Hindus. Females.	Muhammadans. Total.	Muhammadans. Males.	Muhammadans. Females	Others. Total.	Others. Males.	Others. Females.
1	2	3	4	5	6	7	8	9	10	11	12	13	14	15
Cawnpore—(concld).	23	Sachendi	38,535	20,825	17,710	37,069	20,020	17,049	1,257	684	573	209	121	88
	24	Sajeti	33,884	18,124	15,760	32,280	17,282	14,998	1,591	835	756	13	7	6
	25	Sikandra	44,463	23,734	20,729	41,876	22,373	19,503	2,559	1,341	1,218	28	20	8
		Fatehpur	*676,939*	*350,207*	*326,732*	*597,966*	*310,830*	*287,136*	*78,308*	*39,052*	*39,256*	*665*	*325*	*340*
Fatehpur.	1	Bindki	46,244	24,423	21,821	40,315	21,391	18,924	5,893	3,013	2,880	36	19	17
	2	Chandpur	43,927	23,043	20,884	40,925	21,494	19,431	2,999	1,546	1,453	3	3	..
	3	Ghazipur	52,442	27,397	25,045	49,877	26,068	23,809	2,560	1,326	1,234	5	3	2
	4	Husainganj	52,822	26,991	25,831	50,115	25,636	24,479	2,698	1,350	1,348	9	5	4
	5	Fatehpur	57,167	29,914	27,253	44,961	23,777	21,204	11,963	6,042	5,921	223	95	128
	6	Jahanabad	53,286	28,140	25,146	49,086	25,980	23,106	4,144	2,130	2,014	56	30	26
	7	Hathgaon	74,332	37,547	36,785	58,905	30,041	28,864	15,419	7,501	7,918	8	5	3
	8	Khakhreru	77,219	39,005	38,214	66,391	33,799	32,592	10,595	5,094	5,501	233	112	121
	9	Khaga	71,626	36,506	35,120	63,295	32,331	30,964	8,287	4,146	4,141	44	29	15
	10	Kalyanpur	43,536	23,122	20,414	41,569	22,099	19,470	1,965	1,022	943	2	1	1
	11	Lalauli	46,140	23,976	22,164	41,143	21,453	19,690	4,961	2,506	2,455	36	17	19
	12	Tharison	58,198	30,143	28,055	51,364	26,761	24,603	6,824	3,376	3,448	10	6	4
		Banda	*651,237*	*332,161*	*325,076*	*619,300*	*313,268*	*306,032*	*37,068*	*18,435*	*18,633*	*869*	*458*	*411*
Banda.	1	Matsundh	19,851	10,059	9,792	18,610	9,425	9,185	1,238	633	605	3	1	2
	2	Khanna	21,604	10,894	10,710	20,683	10,424	10,259	906	460	446	15	10	5
	3	Banda	55,803	28,130	27,673	48,041	24,374	23,667	7,313	3,521	3,792	449	235	214
	4	Pailani	47,917	24,580	23,337	44,564	22,951	21,613	3,353	1,629	1,724	..	..	..
	5	Tendwari	32,394	16,411	15,983	30,184	15,345	14,839	2,210	1,066	1,144	..	..	..
	6	Rajapur	38,907	19,674	19,233	37,894	19,162	18,732	945	482	463	68	30	38
	7	Raipura	26,955	13,939	13,016	26,381	13,629	12,752	574	310	264	..	..	..
	8	Mau	39,342	20,053	19,289	38,040	19,374	18,666	1,242	647	595	60	32	28
	9	Marka	26,221	13,328	12,893	25,469	12,963	12,506	752	365	387	..	..	..
	10	Bisanda	50,360	24,995	25,365	47,553	23,577	23,976	2,806	1,417	1,389	1	1	..
	11	Baberu	37,439	18,826	18,613	34,626	17,380	17,246	2,741	1,408	1,333	72	38	34
	12	Badausa	44,188	22,383	21,805	42,354	21,441	20,913	1,823	936	887	11	6	5
	13	Kalinjar	24,524	12,467	12,057	23,621	11,993	11,628	878	463	415	25	11	14
	14	Pangara	33,689	16,530	17,159	29,549	14,540	15,009	4,131	1,985	2,146	9	5	4
	15	Karwi	38,208	19,336	18,872	35,836	18,164	17,672	2,270	1,118	1,152	102	54	48
	16	Manikpur	17,646	9,030	8,616	17,242	8,809	8,433	371	201	170	33	20	13
	17	Itwan	9,468	4,790	4,678	9,158	4,619	4,539	302	165	137	8	6	2
	18	Pahari	30,897	15,541	15,356	30,208	15,189	15,019	685	348	337	4	4	..
	19	Girwan	28,807	14,464	14,343	27,352	13,723	13,629	1,448	737	711	7	4	3
	20	Kamasin	33,017	16,731	16,286	31,935	16,186	15,749	1,080	544	536	2	1	1
		Hamirpur	*465,223*	*234,842*	*230,381*	*434,024*	*219,756*	*214,268*	*30,455*	*14,777*	*15,678*	*744*	*309*	*435*
Hamirpur.	1	Ajnar	26,243	13,174	13,069	25,653	12,872	12,781	514	263	251	76	39	37
	2	Bewar	26,486	13,450	13,036	24,120	12,315	11,805	2,365	1,134	1,231	1	1	..

District	No.	Thana											
Hamirpur.	3	Hamirpur	7,833	4,143	3,690	6,159	3,279	2,880	1,559	802	757	115	62	53
	4	Jalalpur	21,157	10,780	10,377	20,163	10,289	9,874	990	487	503	4	4	..
	5	Jariya	28,987	14,616	14,371	27,874	14,041	13,833	1,112	574	538	1	1	..
	6	Kashipur	22,918	11,503	11,415	22,055	11,060	10,995	854	437	417	9	6	3
	7	Kulpahar	21,025	10,546	10,479	19,556	9,864	9,692	1,372	662	710	97	20	77
	8	Kabrai	18,644	9,588	9,056	18,083	9,307	8,776	561	281	280	..	..	..
	9	Kurara	21,442	11,076	10,366	20,814	10,749	10,065	628	327	301	..	..	..
	10	Lalpura	22,751	11,613	11,138	21,677	11,091	10,586	1,059	514	545	15	8	7
	11	Mahoba	32,410	16,308	16,102	28,450	14,435	14,015	3,730	1,817	1,913	230	56	174
	12	Maudaha	31,175	15,527	15,648	25,962	13,143	12,819	5,190	2,374	2,816	23	10	13
	13	Muskara	31,482	15,838	15,644	29,914	15,057	14,857	1,532	765	767	36	16	20
	14	Majhgawan	34,776	17,357	17,419	33,186	16,595	16,591	1,587	759	828	3	3	..
	15	Panwari	27,254	13,687	13,567	25,523	12,856	12,667	1,730	830	900	1	1	..
	16	Rath	37,614	18,591	19,023	33,746	16,773	16,973	3,782	1,771	2,011	86	47	39
	17	Sumerpur	29,570	15,208	14,362	28,211	14,499	13,712	1,314	675	639	45	34	11
	18	Srinagar	23,456	11,837	11,619	22,878	11,531	11,347	576	305	271	2	1	1
		Allahabad	*1,461,136*	*744,382*	*722,754*	*1,260,092*	*638,541*	*621,551*	*197,621*	*100,082*	*97,539*	*9,423*	*5,759*	*3,664*
Allahabad.	1	Barah	32,926	16,537	16,389	32,008	16,039	15,969	915	497	418	3	1	2
	2	Cannington	10,093	6,235	3,858	6,752	4,311	2,441	1,451	1,011	440	1,890	913	977
	3	Cantonment	11,213	7,237	3,976	6,879	4,077	2,802	1,686	1,089	597	2,648	2,071	577
	4	Colonelganj	34,767	19,408	15,359	24,193	13,427	10,766	8,341	4,768	3,573	2,233	1,213	1,020
	5	Daraganj	13,560	7,474	6,086	11,603	6,437	5,166	1,930	1,024	906	27	13	14
	6	Dando	19,514	9,971	9,543	19,026	9,683	9,343	483	285	198	5	3	2
	7	Ghurpur	34,337	17,153	17,184	30,018	15,040	14,978	4,298	2,100	2,198	21	13	8
	8	Handia	79,125	39,418	39,707	71,917	36,011	35,906	7,196	3,397	3,799	12	10	2
	9	Kotwali	97,566	52,303	45,263	60,893	32,932	27,961	35,280	18,582	16,698	1,393	789	604
	10	Kydganj	10,398	6,021	4,377	7,520	4,349	3,171	2,713	1,551	1,162	165	121	44
	11	Kokhraj	66,789	33,644	33,145	56,961	28,847	28,114	9,778	4,766	5,012	50	31	19
	12	Kuraon	48,003	23,960	24,043	46,246	23,083	23,163	1,757	877	880	..	..	..
	13	Khiri	19,781	9,999	9,782	19,232	9,720	9,512	548	278	270	1	1	..
	14	Karchhana	73,061	36,689	36,372	69,417	34,852	34,565	3,636	1,832	1,804	8	5	3
	15	Manjhanpur	63,951	32,374	31,577	54,873	27,935	26,938	9,062	4,428	4,634	16	11	5
	16	Meja	62,007	30,550	31,457	58,189	28,620	29,569	3,635	1,847	1,788	183	83	100
	17	Manda	39,747	19,657	20,090	36,333	17,915	18,418	3,409	1,739	1,670	5	3	2
	18	Muthiganj	19,545	11,381	8,164	15,221	8,841	6,380	3,874	2,231	1,643	450	309	141
	19	Nawabganj	74,324	36,267	38,057	65,564	32,019	33,545	8,760	4,248	4,512	..	..	..
	20	Pura Mufti	53,527	26,223	27,304	42,319	20,880	21,439	11,199	5,340	5,859	9	3	6
	21	Pachim Sarira	77,436	39,647	37,789	71,150	36,492	34,658	6,239	3,132	3,107	47	23	24
	22	Mau Aima	68,925	33,603	35,322	56,929	27,823	29,106	11,996	5,780	6,216	..	..	..
	23	Phulpur	76,274	38,319	37,955	66,323	33,393	32,930	9,942	4,919	5,023	9	7	2
	24	Raniganj*	13,751	6,632	7,119	11,281	5,430	5,851	2,470	1,202	1,268	..	..	..
	25	Sarai Memrez	70,833	35,307	35,526	65,396	32,590	32,806	5,436	2,716	2,720	1	1	..
	26	Sarai Akil	76,469	37,922	38,547	65,205	32,407	32,798	11,180	5,474	5,706	84	41	43
	27	Saini	64,351	32,615	31,736	52,055	26,628	25,427	12,236	5,955	6,281	60	32	28
	28	Soraon	66,172	32,749	33,423	61,154	30,280	30,874	4,999	2,458	2,541	19	11	8
	29	Sarai Inayat	71,920	36,368	35,552	60,011	30,478	29,533	11,858	5,860	5,998	51	30	21
	30	Shankargarh	16,771	8,719	8,052	15,424	8,002	7,422	1,314	696	618	33	21	12
		Jhansi	*680,688*	*350,192*	*330,496*	*629,671*	*322,423*	*307,248*	*34,169*	*18,166*	*16,003*	*16,848*	*9,603*	*7,245*
Jhansi.	1	Babina	23,784	12,466	11,318	23,089	12,055	11,034	297	184	113	398	227	171
	2	Baragaon	17,397	8,696	8,701	17,090	8,531	8,559	293	159	134	14	6	8
	3	Barwa Sagar	19,657	10,069	9,588	18,926	9,680	9,246	460	246	214	271	143	128
	4	Baghera	14,842	7,619	7,223	14,397	7,372	7,025	320	180	140	125	67	58
	5	Birdha	16,655	8,462	8,193	15,945	8,100	7,845	383	191	192	327	171	156
	6	Bansi	10,240	5,239	5,001	9,948	5,085	4,863	86	48	38	206	106	100
	7	Banpur	19,036	9,683	9,353	17,955	9,143	8,812	349	159	190	732	381	351
	8	Bar	31,329	16,025	15,304	30,022	15,560	14,662	289	150	139	1,018	515	503
	9	Chirgaon	21,938	11,225	10,713	21,168	10,799	10,369	692	378	314	78	48	30
	10	Dudhai	10,445	5,388	5,057	9,941	5,112	4,829	267	149	118	237	127	110

* Thana Raniganj situated in Partabgarh district.

Population of the Police Circles Distributed by Religion.

Name of district.	Serial number of Thana.	Name of thana.	Population. Total.	Population. Males.	Population. Females.	Hindus. Total.	Hindus. Males.	Hindus. Females.	Muhammadans. Total.	Muhammadans. Males.	Muhammadans. Females.	Others. Total	Others. Males.	Others. Females.
1	2	3	4	5	6	7	8	9	10	11	12	13	14	15
Jhansi—(concluded).	11	Ghat Lahchura	17,586	8,733	8,853	17,064	8,456	8,608	517	275	242	5	2	3
	12	Garautha	18,882	9,574	9,308	17,994	9,137	8,857	885	436	449	3	1	2
	13	Gursarai	15,164	7,607	7,557	14,289	7,168	7,121	730	372	358	145	67	78
	14	Girar	8,868	4,564	4,304	8,589	4,423	4,166	36	18	18	243	123	120
	15	Irichh	14,915	7,644	7,271	14,031	7,194	6,837	863	441	422	21	9	12
	16	Jakhlaun	11,650	5,993	5,657	11,206	5,768	5,438	245	123	122	199	102	97
	17	Jakhaura	19,277	9,924	9,353	18,339	9,446	8,893	202	113	89	736	365	371
	18	Kotwali	44,835	22,849	21,986	34,972	17,842	17,130	8,719	4,372	4,347	1,144	635	509
	19	Katera	15,568	8,042	7,526	14,905	7,690	7,215	374	197	177	289	155	134
	20	Kakarwai	11,424	5,871	5,553	11,005	5,668	5,337	393	193	200	26	10	16
	21	Kailwara	10,243	5,272	4,971	9,866	5,075	4,791	106	56	50	271	141	130
	22	Lalitpur	37,900	19,350	18,550	33,257	16,971	16,286	2,157	1,113	1,044	2,486	1,266	1,220
	23	Moth	19,951	10,073	9,878	19,296	9,720	9,576	620	336	284	35	17	18
	24	Mau	45,922	23,186	22,736	42,792	21,590	21,202	2,400	1,201	1,199	730	395	335
	25	Mahroni	20,897	10,626	10,271	19,601	9,977	9,624	523	265	258	773	384	389
	26	Maraura	18,551	9,452	9,099	17,393	8,819	8,574	272	153	119	886	480	406
	27	New Jhansi	30,912	16,558	14,354	23,301	12,461	10,840	6,245	3,386	2,859	1,366	711	655
	28	Nathi Khera	13,975	7,170	6,805	13,667	7,005	6,662	62	32	30	246	133	113
	29	Narhat	16,121	8,238	7,883	15,196	7,737	7,459	443	237	206	482	264	218
	30	Pandwaha	18,297	9,257	9,040	17,735	8,963	8,772	542	281	261	20	13	7
	31	Raksa	15,261	8,069	7,192	15,066	7,939	7,127	175	119	56	20	11	9
	32	Sadr Bazar	11,972	8,180	3,792	6,402	4,097	2,305	3,181	2,051	1,130	2,389	2,032	357
	33	Sojhna	12,521	6,393	6,128	11,961	6,103	5,858	15	8	7	545	282	263
	34	Talbehat	24,128	12,339	11,789	23,441	11,978	11,463	377	199	178	310	162	148
	35	Uldan	20,545	10,356	10,189	19,822	9,959	9,863	651	345	306	72	52	20
		Jalaun ..	*404,775*	*209,525*	*195,250*	*376,150*	*195,141*	*181,609*	*27,408*	*14,040*	*13,368*	*617*	*344*	*273*
Jalaun.	1	Ata	21,984	11,304	10,680	20,826	10,690	10,136	1,153	609	544	5	5	..
	2	Ait	28,960	14,686	14,274	27,315	13,844	13,471	1,573	803	770	72	39	33
	3	Churkhi	27,436	14,286	13,150	26,664	13,879	12,785	748	393	355	24	14	10
	4	Dakor	16,942	8,653	8,289	15,736	8,061	7,675	1,184	579	605	22	13	9
	5	*Gopalpur* (1)	5,829	3,018	2,811	5,584	2,896	2,688	240	119	121	5	3	2
	6	Jagamanpura (1)	14,655	7,811	6,844	14,119	7,538	6,581	536	273	263	..	..	..
	7	Jalaun	47,988	24,608	23,380	44,987	23,072	21,915	2,966	1,517	1,449	35	19	16
	8	Kalpi	28,812	14,690	14,122	23,977	12,266	11,711	4,755	2,372	2,383	80	52	28
	9	Kailya	18,721	9,588	9,133	18,132	9,278	8,854	548	289	259	41	21	20
	10	Kunch	42,906	22,020	20,886	38,417	19,695	18,722	4,450	2,304	2,146	39	21	18
	11	Kuthaund	43,339	22,800	20,539	40,624	21,390	19,234	2,700	1,402	1,298	15	8	7
	12	Madhogarh	40,562	21,134	19,428	38,789	20,318	18,471	1,551	802	749	22	14	8
	13	Orai	29,530	15,257	14,273	25,737	13,319	12,418	3,546	1,808	1,738	247	130	117
	14	Rendhar	22,798	11,886	10,912	21,991	11,469	10,522	804	415	389	3	2	1
	15	Rampura (1)	14,513	7,784	6,729	13,852	7,426	6,426	654	355	299	7	3	4
		Benares Division ..	*4,809,478*	*2,402,245*	*2,407,233*	*4,404,920*	*2,201,750*	*2,203,170*	*395,898*	*195,982*	*199,916*	*8,660*	*4,513*	*4,147*
		Benares ..	*897,035*	*452,067*	*444,968*	*796,925*	*400,773*	*396,152*	*96,857*	*49,516*	*47,341*	*3,253*	*1,778*	*1,475*

Benares.	1	Adampur ..	22,423	11,317	11,106	13,545	6,906	6,639	8,816	4,382	4,434	62	29	33
	2	Alinagar ..	33,997	17,650	16,347	29,790	15,453	14,337	3,943	2,060	1,883	264	137	127
	3	Baragaon ..	62,418	31,138	31,280	59,469	29,634	29,835	2,934	1,496	1,438	15	8	7
	4	Bhelupura ..	42,745	21,570	21,175	36,160	18,242	17,918	6,460	3,251	3,209	125	77	48
	5	Ballua ..	44,258	21,347	22,911	40,542	19,664	20,878	3,689	1,672	2,017	27	11	16
	6	Chetganj ..	20,985	10,835	10,150	14,886	7,637	7,249	5,946	3,117	2,829	153	81	72
	7	Chowk ..	24,683	12,955	11,728	19,464	10,272	9,192	4,990	2,544	2,446	229	139	90
	8	Cholapur ..	88,683	43,853	44,830	86,299	42,692	43,607	2,359	1,147	1,212	25	14	11
	9	Chandauli ..	46,113	23,256	22,857	42,803	21,598	21,205	3,308	1,656	1,652	2	2	..
	10	Cantonment	7,287	4,377	2,910	5,036	2,772	2,264	1,465	1,000	465	786	605	181
	11	Dasasumedh	45,000	22,510	22,490	35,714	17,854	17,860	8,833	4,574	4,259	453	82	371
	12	Jaitpur ..	22,869	11,673	11,196	7,923	4,072	3,851	14,682	7,473	7,209	264	128	136
	13	Kotwali ..	32,430	16,877	15,553	28,526	14,813	13,713	3,782	1,990	1,792	122	74	48
	14	Mirza Murad	74,573	37,181	37,392	71,448	35,643	35,805	3,123	1,537	1,586	2	1	1
	15	Phulpur ..	63,253	31,478	31,775	59,779	29,711	30,068	3,251	1,652	1,599	223	115	108
	16	Ramnagar ..	28,019	14,202	13,817	23,747	12,114	11,633	4,253	2,077	2,176	19	11	8
	17	Rohnia ..	63,522	31,608	31,914	59,320	29,435	29,885	4,160	2,149	2,011	42	24	18
	18	Sikraul ..	82,236	42,876	39,360	76,178	39,465	36,713	5,635	3,181	2,454	423	230	193
	19	Said Raja ..	50,363	24,986	25,377	47,024	23,348	23,676	3,332	1,636	1,696	7	2	5
	20	Sakaldiha ..	41,178	20,378	20,800	39,272	19,448	19,824	1,896	922	974	10	8	2
		Mirzapur ..	*1,071,046*	*530,214*	*540,832*	*1,001,022*	*494,931*	*506,091*	*68,507*	*34,541*	*33,966*	*1,517*	*742*	*775*
Mirzapur.	1	Ahraura ..	33,433	16,685	16,748	30,786	15,358	15,428	2,566	1,286	1,280	81	41	40
	2	Aurai ..	66,829	32,796	34,033	60,266	29,476	30,790	6,548	3,313	3,235	15	7	8
	3	Bindhachal..	63,508	30,465	33,043	59,008	28,251	30,757	4,474	2,201	2,273	26	13	13
	4	Bhadohi ..	73,510	36,426	37,084	66,063	32,628	33,435	7,430	3,791	3,639	17	7	10
	5	Chunar ..	68,346	33,738	34,608	62,480	30,908	31,572	5,547	2,686	2,861	319	144	175
	6	Chopan ..	32,212	16,153	16,059	31,735	15,909	15,826	477	244	233	..	..	..
	7	Chakia ..	70,383	35,342	35,041	65,024	32,613	32,411	5,354	2,725	2,629	5	4	1
	8	Dudhi ..	44,617	22,313	22,304	43,482	21,701	21,781	1,001	536	465	134	76	58
	9	Ghorawal ..	30,913	15,393	15,520	30,055	14,973	15,082	858	420	438	..	..	..
	10	Gopiganj ..	98,652	48,562	50,090	93,146	45,754	47,392	5,438	2,776	2,662	68	32	36
	11	Hallia ..	37,989	19,141	18,848	36,115	18,147	17,968	1,874	994	880	..	..	..
	12	Kotwali ..	66,619	33,549	33,070	68,013	28,988	29,025	8,127	4,310	3,817	479	251	228
	13	Khairwa ..	35,966	18,084	17,882	34,643	17,418	17,225	1,313	660	653	10	6	4
	14	Kon ..	14,123	7,011	7,112	13,287	6,593	6,694	836	418	418	..	..	..
	15	Kachwa ..	46,029	22,117	23,912	44,256	21,254	23,002	1,494	748	746	279	115	164
	16	Lalganj ..	30,413	15,478	14,935	29,378	14,913	14,465	1,034	564	470	1	1	..
	17	Marihan ..	24,090	12,134	11,956	23,455	11,799	11,656	633	333	300	2	2	..
	18	Mirzapur Khurd	56,065	27,443	28,622	51,344	25,162	26,182	4,648	2,241	2,407	73	40	33
	19	Pandri ..	29,117	14,540	14,577	28,055	14,011	14,044	1,054	526	528	8	3	5
	20	Pannuganj	35,559	17,383	18,176	34,371	16,809	17,562	1,188	574	614	..	..	..
	21	Robertsganj	49,281	24,004	25,277	46,261	22,574	23,687	3,020	1,430	1,590	..	..	..
	22	Suriawan ..	63,392	31,457	31,935	59,799	29,692	30,107	3,593	1,765	1,828	..	..	..
		Jaunpur ..	*1,156,254*	*576,070*	*580,184*	*1,053,003*	*524,876*	*528,127*	*101,296*	*50,195*	*51,101*	*1,955*	*999*	*956*
Jaunpur.	1	Bakhsha ..	69,064	34,973	34,091	65,303	33,094	32,209	3,734	1,862	1,872	27	17	10
	2	Badlapur ..	92,929	46,711	46,218	87,757	44,129	43,628	5,129	2,557	2,572	43	25	18
	3	Badshahpur	56,433	28,399	28,034	53,364	26,826	26,538	3,068	1,572	1,496	1	1	..
	4	Bamniaon ..	68,505	34,045	34,460	64,753	32,132	32,621	3,749	1,910	1,839	3	3	..
	5	Chandwak ..	51,153	25,475	25,678	47,299	23,586	23,713	3,744	1,828	1,916	110	61	49
	6	Jaunpur ..	82,124	41,649	40,475	62,246	31,669	30,577	19,512	9,802	9,710	366	178	188
	7	Jalalpur ..	69,913	34,540	35,373	67,050	33,155	33,895	2,839	1,368	1,471	24	17	7
	8	Kirakat ..	117,259	58,057	59,202	110,151	54,572	55,579	5,822	2,843	2,979	1,286	642	644
	9	Machhlishahr	78,109	38,852	39,257	71,156	35,460	35,696	6,908	3,366	3,542	45	26	19
	10	Mariahu ..	94,640	46,361	48,279	88,655	43,439	45,216	5,983	2,920	3,063	2	2	..
	11	Rampur ..	72,990	35,668	37,302	69,058	33,672	35,386	3,930	2,014	1,916	2	2	..

(1) These are semi-independent jagirs with their own police.

PROVINCIAL TABLE III.

Population of the Police Circles Distributed by Religion—(continued).

Number of district.	Serial number of thana.	Name of thana.	Population. Total.	Population. Males.	Population. Females.	Hindus. Total.	Hindus. Males.	Hindus. Females.	Muhammadans. Total.	Muhammadans. Males.	Muhammadans. Females.	Others. Total.	Others. Males.	Others. Females.
1	2	3	4	5	6	7	8	9	10	11	12	13	14	15
Jaunpur—(concluded).	12	Shahganj ..	60,960	30,214	30,746	47,994	23,857	24,137	12,949	6,347	6,602	17	10	7
	13	Sarai Khwaja	79,060	39,633	39,427	68,450	34,378	34,072	10,597	5,249	5,348	13	6	7
	14	Sarpataha ..	78,152	39,715	38,437	70,440	35,962	34,478	7,711	3,752	3,959	1	1	..
	15	Sujanganj ..	84,963	41,758	43,205	79,327	38,945	40,382	5,621	2,805	2,816	15	8	7
		Ghazipur ..	*839,725*	*420,200*	*419,525*	*762,435*	*383,730*	*378,705*	*76,561*	*36,090*	*40,471*	*729*	*380*	*349*
Ghazipur.	1	Birnoo ..	39,460	20,295	19,165	37,759	19,478	18,281	1,701	817	884	..	..	..
	2	Dildarnagar	46,425	22,251	24,174	36,457	17,8[illegible]8	18,629	9,835	4,362	5,473	133	61	72
	3	Dhanapur ..	45,876	22,518	23,358	42,927	21,084	21,843	2,949	1,434	1,515	..	..	..
	4	Gahmar ..	40,421	19,520	20,901	37,741	18,314	19,427	2,679	1,205	1,474	1	1	..
	5	Karimuddinpur	70,172	34,997	35,175	64,898	32,475	32,423	5,044	2,404	2,640	230	118	112
	6	Kotwali ..	71,933	37,057	34,876	59,968	31,205	28,763	11,721	5,720	6,001	244	132	112
	7	Murdah ..	34,444	17,733	16,711	32,961	16,979	15,982	1,481	752	729	2	2	..
	8	Muhammadabad	91,079	45,060	46,019	80,375	40,168	40,213	10,698	4,895	5,803	6	3	3
	9	Nandganj ..	58,081	28,351	29,730	53,717	26,277	27,440	4,328	2,050	2,278	36	24	12
	10	Kasimabad ..	63,231	32,443	30,788	57,408	29,561	27,847	5,823	2,882	2,941	..	..	..
	11	Shadiabad ..	86,753	44,382	42,371	82,375	42,201	40,174	4,362	2,175	2,187	16	6	10
	12	Saidpur ..	94,798	47,439	47,359	89,349	44,798	44,551	5,429	2,6[illegible]8	2,801	20	13	7
	13	Sadat ..	36,540	18,557	17,983	33,777	17,233	16,544	2,734	1,311	1,423	29	13	16
	14	Zamaniah ..	60,512	29,597	30,915	52,723	26,135	26,588	7,777	3,455	4,322	12	7	5
		Ballia ..	*845,418*	*423,694*	*421,724*	*791,535*	*397,440*	*394,095*	*52,677*	*25,640*	*27,037*	*1,206*	*614*	*592*
Ballia.	1	Ballia ..	106,466	52,246	54,220	98,154	48,091	50,063	8,117	4,057	4,060	195	98	97
	2	Bairia ..	83,908	41,524	42,384	81,710	40,436	41,274	2,191	1,083	1,108	7	5	2
	3	Bansdih ..	108,481	53,550	54,931	103,434	51,113	52,321	4,945	2,385	2,560	102	52	50
	4	Garwar ..	70,460	36,243	34,217	65,096	33,692	31,404	5,261	2,500	2,761	103	51	52
	5	Haldharpur	45,759	23,993	21,766	43,676	22,905	20,771	1,943	1,016	927	140	72	68
	6	Haldi ..	49,503	23,163	26,340	47,195	22,065	25,130	2,308	1,098	1,210	..	..	..
	7	Korantadih	57,822	28,396	29,426	55,307	27,161	28,146	2,501	1,226	1,275	14	9	5
	8	Nagra ..	66,405	34,608	31,797	62,997	32,845	30,152	3,408	1,763	1,645	..	..	..
	9	Reoti ..	54,275	26,512	27,763	52,473	25,621	26,852	1,801	890	911	1	1	..
	10	Rasra ..	58,061	30,582	27,479	52,190	27,781	24,409	5,236	2,480	2,756	655	321	314
	11	Sikandarpur	90,881	45,768	45,113	81,699	41,460	40,239	9,175	4,305	4,870	7	3	4
	12	Ubhaon ..	53,397	27,109	26,288	47,604	24,270	23,334	5,791	2,837	2,954	2	2	..
		Gorakhpur Division ..	*6,524,419*	*3,280,721*	*3,243,698*	*5,705,369*	*2,868,612*	*2,836,757*	*814,465*	*409,617*	*404,848*	*4,585*	*2,492*	*2,093*
		Gorakhpur ..	*3,201,180*	*1,604,635*	*1,596,545*	*2,875,402*	*1,440,546*	*1,434,856*	*322,946*	*162,535*	*160,411*	*2,832*	*1,554*	*1,278*
	1	Bansgaon ..	113,957	57,055	56,902	107,136	53,659	53,477	6,810	3,391	3,419	11	5	6
	2	Barhalganj ..	85,429	41,839	43,590	80,034	39,166	40,868	5,394	2,672	2,722	1	1	..
	3	Belghat ..	98,641	49,041	49,600	92,355	45,878	46,477	6,153	3,098	3,055	133	65	68
	4	Barhaj ..	69,677	34,772	34,905	65,286	32,502	32,784	4,368	2,252	2,116	23	18	5
	5	Barhi ..	80,698	39,797	40,901	77,716	38,271	39,445	2,962	1,510	1,452	20	16	4

District	No.	Tahsil												
Gorakhpur	6	Bishunpura	50,025	24,621	25,404	43,388	21,358	22,030	6,636	3,262	3,374	1	1	..
	7	Biraicha	65,910	33,160	32,750	58,253	29,285	28,968	7,655	3,873	3,782	2	2	..
	8	Chaura	84,793	42,848	41,945	80,762	40,805	39,957	3,992	2,027	1,965	39	16	23
	9	Deoria	115,942	62,578	53,364	107,430	58,047	49,383	8,429	4,471	3,958	83	60	23
	10	Gola	89,981	44,064	45,917	83,990	41,105	42,885	5,969	2,945	3,024	22	14	8
	11	Hata	148,183	74,451	73,732	135,669	68,154	67,515	12,514	6,297	6,217	..	..	..
	12	Kazipur	100,397	49,397	51,000	83,558	41,136	42,422	16,824	8,253	8,571	15	8	7
	13	Khampar	129,201	62,892	66,309	118,838	57,854	60,984	10,356	5,033	5,323	7	5	2
	14	Khajni	93,424	47,064	46,360	88,502	44,591	43,911	4,917	2,470	2,447	5	3	2
	15	Kotwali	152,334	79,238	73,096	125,795	65,385	60,410	24,735	12,880	11,855	1,804	973	831
	16	Kasia	104,847	52,374	52,473	88,470	44,035	44,435	16,364	8,327	8,037	13	12	1
	17	Kothibhar	120,880	60,440	60,440	105,607	52,804	52,803	15,269	7,632	7,637	4	4	..
	18	Musaila	99,047	49,635	49,412	93,421	46,739	46,682	5,621	2,883	2,738	5	3	2
	19	Maharajganj	103,690	52,632	51,058	91,213	45,449	45,764	14,476	7,182	7,294	1	1	..
	20	Mansurganj	69,568	35,047	34,521	61,923	31,200	30,723	7,640	3,843	3,797	5	4	1
	21	Nichlaul	52,531	26,503	26,028	46,344	23,245	23,099	6,178	3,253	2,925	9	5	4
	22	Paisia	57,082	29,113	27,969	49,831	25,402	24,429	7,251	3,711	3,540	..	..	..
	23	Panera	38,456	19,647	18,809	36,274	18,492	17,782	2,182	1,155	1,027	..	..	..
	24	Pipraich	107,127	54,325	52,802	98,828	50,097	48,731	8,286	4,217	4,069	13	11	2
	25	Padrauna	111,749	55,585	56,164	93,681	46,608	47,073	18,066	8,975	9,091	2	2	..
	26	Rigauli	86,327	43,104	43,223	81,823	40,817	41,006	4,486	2,277	2,209	18	10	8
	27	Ramkola	85,590	43,244	42,346	74,961	37,791	37,170	10,614	5,446	5,168	15	7	8
	28	Rudarpur	123,157	61,297	61,860	116,526	57,988	58,538	6,623	3,305	3,318	8	4	4
	29	Salempur	114,516	55,310	59,206	99,991	48,424	51,567	13,976	6,599	7,377	549	287	262
	30	Sahjanwa	81,588	41,071	40,517	76,957	38,717	38,240	4,626	2,350	2,276	5	4	1
	31	Semra	128,887	64,924	63,963	111,464	56,138	55,326	17,411	8,780	8,631	12	6	6
	32	Tairiya-Sujan	79,390	38,621	40,769	67,580	32,897	34,683	11,806	5,720	6,086	4	4	..
	33	Thuthibari	30,941	15,758	15,183	26,229	13,315	12,914	4,712	2,443	2,269	..	..	..
	34	Tarkulwa	125,215	63,198	62,017	105,567	53,192	52,375	19,645	10,003	9,642	3	3	..
		Basti	*1,830,421*	*926,286*	*904,135*	*1,525,385*	*771,991*	*753,394*	*304,676*	*154,063*	*150,613*	*360*	*232*	*128*
Basti	1	Chillia	106,532	53,487	53,045	82,370	41,311	41,059	24,158	12,172	11,986	4	4	..
	2	Basti	112,555	57,702	54,853	96,374	49,294	47,080	16,043	8,327	7,716	138	81	57
	3	Bansi	107,830	54,287	53,543	85,068	42,854	42,214	22,732	11,418	11,314	30	15	15
	4	Budhabandh	77,330	39,208	38,122	67,700	34,341	33,359	9,630	4,867	4,763	..	..	..
	5	Captainganj	83,998	42,235	41,763	78,283	39,379	38,904	5,705	2,850	2,855	10	6	4
	6	Chhaoni	81,829	41,419	40,410	76,775	38,822	37,953	5,054	2,597	2,457	..	..	..
	7	Dhebarua	71,008	36,308	34,700	50,452	25,763	24,689	20,546	10,539	10,007	10	6	4
	8	Domariaganj	84,997	42,848	42,149	55,350	28,092	27,258	29,647	14,756	14,891	..	..	..
	9	Dhanghata	77,935	39,359	38,576	70,983	35,834	35,149	6,952	3,525	3,427	..	..	..
	10	Dudhara	76,270	38,279	37,991	45,223	22,687	22,536	31,047	15,592	15,455	..	..	..
	11	Itwa	89,444	45,241	44,203	71,942	36,394	35,548	17,500	8,845	8,655	2	2	..
	12	Kalwari	78,238	39,404	38,834	69,585	35,134	34,451	8,652	4,269	4,383	1	1	..
	13	Khalilabad	81,004	41,328	39,676	70,643	35,921	34,722	10,303	5,369	4,934	58	38	20
	14	Lotan	55,996	28,250	27,746	47,607	23,922	23,685	8,388	4,327	4,061	1	1	..
	15	Mahuli	85,002	42,713	42,289	77,778	39,098	38,680	7,201	3,598	3,603	23	17	6
	16	Mehdawal	89,759	45,963	43,796	72,496	37,230	35,266	17,240	8,713	8,527	23	20	3
	17	Paikaulia	80,392	40,985	39,407	71,938	36,698	35,240	8,439	4,277	4,162	15	10	5
	18	Parasrampur	71,925	36,314	35,611	64,879	32,765	32,114	7,041	3,546	3,495	5	3	2
	19	Rudhauli	67,620	34,257	33,363	56,910	28,827	28,083	10,707	5,427	5,280	3	3	..
	20	Sonhan	94,708	47,732	46,976	81,738	41,256	40,482	12,949	6,462	6,487	21	14	7
	21	Tilokpur	73,020	37,012	36,008	57,038	28,862	28,176	15,978	8,146	7,832	4	4	..
	22	Uska	83,029	41,955	41,074	74,253	37,507	36,746	8,764	4,441	4,323	12	7	5
		Azamgarh	*1,492,818*	*749,800*	*743,018*	*1,304,582*	*656,075*	*648,507*	*186,843*	*93,019*	*93,824*	*1,393*	*706*	*687*
Azamgarh	1	Atraulia	81,618	41,197	40,421	75,768	38,187	37,581	5,820	2,995	2,825	30	15	15
	2	Azamgarh	62,565	31,807	30,758	54,749	27,795	26,954	7,610	3,904	3,706	206	108	98
	3	Ahraula	92,255	46,472	45,783	80,532	40,671	39,861	11,719	5,798	5,921	4	3	1
	4	Barda	58,272	28,843	29,429	51,580	25,560	26,020	6,691	3,282	3,409	1	1	..
	5	Chiriakote	84,916	43,256	41,660	79,857	40,706	39,151	4,881	2,470	2,411	178	80	98

PROVINCIAL TABLE III.

Population of the Police Circles Distributed by Religion—(*continued*).

Name of district.	Serial number of thana.	Name of thana.	Population. Total.	Population. Males.	Population. Females.	Hindus. Total.	Hindus. Males.	Hindus. Females.	Muhammadans. Total.	Muhammadans. Males.	Muhammadans. Females.	Others. Total.	Others. Males.	Others. Females.
1	2	3	4	5	6	7	8	9	10	11	12	13	14	15
Azamgarh—(*concluded*).	6	Deogaon ..	62,552	30,955	31,597	56,333	27,968	28,365	6,028	2,898	3,130	191	89	102
	7	Dohri ..	76,818	38,100	38,718	73,104	36,273	36,831	3,405	1,680	1,725	309	147	162
	8	Didarganj ..	79,465	39,257	40,208	62,050	30,770	31,280	17,386	8,469	8,917	29	18	11
	9	Ghosi ..	75,010	38,262	36,748	65,492	33,490	32,002	9,496	4,759	4,737	22	13	9
	10	Gambhirpur ..	63,057	31,205	31,852	53,373	26,400	26,973	9,682	4,803	4,879	2	2	..
	11	Kandhrapur ..	66,729	33,484	33,245	59,090	29,578	29,512	7,623	3,896	3,727	16	10	6
	12	Madhuban ..	81,027	40,581	40,446	73,128	36,674	36,454	7,883	3,899	3,984	16	8	8
	13	Maharajganj ..	78,686	39,663	39,023	74,227	37,336	36,891	4,440	2,322	2,118	19	5	14
	14	Muhammadabad ..	86,266	43,754	42,512	73,164	37,194	35,970	13,010	6,509	6,501	92	51	41
	15	Mau ..	92,989	47,246	45,743	76,239	38,924	37,315	16,702	8,295	8,407	48	27	21
	16	Mubarakpur ..	82,874	41,104	41,770	58,610	29,036	29,574	24,244	12,056	12,188	20	12	8
	17	Nizamabad ..	85,049	42,550	42,499	69,698	34,999	34,699	15,304	7,524	7,780	47	27	20
	18	Pawai ..	54,304	27,373	26,931	47,663	24,109	23,554	6,641	3,264	3,377	..	..	..
	19	Raunapar ..	57,288	28,847	28,441	52,426	26,322	26,104	4,836	2,509	2,327	26	16	10
	20	Tarwa ..	71,076	35,844	35,234	67,499	34,083	33,416	3,442	1,687	1,755	137	74	63
		Kumaun Division ..	*1,328,790*	*685,209*	*643,581*	*1,241,244*	*634,293*	*606,951*	*79,043*	*45,980*	*33,063*	*8,503*	*4,936*	*3,567*
		Naini Tal ..	*323,519*	*182,875*	*140,644*	*247,545*	*139,356*	*108,189*	*71,883*	*41,238*	*30,645*	*4,091*	*2,281*	*1,810*
Naini Tal.	1	Baspur ..	20,791	11,629	9,162	10,055	5,632	4,423	10,660	5,953	4,707	76	44	32
	2	Bisjula ..	1,910	1,008	902	1,909	1,007	902	1	1	..	..	..	..
	3	Chaugarh ..	3,629	1,969	1,660	3,629	1,969	1,660	..	..	..	..	..	..
	4	Chaubhansi ..	521	263	258	521	263	258	..	..	..	..	..	..
	5	Dhaniakot ..	2,424	1,440	984	2,366	1,387	979	52	47	5	6	6	..
	6	Gadarpur ..	13,319	7,652	5,667	6,120	3,537	2,583	7,147	4,080	3,067	52	35	17
	7	Haldwani ..	48,591	27,554	21,037	42,540	23,785	18,755	5,491	3,474	2,017	560	295	265
	8	Jaspur ..	21,240	11,661	9,579	13,816	7,569	6,247	6,907	3,800	3,107	517	292	225
	9	Kichha ..	21,899	12,307	9,592	12,016	6,863	5,153	9,795	5,385	4,410	88	59	29
	10	Kashipur ..	40,268	21,420	18,848	24,348	12,919	11,4:9	15,668	8,366	7,302	252	135	117
	11	Khatima ..	30,162	16,684	13,478	28,533	15,512	13,021	1,599	1,154	445	30	18	12
	12	Ramnagar ..	36,753	21,288	15,465	32,094	18,376	13,718	4,218	2,656	1,562	441	256	185
	13	Simalkha ..	507	229	278	502	225	277	5	4	1	..	..	..
	14	Sitarganj ..	24,963	13,879	11,084	17,913	9,950	7,963	7,041	3,922	3,119	9	7	2
	15	Tanakpur ..	6,902	4,006	2,896	5,839	3,327	2,512	913	606	307	150	73	77
	16	Uchakot ..	2,489	1,292	1,197	2,489	1,292	1,197	..	..	..	..	..	..
	17	Purbiagar ..	2,102	1,115	987	2,097	1,112	985	5	3	2	..	..	..
	18	Paschimiagar ..	646	342	304	646	342	304	..	..	..	..	..	..
	19	Ramgarh Malla ..	803	548	255	730	503	227	45	30	15	28	15	13
	20	Ramgarh Talla ..	118	65	53	118	65	53	..	..	..	..	..	..
	21	Kota Malla ..	2,619	1,634	985	2,578	1,612	966	2	2	..	39	20	19
	22	Kota Talla ..	2,650	1,405	1,245	2,642	1,398	1,244	1	1	..	7	6	1
	23	Malli Rao ..	931	411	520	931	411	520	..	..	..	..	..	..
	24	Mhruri Bichali ..	1,601	1,182	419	1,525	1,127	398	35	29	6	41	26	15
	25	Mhruri Talli ..	528	358	170	482	334	148	33	19	14	13	5	8
	26	Purbi Chhakata ..	4,163	2,312	1,851	4,155	2,305	1,850	6	6	..	2	1	1
	27	Paschimi Chhakata ..	8,333	5,471	2,862	7,277	4,722	2,555	845	649	196	211	100	111
	28	Kutauli Malli ..	1,062	519	543	1,059	516	543	3	3	..	..	..	..

29	Kutauli Talli	1,847	845	802	1,845	843	802	2	2	..	..	..	..
30	Bisaud Bichla	563	274	289	563	274	289	..	..	..	..	..	..
31	Bisaud Talla	526	299	227	510	284	226	1	1	..	15	14	1
32	Kosian Talla	1,329	688	641	1,316	678	638	..	..	..	13	10	3
33	Kosian Malla	1,038	544	494	1,025	535	490	13	9	4	..	..	..
34	Purbi Chauthan	1,650	796	854	1,650	796	854	..	..	..	..	..	..
35	Paschimi Chauthan	2,406	1,158	1,248	2,346	1,130	1,216	11	8	3	49	20	29
36	Naini Tal (Malli and Talli Tal)	12,436	8,628	3,808	9,560	6,756	2,804	1,384	1,028	356	1,492	844	648
	Almora ..	*525,104*	*266,516*	*258,588*	*518,166*	*262,267*	*255,899*	*3,546*	*2,142*	*1,404*	*3,392*	*2,107*	*1,285*
	Almora.												
1	Askot Malla	8,790	4,121	4,669	8,606	4,037	4,569	50	20	30	134	64	70
2	Askot Talla	9,526	4,820	4,706	9,496	4,805	4,691	10	7	3	20	8	12
3	Barbisi	7,551	3,835	3,716	7,511	3,811	3,700	13	6	7	27	18	9
4	Maili Athlusi Talli	6,722	3,443	3,279	6,705	3,433	3,272	3	2	1	14	8	6
5	Dindihat Athbisi Malli	5,122	2,605	2,517	5,110	2,600	2,510	12	5	7	..	..	..
6	Dharma Malla	364	175	189	350	165	185	..	..	..	14	10	4
7	Byans	72	31	41	70	29	41	..	..	..	2	2	..
8	Chaudans	3,282	1,531	1,751	3,270	1,527	1,748	..	..	..	12	4	8
9	Johar Talla Desh	8,897	4,422	4,475	8,884	4,414	4,470	7	4	3	6	4	2
10	Goriphat	6,165	3,111	3,054	6,165	3,111	3,054	..	..	..	..	..	..
11	Chalsi	5,762	2,949	2,813	5,762	2,949	2,813	..	..	..	..	..	..
12	Begruban	7,799	3,970	3,829	7,792	3,964	3,828	6	5	1	1	1	..
13	Sipti Farka	1,156	575	581	1,156	575	581	..	..	..	..	..	..
14	Talla Des	4,477	2,233	2,244	4,477	2,233	2,244	..	..	..	..	..	..
15	Palbilon Malla	4,094	2,226	1,868	4,086	2,221	1,865	3	3	..	5	2	3
16	Palbilon Talla	2,177	1,180	997	2,177	1,180	997	..	..	..	..	..	..
17	Gum Des	7,172	3,559	3,613	7,129	3,539	3,590	..	..	..	43	20	23
18	Talla Rao	1,914	992	922	1,913	991	922	1	1	..	..	..	..
19	Asi	914	471	443	914	471	443	..	..	..	..	..	..
20	Talla Charal	2,087	1,171	916	2,057	1,155	902	..	..	..	30	16	14
21	Khilpati Phat	3,519	1,788	1,731	3,519	1,788	1,731	..	..	..	..	..	..
22	Bisung Gonol	3,763	1,918	1,845	3,634	1,855	1,779	33	18	15	96	45	51
23	Mahar	6,256	3,012	3,244	5,780	2,826	2,954	158	77	81	318	109	209
24	Rawal	7,314	3,745	3,569	7,308	3,742	3,566	2	1	1	4	2	2
25	Talla Waldiya	5,942	3,001	2,941	5,938	3,000	2,938	4	1	3	..	..	..
26	Seti Talli and Malli	5,174	2,571	2,603	5,076	2,542	2,534	6	3	3	92	26	66
27	Khadait	5,682	2,916	2,766	5,639	2,895	2,744	13	6	7	30	15	15
28	Saun Naya Des	7,760	3,757	4,003	7,752	3,754	3,998	..	..	..	8	3	5
29	Ranikhet	5,781	4,423	1,358	3,310	2,464	846	1,050	735	315	1,421	1,224	197
30	Talla Silour	5,274	2,481	2,793	5,274	2,481	2,793	..	..	..	..	..	..
31	Malla Silour	6,176	3,065	3,111	6,100	3,031	3,069	58	28	30	18	6	12
32	Giwar Walla	7,132	3,695	3,437	7,101	3,680	3,421	17	7	10	14	8	6
33	Giwar Palla	8,112	4,339	3,773	8,090	4,327	3,763	16	10	6	6	2	4
34	Giwar Talla	8,021	3,908	4,113	7,984	3,892	4,092	33	14	19	4	2	2
35	Dora Malla	7,462	3,693	3,769	7,358	3,649	3,709	6	4	2	98	40	58
36	Dora Talla	6,610	3,185	3,425	6,610	3,185	3,425	..	..	..	..	..	..
37	Dora Bichla	9,659	4,790	4,869	9,656	4,789	4,867	3	1	2	..	..	..
38	Kakalsun Malla	7,349	3,524	3,825	7,336	3,512	3,824	13	12	1	..	..	..
39	Kakalsun Talla and Walla Naya	6,904	3,378	3,526	6,858	3,358	3,500	46	20	26	..	..	..
40	Naya Palla	5,910	2,924	2,986	5,910	2,924	2,986	..	..	..	..	..	..
41	Shalt Talla	8,721	4,513	4,208	8,660	4,455	4,205	61	58	3	..	..	..
42	Shalt Malla	7,802	3,754	4,048	7,783	3,745	4,038	19	9	10	..	..	..
43	Walla Salt and Palla Shalt	11,305	5,490	5,813	11,261	5,467	5,794	42	23	19	..	..	..
44	Talla Chaukot	8,828	4,312	4,516	8,827	4,312	4,515	1	..	1	..	..	..
45	Bichla Chaukot	9,500	4,634	4,866	9,500	4,634	4,866	..	..	..	..	..	..
46	Malla Chaukot	8,195	4,036	4,159	8,177	4,026	4,151	12	8	4	6	2	4
47	Dug	6,309	3,268	3,041	6,203	3,220	2,983	87	39	48	19	9	10
48	Danpur Talla	7,834	3,980	3,854	7,812	3,969	3,843	8	5	3	14	6	8
49	Danpur Bichla	4,611	2,336	2,275	4,611	2,336	2,275	..	..	..	..	..	..
50	Danpur Malla	6,774	3,353	3,421	6,773	3,352	3,421	1	1	..	..	..	..
51	Talla Katyur	5,935	3,038	2,897	5,865	3,001	2,864	57	30	27	13	7	6

PROVINCIAL TABLE III.

Population of the Police Circles Distributed by Religion—(*continued*).

Name of district.	Serial number of thana.	Name of thana.	Population. Total.	Population. Males.	Population. Females.	Hindus. Total.	Hindus. Males.	Hindus. Females.	Muhammadans. Total.	Muhammadans. Males.	Muhammadans. Females.	Others. Total.	Others. Males.	Others. Females.
1	2	3	4	5	6	7	8	9	10	11	12	13	14	15
Almora—(*concluded*).	52	Nakuri	5,422	2,738	2,684	5,418	2,735	2,683	..	..	..	4	3	1
	53	Bichla Katyur	7,544	3,883	3,661	7,453	3,827	3,626	65	38	27	26	18	8
	54	Malla Katyur	9,709	5,024	4,685	9,565	4,938	4,627	53	34	19	91	52	39
	55	Chaugaon	4,205	2,141	2,064	4,183	2,122	2,061	22	19	3	..	..	..
	56	Kandarkua	3,014	1,473	1,541	3,010	1,470	1,540	3	2	1	1	1	..
	57	Malli Doti	5,706	2,787	2,919	5,671	2,769	2,902	35	18	17	..	..	..
	58	Talla Lakhanpur	4,818	2,456	2,362	4,808	2,449	2,359	5	4	1	5	3	2
	59	Darun	6,269	3,225	3,044	6,269	3,225	3,044	..	..	..	..	..	..
	60	Rangor	8,994	4,738	4,256	8,993	4,737	4,256	..	..	..	1	1	..
	61	Rithagarh	6,107	3,148	2,959	6,095	3,141	2,954	7	4	3	5	3	2
	62	Salam Talla	5,900	2,951	2,949	5,900	2,951	2,949	..	..	..	..	..	..
	63	Salam Malla	5,631	2,853	2,778	5,631	2,853	2,778	..	..	..	..	..	..
	64	Lakhanpur Malla	5,853	2,966	2,887	5,849	2,963	2,886	4	3	1	..	..	..
	65	Kharai	4,129	2,096	2,033	4,113	2,088	2,025	16	8	8	..	..	..
	66	Almora	10,560	6,540	4,020	9,232	5,831	3,401	961	561	400	367	148	219
	67	Athaguli Walla	5,467	2,584	2,883	5,455	2,581	2,874	12	3	9	..	..	..
	68	Athaguli Palla	4,572	2,228	2,344	4,572	2,228	2,344	..	..	..	..	..	..
	69	Rioni Dwar Sown	5,786	2,853	2,933	5,743	2,827	2,916	41	25	16	2	1	1
	70	Borarau Palla	7,459	3,800	3,659	7,414	3,776	3,638	36	18	18	9	6	3
	71	Borarau Walla	6,149	3,147	3,002	6,033	3,089	2,944	96	49	47	20	9	11
	72	Kairarau	5,079	2,503	2,576	5,057	2,491	2,566	16	8	8	6	4	2
	73	Bisaud	1,932	959	973	1,930	958	972	2	1	1	..	..	..
	74	Syunara Malla	6,315	3,129	3,186	6,289	3,113	3,176	25	15	10	1	1	..
	75	Syunara Talla	6,248	3,118	3,130	6,226	3,109	3,117	18	7	11	4	2	2
	76	Tikhun Malla	5,216	2,501	2,715	5,196	2,490	2,706	20	11	9	..	..	..
	77	Tikhun Talla	5,586	2,724	2,862	5,584	2,722	2,862	1	1	..	1	1	..
	78	Uchyur	4,825	2,382	2,443	4,817	2,377	2,440	1	1	..	7	4	3
	79	Khasparja	7,752	3,960	3,792	7,454	3,805	3,649	78	49	29	220	106	114
	80	Kamsyr Walla	5,033	2,601	2,432	5,003	2,587	2,416	30	14	16	..	..	..
	81	Kamsyr Palla	5,447	2,778	2,669	5,430	2,767	2,663	17	11	6	..	..	..
	82	Bherang	5,412	2,752	2,660	5,408	2,750	2,658	..	..	..	4	2	2
	83	Bel	6,603	3,434	3,169	6,603	3,434	3,169	..	..	..	..	..	..
	84	Baraon Talla	6,294	3,231	3,063	6,246	3,206	3,040	21	11	10	27	14	13
	85	Baraon Malla	5,402	2,829	2,573	5,236	2,735	2,501	63	40	23	103	54	49
	86	Athigaun Palla	5,588	2,908	2,680	5,562	2,894	2,668	7	3	4	19	11	8
	87	Athigaun Walla	4,659	2,428	2,231	4,625	2,409	2,216	34	19	15	..	..	..
	88	Pungraon	4,764	2,401	2,363	4,759	2,399	2,359	6	2	4	..	..	..
		Garhwal ..	*480,167*	*235,818*	*244,349*	*475,533*	*232,670*	*242,863*	*3,674*	*2,600*	*1,014*	*1,020*	*548*	*472*
	1	Paidulsyun Nandalsyun	10,942	5,254	5,688	10,503	5,024	5,479	127	78	49	312	152	160
	2	Kandwalsyun	4,596	2,116	2,481	4,574	2,095	2,479	22	20	2	..	..	..
	3	Patwalyun Gagwarsyun	6,818	3,274	3,544	6,792	3,262	3,530	26	12	14	..	..	..
	4	Manyarsyun East	2,978	1,509	1,469	2,955	1,495	1,460	7	7	..	16	7	9
	5	Maniayarsyun West	4,174	1,975	2,199	4,174	1,975	2,199	..	..	..	..	..	..
	6	Idwalsyun	5,268	2,466	2,802	5,268	2,466	2,802	..	..	..	..	..	..
	7	Sitonsyun	5,783	2,723	3,060	5,783	2,723	3,060	..	..	..	..	..	..
	8	Kapalsyun Khetsyun	7,317	3,418	4,104	7,489	3,400	4,089	..	..	..	33	13	20

PROVINCIAL TABLE III.

District	No.	Pargana																	
Garhwal	9	Banelsyun ..	..	..	..	3,301	1,600	1,701	3,301	1,600	1,701	..	..	..	..	..	..		
	10	Bangarsyun Rawatsyun		..	..	5,083	2,404	2,679	5,083	2,404	2,679	..	..	..	..	..	..		
	11	Aswalsyun ..	..	..	..	7,281	3,241	4,040	7,267	3,234	4,033	14	7	7	..	..	..		
	12	Badalpur Bichla	..	..	..	5,596	2,669	2,927	5,596	2,669	2,927	..	..	..	..	..	..		
	13	Badalpur Talla	..	..	..	5,916	2,898	3,018	5,916	2,898	3,018	..	..	..	..	..	..		
	14	Chandpur Malla	..	..	..	8,053	3,925	4,128	7,994	3,896	4,098	59	29	30	..	..	..		
	15	Chandpur Bichla	..	..	..	5,856	2,822	3,034	5,827	2,811	3,016	25	7	16	6	4	2		
	16	Chandpur Talla	..	..	..	4,751	2,246	2,505	4,664	2,208	2,456	87	38	49	..	..	..		
	17	Khansar ..	..	..	..	4,724	2,310	2,414	4,716	2,306	2,410	8	4	4	..	..	..		
	18	Chauthan ..	..	..	..	5,532	2,682	2,650	5,318	2,674	2,644	5	3	2	9	5	4		
	19	Sirgurkarakot	..	..	..	6,430	3,140	3,290	6,430	3,140	3,290	..	..	..	..	..	..		
	20	Dhaijyuli ..	..	..	..	5,211	2,498	2,713	5,201	2,492	2,709	..	..	..	10	6	4		
	21	Lohba ..	..	..	..	6,167	2,932	3,235	6,086	2,890	3,196	56	27	29	25	15	10		
	22	Choparakot	..	..	..	4,982	2,467	2,515	4,954	2,452	2,502	13	7	6	15	8	7		
	23	Khatali Walli	..	..	..	7,232	3,582	3,650	7,232	3,582	3,650	..	..	..	..	..	..		
	24	Khatali Palli	..	..	..	8,460	4,180	4,280	8,430	4,180	4,280	..	..	..	..	..	..		
	25	Kolagarh ..	..	..	..	2,624	1,218	1,406	2,624	1,218	1,406	..	..	..	..	..	..		
	26	Iriakot Talla	..	..	..	5,281	2,489	2,792	5,281	2,489	2,792	..	..	..	..	..	..		
	27	Iriakot Malla	..	..	..	5,801	2,717	3,084	5,800	2,716	3,084	1	1	..	..	..	..		
	28	Sahali West	..	..	..	5,407	2,572	2,835	5,402	2,569	2,833	..	..	..	5	3	2		
	29	Gujru ..	..	..	..	6,470	3,076	3,394	6,469	3,076	3,393	1	..	1	..	..	..		
	30	Bangarsyun	..	..	..	3,317	1,608	1,709	3,317	1,608	1,709	..	..	..	..	..	..		
	31	Sahali East	..	..	..	4,046	1,919	2,127	3,945	1,874	2,071	8	3	5	95	42	51		
	32	Dhaundyalsyun	..	..	..	3,519	1,682	1,837	3,519	1,682	1,837	..	..	..	..	..	..		
	33	Talain ..	..	..	..	5,790	2,781	3,009	5,783	2,774	3,009	5	5	..	2	2	..		
	34	Kandia Palla	..	..	..	2,398	1,192	1,206	2,398	1,192	1,206	..	..	..	..	..	..		
	35	Paino ..	..	..	..	4,910	2,277	2,633	4,893	2,270	2,623	15	7	8	2	..	2		
	36	Kandia Walla	..	..	..	3,053	1,491	1,532	3,051	1,490	1,561	2	1	1	..	..	..		
	37	Sila ..	..	..	..	6,329	3,425	2,904	6,003	3,248	2,758	318	175	143	5	2	3		
	38	Bungi ..	..	..	..	4,651	2,189	2,442	4,623	2,186	2,437	5	2	3	3	1	2		
	39	Badalpur Malla	..	..	..	5,806	2,785	3,071	5,799	2,730	3,069	7	5	2	..	..	..		
	40	Mawalsyun	..	..	..	5,908	2,755	3,153	5,908	2,755	3,153	..	..	..	..	..	..		
	41	Bijlot ..	..	..	..	4,546	2,136	2,410	4,545	2,136	2,409	1	..	1	..	..	..		
	42	Lansdowne ..	..	..	..	6,281	5,182	1,149	5,862	4,835	1,027	275	201	74	144	96	48		
	43	Nagpur Malla	..	..	..	8,269	3,969	4,300	8,269	3,969	4,300	..	..	..	..	..	..		
	44	Nagur Bichla	..	..	..	5,912	2,901	3,011	5,892	2,893	2,999	20	8	12	..	..	..		
	45	Khaderh ..	..	..	..	5,575	2,684	2,941	5,570	2,629	2,941	5	5	..	..	..	..		
	46	Nagpur Talla	..	..	..	9,171	4,420	4,751	9,166	4,419	4,747	5	1	4	..	..	..		
	47	Khaliphat Malla	..	..	..	10,996	5,355	5,641	10,995	5,354	5,641	1	1	..	..	..	..		
	48	Kaliphat Talla	..	..	..	14,038	6,906	7,132	13,794	6,791	7,008	244	115	129	..	..	..		
	49	Dasjala ..	..	..	..	7,928	3,868	4,060	7,928	3,838	4,060	..	..	..	..	..	..		
	50	Badhan Talla	..	..	..	5,392	2,735	2,657	5,325	2,700	2,626	64	33	31	2	2	..		
	51	Badhan Walla	..	..	..	5,860	2,809	3,051	5,827	2,793	3,031	33	13	20	..	..	..		
	52	Pandarpar Badhan	..	..	..	12,878	6,352	6,526	12,853	6,340	6,518	25	12	13	..	..	..		
	53	Painkhanda Talla	..	..	..	5,185	2,535	2,650	5,185	2,535	2,650	..	..	..	..	..	..		
	54	Painkhanda Malla	..	..	..	1,676	825	851	1,676	825	851	..	..	..	..	..	..		
	55	Danpur ..	..	..	..	2,919	1,444	1,475	2,913	1,444	1,475	..	..	..	..	..	..		
	56	Bidolsyun ..	..	..	..	7,644	3,611	4,033	7,557	3,564	3,993	..	..	..	87	47	40		
	57	Kandarsyun	..	..	..	10,315	4,896	5,419	10,280	4,876	5,404	..	..	..	35	20	15		
	58	Ranigarh ..	..	..	..	5,610	2,747	2,863	5,603	2,742	2,861	5	3	2	2	2	..		
	59	Kathulsyun	..	..	..	4,756	2,226	2,530	4,756	2,226	2,530	..	..	..	..	..	..		
	60	Chalansyun	..	..	..	6,121	2,994	3,127	6,121	2,994	3,127	..	..	..	..	..	..		
	61	Bachhansyun	..	..	..	5,329	2,625	2,704	5,316	2,619	2,697	..	..	..	13	6	7		
	62	Srinagar ..	..	..	..	2,357	1,252	1,105	2,228	1,177	1,051	80	45	35	49	30	19		
	63	Kimgadigarh	..	..	..	4,564	2,123	2,441	4,564	2,123	2,441	..	..	..	..	..	..		
	64	Pingla Pakha	..	..	..	1,831	866	965	1,830	865	965	..	..	..	1	1	..		
	65	Guradsyun ..	..	..	..	4,839	2,164	2,675	4,832	2,162	2,670	1	..	1	6	2	4		
	66	Ringwarsyun	..	..	..	2,022	930	1,092	2,018	928	1,090	..	..	..	4	2	2		
	67	Jaintolsyun ..	..	..	..	2,430	1,136	1,294	2,430	1,136	1,294	..	..	..	..	..	..		
	68	Mandarsyun South	..	..	..	4,336	1,983	2,353	4,333	1,983	2,350	3	..	3	..	..	..		
	69	Mandarsyun North	..	..	..	2,378	1,061	1,317	2,378	1,061	1,317	..	..	..	..	..	..		
	70	Dasoli Malli	..	..	..	8,860	4,316	4,544	8,833	4,302	4,531	20	10	10	7	4	3		

Population of the Police Circles Distributed by Religion—(*continued*).

Name of district.	Serial number of thana.	Name of thana.	Population.			Hindūs.			Muhammadans.			Others.		
			Total.	Males.	Females.	Total.	Males.	Females.	Total.	Males.	Males.	Total.	Males.	Females.
1	2	3	4	5	6	7	8	9	10	11	12	13	14	15
Garhwal—(*concluded*).	71	Dasoli Talli	13,629	6,653	6,979	13,605	6,642	6,963	12	7	5	12	4	8
	72	Kotdwara	13,705	9,454	4,251	11,940	7,856	4,084	1,870	1,538	132	95	60	35
	73	Udepur Talla	4,878	2,427	2,451	4,870	2,425	2,445	8	2	6	..	..	..
	74	Udepur Malla	4,696	2,231	2,465	4,696	2,281	2,465	..	..	..	..	..	..
	75	Udepur Walla	5,995	2,748	3,247	5,993	2,746	3,247	2	2	..	..	..	..
	76	Udepur Palla	3,600	1,740	1,860	3,600	1,740	1,860	..	..	..	..	..	..
	77	Lagur Walla	3,713	1,829	1,884	3,708	1,826	1,881	5	3	2	..	..	..
	78	Lagur Palla	7,343	3,458	3,885	7,259	3,421	3,838	83	36	47	1	1	..
	79	Dhangoo Talla	2,839	1,388	1,451	2,839	1,388	1,451	..	..	..	..	..	..
	80	Dhangoo Bichla	3,423	1,674	1,749	3,421	1,672	1,749	1	1	..	1	1	..
	81	Dhangoo Malla	4,145	1,966	2,179	4,145	1,966	2,179	..	..	..	..	..	..
	82	Dabbralsyun	5,534	2,591	2,943	5,528	2,589	2,939	..	..	..	6	2	4
	83	Ajmere Walla	5,602	2,704	2,598	5,347	2,672	2,775	236	124	112	19	8	11
	84	Ajmere Palla	3,306	1,553	1,753	3,300	1,551	1,749	6	2	4	..	..	..
		Oudh	*12,558,004*	*6,484,700*	*6,073,304*	*10,832,484*	*5,599,852*	*5,232,632*	*1,700,687*	*869,329*	*831,358*	*24,833*	*15,519*	*9,374*
		Lucknow Division	*5,911,642*	*3,128,767*	*2 782,875*	*5,139,230*	*2,722,618*	*2,416,612*	*753,896*	*394,446*	*359,450*	*18,516*	*11,703*	*6,813*
		Lucknow	*764,411*	*411,799*	*352,612*	*592,260*	*319,465*	*272,795*	*160,697*	*84,572*	*76,125*	*11,454*	*7,762*	*3,692*
Lucknow.	1	Banthra	65,216	34,804	30,412	60,364	32,296	28,068	4,841	2,499	2,342	11	9	2
	2	Chauk (Lucknow)	62,344	34,417	27,927	33,829	19,373	14,456	27,618	14,492	13,126	897	552	345
	3	Daulatganj	29,375	15,225	14,150	16,005	8,582	7,423	13,313	6,610	6,703	57	33	24
	4	Dilkusha	19,782	13,283	6,499	10,714	6,415	4,299	4,461	2,911	1,550	4,607	3,957	650
	5	Goshainganj	71,688	37,743	33,945	64,555	34,103	30,452	7,118	3,632	3,483	15	8	7
	6	Hasanganj	26,411	15,022	11,389	19,461	11,168	8,293	6,778	3,752	3,026	172	102	70
	7	Itaunja	56,232	29,714	26,518	51,441	27,192	24,249	4,690	2,470	2,220	101	52	49
	8	Kakori	59,906	31,475	28,431	50,508	26,824	23,684	9,369	4,638	4,731	29	13	16
	9	Malihabad	92,061	48,871	43,190	76,967	41,089	35,878	15,066	7,766	7,300	28	16	12
	10	Mandiaon	70,852	37,393	33,459	61,903	32,805	29,098	8,901	4,561	4,340	48	27	21
	11	Mohanlalganj	80,167	41,504	38,663	73,875	38,380	35,495	6,249	3,094	3,155	43	30	13
	12	Sadatganj	25,073	13,019	12,054	15,324	8,223	7,101	9,636	4,730	4,906	113	66	47
	13	Wazirganj	42,639	23,374	19,265	20,449	11,498	8,951	21,448	11,429	10,019	742	447	295
	14	Hazratganj	62,665	35,955	26,710	36,865	21,517	15,348	21,209	11,988	9,221	4,591	2,450	2,141
		Unao	*910,915*	*478,585*	*432,330*	*834,067*	*438,163*	*395,904*	*76,033*	*39,959*	*36,074*	*815*	*463*	*352*
Unao.	1	Achalganj	66,091	34,348	31,743	62,647	32,517	30,130	3,303	1,764	1,539	141	67	74
	2	Fatehpur Chaurasi	68,152	36,625	31,527	63,164	33,923	29,241	4,985	2,702	2,283	3	..	3
	3	Bangarmau	89,128	48,049	41,079	75,598	40,905	34,693	13,524	7,142	6,382	6	2	4
	4	Purwa	59,362	30,481	28,981	54,546	27,961	26,585	4,725	2,419	2,306	91	51	40
	5	Mauravan	65,068	33,467	31,601	60,461	31,154	29,307	4,597	2,304	2,293	10	9	1
	6	Bara	66,452	33,141	33,311	64,489	32,100	32,389	1,888	999	889	75	42	33
	7	Behar	55,855	27,574	28,281	53,377	26,300	27,077	2,463	1,262	1,201	15	12	3
	8	Hasanganj	74,311	39,468	34,843	66,990	35,639	31,351	7,285	3,806	3,479	36	23	13
	9	Auras	78,951	42,367	36,584	70,150	37,669	32,481	8,787	4,690	4,097	14	8	6

	No.	Name													
	10	Ajgain	74,806	39,673	34,633	69,752	37,282	32,470	4,351	2,292	2,089	205	100	94
	11	Asoha	54,449	28,368	26,081	51,652	26,917	24,735	2,759	1,431	1,328	38	20	18
	12	Unao	86,038	46,233	39,805	77,778	41,763	36,015	8,108	4,371	3,737	152	99	53
	13	Safipur	72,752	38,841	33,911	63,463	34,033	29,430	9,258	4,787	4,471	31	21	10
		Rae Bareli ..	*1,016,864*	*510,665*	*506,199*	*928,787*	*467,038*	*461,749*	*87,566*	*43,326*	*44,240*	*511*	*301*	*210*
Rae Bareli	1	Dalmau	79,366	39,792	39,574	75,304	37,742	37,562	4,009	2,023	1,986	53	27	26
	2	Sareni	88,185	43,739	44,446	85,061	42,119	42,942	3,114	1,616	1,498	10	4	6
	3	Gurbakhshganj	81,523	40,726	40,797	77,944	38,909	39,035	3,529	1,782	1,747	50	85	15
	4	Rae Bareli..	106,357	54,238	52,119	94,143	48,035	46,108	11,953	6,057	5,896	261	146	115
	5	Sheoratanganj	69,876	35,206	34,670	62,363	31,493	30,837	7,500	3,701	3,799	13	9	4
	6	Bachhrawan	92,226	47,137	45,089	87,111	44,485	42,626	5,085	2,634	2,451	30	18	12
	7	Maharajganj	82,421	41,843	40,578	77,178	39,276	37,902	5,237	2,563	2,674	6	4	2
	8	Nasirabad	103,251	51,534	51,717	85,505	42,995	42,510	17,709	8,511	9,198	37	28	9
	9	Salon	82,526	40,799	41,727	72,042	35,724	36,318	10,456	5,061	5,395	28	14	14
	10	Mohanganj	79,047	39,443	39,604	67,882	33,990	33,892	11.165	5,453	5,712	..	..	..
	11	Mustafabad	64,387	32,121	32,266	60,666	30,278	30,388	3,711	1,835	1,876	10	8	2
	12	Jagatpur	87,699	44,087	43,612	83,588	41,989	41,599	4,098	2,090	2,008	13	8	5
		Sitapur ..	*1,138,996*	*606,339*	*532,657*	*965,152*	*515,600*	*450,152*	*171,779*	*89,904*	*81,875*	*1,465*	*835*	*630*
Sitapur	1	Pisawan	42,340	22,769	19,571	37,873	20,403	17,470	4,446	2,852	2,094	21	14	7
	2	Mahsoi	54,104	28,982	25,122	50,627	27,162	23,465	3,472	1,816	1,658	5	4	1
	3	Tambaur	84,326	44,003	40,323	71,263	37,230	34,033	13,061	6,772	6,289	2	1	1
	4	Biswan	75,681	40,233	35,448	59,585	31,794	27,791	16,031	8,407	7,624	65	32	33
	5	Mahmudabad	92,332	49,130	43,202	71,718	38,261	33,457	20,455	10,775	9,680	159	94	65
	6	Sadarpur	69,788	37,298	32,490	59,635	31,926	27,709	10,126	5,353	4,773	27	19	8
	7	Thanagaon..	67,467	35,569	31,898	59,077	31,184	27,893	8,382	4,379	4,003	8	6	2
	8	Sidhauli	89,239	47,011	42,228	78,886	41,541	37,345	10,127	5,305	4,822	228	165	61
	9	Kamalpur	70,004	36,833	33,171	64,652	34,052	30,600	5,303	2,756	2,547	49	25	24
	10	Sitapur	106,050	57,017	49,033	83,675	45,500	38,175	21,658	11,150	10,508	717	367	350
	11	Misrikh	69,721	39,101	30,620	62,097	34,835	27,262	7,585	4,242	3,343	39	24	15
	12	Maholi	77,346	41,795	35,551	72,194	38,946	33,248	5,065	2,804	2,261	87	45	42
	13	Laharpur	79,697	41,788	37,909	64,274	33,943	30,331	15,383	7,822	7,561	40	23	17
	14	Hargaon	73,219	38,574	34,645	60,564	32,000	28,564	12,652	6,571	6,081	3	3	..
	15	Talgaon	87,682	46,236	41,446	69,632	36,823	32,809	18,033	9,400	8,633	17	13	4
		Hardoi ..	*1,121,248*	*609,867*	*511,381*	*999,236*	*545,238*	*453,998*	*119,540*	*63,306*	*56,234*	*2,472*	*1,323*	*1,149*
Hardoi	1	Hardoi	92,614	51,115	41,499	84,489	46,567	37,922	7,435	4,194	3,241	690	354	336
	2	Tundiaon	65,581	35,366	30,215	57,862	31,368	26,494	7,697	3,984	3,713	22	14	8
	3	Pihani	86,405	46,272	40,133	73,181	39,381	33,800	13,127	6,841	6,286	97	50	47
	4	Shahabad	86,966	46,874	40,092	68,430	37,227	31,203	17,939	9,333	8,606	597	314	283
	5	Pali	85,026	46,757	38,269	79,644	43,855	35,789	5,152	2,777	2,375	230	125	105
	6	Behta Gokul	58,222	32,156	26,066	54,918	30,354	24,564	3,067	1,666	1,401	237	136	101
	7	Bilgram	66,786	36,510	30,276	58,051	31,939	26,112	8,627	4,516	4,111	108	55	53
	8	Sandi	66,653	36,438	30,215	61,583	33,731	27,852	4,992	2,657	2,335	78	50	28
	9	Mallanwan..	93,927	50,925	43,002	83,624	45,519	38,105	10,207	5,357	4,850	96	49	47
	10	Harpalpur	81,561	44,832	36,729	77,879	42,781	35,098	3,454	1,925	1,529	228	126	102
	11	Sandila	69,603	37,166	32,437	53,802	29,089	24,713	15,776	8,065	7,711	25	12	13
	12	Beniganj	65,813	35,890	29,923	60,988	33,202	27,786	4,812	2,682	2,130	13	6	7
	13	Ghausganj	61,928	33,153	28,775	54,730	29,312	25,418	7,192	3,837	3,355	6	4	2
	14	Atrauli	72,331	39,080	33,251	66,437	35,922	30,515	5,888	3,155	2,733	6	8	8
	15	Baghauli	67,852	37,333	30,499	63,618	34,991	28,627	4,175	2,317	1,858	59	25	14
		Kheri ..	*959,208*	*511,512*	*447,696*	*819,128*	*437,114*	*382,014*	*138,281*	*73,379*	*64,902*	*1,799*	*1,019*	*780*
Kheri	1	Bhira	53,396	28,786	24,610	48,131	25,815	22,316	5,194	2,917	2,277	71	54	17
	2	Phulbehar	57,600	30,715	26,885	49,071	26,199	22,872	8,522	4,509	4,013	7	7	..
	3	Lakhimpur..	152,739	80,570	72,169	123,973	65,567	58,406	28,389	14,783	13,606	377	220	157
	4	Palia	35,090	20,152	14,938	30,094	17,231	12,863	4,935	2,881	2,054	61	40	21

Population of the Police Circles Distributed by Religion—(*continued*).

Name of district.	Serial number of thana.	Name of thana.	Population. Total.	Population. Males.	Population. Females.	Hindus. Total.	Hindus. Males.	Hindus. Females.	Muhammadans. Total.	Muhammadans. Males.	Muhammadans. Females.	Others. Total.	Others. Males.	Others. Females.
1	2	3	4	5	6	7	8	9	10	11	12	13	14	15
Kheri—(*concluded*).	5	Dhaurahra	75,116	39,152	35,964	64,036	33,350	30,686	11,077	5,799	5,278	3	3	..
	6	Nighasan	109,694	58,574	51,120	94,311	50,311	44,000	15,350	8,240	7,110	33	23	10
	7	Isanagar	66,824	35,140	31,684	59,205	31,142	28,063	7,575	3,977	3,596	46	21	25
	8	Mitauli	74,713	39,908	34,805	67,771	36,184	31,587	6,876	3,687	3,189	66	37	29
	9	Muhamdi	82,106	43,935	38,171	68,409	36,739	31,670	13,376	7,031	6,345	321	165	156
	10	Pasgawan	63,533	34,070	29,463	53,232	28,617	24,615	9,995	5,283	4,712	306	170	136
	11	Gola	117,940	63,462	54,478	100,764	54,234	46,530	16,727	8,981	7,746	449	247	202
	12	Nimgaon	67,844	35,737	32,107	58,048	30,672	27,376	9,737	5,033	4,704	59	32	27
	13	Sujauli (*a*)	2,613	1,311	1,302	2,083	1,053	1,030	530	258	272	..	..	..
		Fyzabad division	*6,646,362*	*3,355,933*	*3,290,429*	*5,693,254*	*2,877,234*	*2,816,020*	*946,791*	*474,883*	*471,908*	*6,317*	*3,816*	*2,501*
		Fyzabad	*1,154,109*	*575,621*	*578,488*	*1,023,556*	*510,594*	*512,962*	*127,954*	*63,137*	*64,817*	*2,599*	*1,890*	*709*
Fyzabad.	1	Ajodhya	14,586	8,084	6,502	12,552	7,008	5,544	2,005	1,056	949	29	20	9
	2	Cantonment	7,136	5,157	1,979	3,706	2,523	1,183	1,725	1,232	493	1,705	1,402	303
	3	Fyzabad	39,043	21,082	17,961	27,255	14,802	12,453	11,303	6,014	5,289	485	266	219
	4	Pura Kalandar	74,306	36,611	37,695	68,173	33,733	34,440	6,089	2,851	3,238	44	27	17
	5	Ramnagar	93,962	46,724	47,238	86,941	43,200	43,741	7,018	3,523	3,495	3	1	2
	6	Akbarpur	92,640	46,350	46,290	78,676	39,412	39,264	13,872	6,891	6,981	92	47	45
	7	Ahrauli	69,693	34,778	34,915	63,994	32,036	31,958	5,680	2,729	2,951	19	13	6
	8	Baskhari	86,913	43,564	43,349	73,824	37,177	36,647	13,084	6,382	6,702	5	5	..
	9	Jalalpur	164,032	82,033	81,999	148,599	74,494	74,105	15,415	7,530	7,885	18	9	9
	10	Tanda	87,860	43,810	44,050	67,837	33,798	34,039	19,905	9,953	9,952	118	59	59
	11	Amona	69,584	34,046	35,538	64,297	31,559	32,738	5,279	2,480	2,799	8	7	1
	12	Bikapur	81,321	38,973	42,348	76,746	36,883	39,863	4,565	2,086	2,479	10	4	6
	13	Haidarganj	43,053	20,797	22,256	40,986	19,847	21,139	2,062	948	1,114	5	2	3
	14	Maharajganj	75,151	36,613	38,538	70,523	34,476	36,047	4,601	2,126	2,475	27	11	16
	15	Milkipur	88,558	44,180	44,378	82,188	41,095	41,093	6,343	3,072	3,271	27	13	14
	16	Raunahi	66,271	32,819	33,452	57,259	28,551	28,708	9,008	4,264	4,744	4	4	..
		Gonda	*1,412,212*	*718,418*	*693,794*	*1,184,607*	*603,433*	*581,174*	*226,907*	*114,652*	*112,255*	*698*	*333*	*365*
Gonda.	1	Itiathok	106,293	53,568	52,730	90,833	45,659	45,224	15,409	7,906	7,503	6	3	3
	2	Kauria	71,514	36,495	35,019	62,939	32,126	30,863	8,521	4,366	4,155	4	3	1
	3	Colonelganj	102,099	52,074	50,025	86,562	44,292	42,270	15,453	7,736	7,717	84	46	38
	4	Gonda	129,833	66,068	63,765	112,152	57,180	54,972	17,233	8,689	8,544	448	199	249
	5	Nawabganj	52,871	26,766	26,105	48,827	24,732	24,095	4,041	2,032	2,009	3	2	1
	6	Paraspur	69,915	35,534	34,381	64,472	32,853	31,619	5,442	2,681	2,761	1	..	1
	7	Tarabganj	94,998	48,056	46,942	89,397	45,310	44,087	5,600	2,745	2,855	1	1	..
	8	Andhiari	79,158	40,210	38,948	71,497	36,389	35,108	7,617	3,803	3,814	44	18	26
	9	Balrampur	89,657	46,056	43,601	72,932	37,564	35,368	16,674	8,460	8,214	51	32	19
	10	Birpur	71,293	36,398	34,895	64,595	33,004	31,591	6,653	3,391	3,302	5	3	2
	11	Lalia	73,243	38,277	34,966	64,969	33,875	31,094	8,274	4,402	3,872	..	..	..
	12	Pachperwa	53,763	27,353	26,410	38,225	19,500	18,725	15,531	7,850	7,681	7	3	4
	13	Sadullahnagar	78,971	39,711	39,260	55,917	28,165	27,752	23,054	11,546	11,508	..	..	..
	14	Srinagar	55,284	28,009	27,275	46,374	23,540	22,834	8,910	4,469	4,441	..	..	..
	15	Tulsipur	101,459	52,383	49,076	79,875	41,126	38,749	21,579	11,253	10,326	5	4	1

	16	Utraula	129,415	65,229	64,186	87,403	44,345	43,058	41,975	20,866	21,109	37	18	19
	17	Wazirganj	52,441	26,231	26,210	47,538	23,773	23,765	4,901	2,457	2,444	2	1	1
		Bahraich ..	*1,047,677*	*544,594*	*503,083*	*844,815*	*439,357*	*405,458*	*201,460*	*104,477*	*96,983*	*1,402*	*760*	*642*
Bahraich.	1	Piyagpur	94,878	48,666	46,212	87,107	44,710	42,397	7,763	3,950	3,813	8	6	2
	2	Ikauna	58,712	30,520	28,192	53,377	27,734	25,643	5,311	2,775	2,536	24	11	13
	3	Bhinga	107,649	55,990	51,659	89,626	46,513	43,113	17,966	9,442	8,524	57	35	22
	4	Fakhrpur	87,998	45,922	42,076	70,444	36,755	33,689	17,514	9,140	8,374	40	27	13
	5	Kaisarganj	79,214	41,220	37,994	57,274	30,081	27,193	21,891	11,111	10,780	49	28	21
	6	Huzurpur	56,204	29,137	27,067	47,091	24,424	22,667	9,093	4,700	4,393	20	13	7
	7	Bahraich	121,842	63,420	58,422	86,475	45,271	41,204	34,983	17,959	17,024	384	190	194
	8	Nanpara	87,054	44,615	42,439	58,120	29,897	28,223	28,318	14,394	13,924	616	324	292
	9	Motipur	46,805	24,972	21,833	38,659	20,528	18,131	8,131	4,435	3,696	15	9	6
	10	Mallipur	54,517	27,891	26,626	41,535	21,274	20,261	12,936	6,590	6,346	46	27	19
	11	Khairighat	50,304	26,051	24,253	43,901	22,748	21,153	6,375	3,284	3,091	28	19	9
	12	Sujauli	20,649	12,104	8,545	16,959	9,763	7,196	3,665	2,323	1,342	25	18	7
	13	Sisaiya	64,112	33,357	30,755	56,479	29,370	27,109	7,586	3,961	3,625	47	26	21
	14	Sonwan	62,047	31,977	30,070	53,730	27,577	26,153	8,317	4,400	3,917	..	..	..
	15	Rupaidih	55,692	28,752	26,940	44,038	22,712	21,326	11,611	6,013	5,598	43	27	16
		Sultanpur .	*1,048,524*	*515,980*	*532,544*	*931,850*	*460,104*	*471,746*	*116,320*	*55,724*	*60,596*	*354*	*152*	*202*
Sultanpur.	1	Sultanpur	97,247	47,593	49,651	74,830	36,909	37,921	22,224	10,618	11,606	193	69	124
	2	Kurebhar	74,426	35,787	38,639	67,604	32,664	34,940	6,817	3,118	3,699	5	5	.
	3	Badlapur*	2,345	1,179	1,166	2,081	1,058	1,023	264	121	143	..	..	..
	4	Aspur†	786	410	376	738	387	351	48	23	25	..	..	..
	5	Dostpur	80,448	40,362	40,086	73,726	37,069	36,657	6,715	3,287	3,428	7	6	1
	6	Jaisinghpur	93,258	46,310	46,948	85,627	42,667	42,960	7,497	3,582	3,915	134	61	73
	7	Kadipur	71,184	35,981	35,203	67,806	34,259	33,547	3,377	1,721	1,656	1	1	..
	8	Lambhua	94,892	46,617	48,245	88,113	43,324	44,789	6,779	3,323	3,456	..	..	..
	9	Bazar Shukul	53,502	26,818	26,684	39,497	20,054	19,443	14,005	6,764	7,241	..	..	..
	10	Haliapur	71,277	31,950	36,327	62,484	30,926	31,558	8,793	4,024	4,769	..	.	..
	11	Jagdispur	92,613	45,719	46,894	79,585	39,469	40,116	13,028	6,250	6,778	..	..	..
	12	Gauriganj	67,160	33,009	34,151	61,047	29,956	31,091	6,111	3,051	3,060	2	2	..
	13	Musafirkhana	85,393	41,483	43,910	75,041	36,622	38,419	10,351	4,860	5,491	1	1	.
	14	Raipur	87,498	42,584	44,914	83,444	40,576	42,868	4,048	2,004	2,044	6	4	2
	15	Piparpur	76,495	37,145	39,350	70,227	34,164	36,063	6,263	2,978	3,285	5	3	2
		Partabgarh ..	*899,973*	*437,183*	*462,790*	*806,129*	*392,062*	*414,067*	*93,613*	*44,985*	*48,628*	*231*	*136*	*95*
Partabgarh.	1	Chandika	67,176	32,033	35,143	61,161	29,256	31,905	6,015	2,777	3,238	..	.	..
	2	Jaitwara	76,750	36,379	40,371	63,802	30,279	33,523	12,948	6,100	6,848	..	..	..
	3	Mao Andrewganj	86,574	42,078	44,496	74,340	35,969	38,371	12,044	6,006	6,038	190	103	87
	4	Sangipur	79,383	38,330	41,053	74,930	36,146	38,784	4,440	2,173	2,267	13	11	2
	5	Kunda	88,771	43,691	45,080	77,160	38,185	38,975	11,604	5,499	6,105	7	7	..
	6	Raipur Bhagdara	70,229	34,269	35,960	65,082	31,687	33,395	5,143	2,578	2,565	4	4	..
	7	Pura Bagh Rae	72,867	35,594	37,273	65,999	32,287	33,712	6,865	3,305	3,560	3	2	1
	8	Sangramgarh	82,483	40,749	41,734	76,897	37,990	38,907	5,585	2,758	2,827	1	1	..
	9	Soraon‡	294	140	154	294	140	154	..	..	..	..	..	..
	10	Aspur	63,111	31,318	31,793	59,668	29,631	30,037	3,443	1,687	1,756	..	..	..
	11	Badshahpur§	5,967	2,930	3,037	5,767	2,824	2,943	200	106	94	..	..	..
	12	Kandhai Hanumanganj .. .	72,136	34,834	37,302	62,831	30,383	32,448	9,304	4,450	4,854	1	1	..
	13	Mau Aima‖	2,683	1,310	1,373	2,361	1,152	1,209	322	158	164	..	..	..
	14	Patti	67,933	32,811	35,122	60,236	29,183	31,053	7,689	3,625	4,064	8	3	5
	15	Raniganj	63,616	30,717	32,899	55,601	26,950	28,651	8,011	3,763	4,248	4	4	..
		Bara Banki ..	*1,063,867*	*564,137*	*519,730*	*902,297*	*471,684*	*430,613*	*180,537*	*91,908*	*88,629*	*1,033*	*545*	*488*
Bara-Banki.	1	Bhilsar	5,467	2,769	2,698	4,505	2,307	2,198	962	462	500	..	..	..
	2	Mowai	146,436	73,878	72,558	115,065	58,498	56,567	31,353	15,372	15,981	18	8	10
	3	Ramsanehighat	73,060	37,686	35,374	65,182	33,660	31,522	7,757	3,972	3,785	141	74	67

(a) Thana Sujauli situated in Bahraich district. * Thana Badlapur situated in Jaunpur district. † Thana Aspur situated in Partabgarh district. ‡ Thana Soraon situated in Allahabad district.

PROVINCIAL TABLE III.

Population of the Police Circles Distributed by Religion—(*concluded*).

Name of district.	Serial number of thana.	Name of thana.	Population.			Hindus.			Muhammadans.			Others.		
			Total.	Males.	Females.	Total.	Males.	Females.	Total.	Males.	Females.	Total.	Males.	Females.
1	2	3	4	5	6	7	8	9	10	11	12	13	14	15
Bara Banki—(*concluded*).	4	Nawabganj	**89,670**	47,647	42,023	**71,574**	38,195	33,379	**17,718**	9,256	8,463	**378**	197	181
	5	Safdarganj	**124,874**	65,068	59,806	**94,003**	49,308	44,095	**30,867**	15,757	15,110	**4**	3	1
	6	Fatehpur	**94,367**	49,671	44,696	**75,603**	40,039	35,564	**18,695**	9,597	9,098	**69**	35	34
	7	Kursi	**83,357**	44,066	39,291	**68,636**	36,462	32,174	**14,718**	7,603	7,115	**3**	1	2
	8	Lalpur	**20,135**	10,619	9,516	**17,283**	9,131	8,152	**2,850**	1,487	1,363	**2**	1	1
	9	Muhammadpur	**57,822**	30,810	27,012	**48,156**	25,313	22,843	**9,561**	4,942	4,619	**105**	55	50
	10	Ramnagar	**94,184**	49,950	44,234	**78,551**	41,784	36,767	**15,505**	8,088	7,417	**128**	78	50
	11	Tikaitnagar	**70,935**	36,953	33,982	**63,157**	33,030	30,127	**7,605**	3,836	3,769	**173**	87	86
	12	Loni Katra	**65,698**	33,927	31,771	**60,654**	31,392	29,262	**5,032**	2,529	2,503	**12**	6	6
	13	Suboha	**66,536**	33,979	32,557	**61,006**	31,200	29,806	**5,530**	2,779	2,751	..	..	..
	14	Siddhaur	**91,784**	47,334	44,450	**79,378**	41,085	38,293	**12,406**	6,249	6,157	..	..	..

PROVINCIAL TABLE IV.

The ages of the population of Municipalities with above 10,000 inhabitants.

PROVINCIAL TABLE IV.

The ages of the population of

Serial number of district.	Name of district.	Serial number of municipality.	Name of municipality.	Population. Persons.	Population. Males	Population. Females.	0—5. Males	0—5. Females	5—10 Males.	5—10 Females.
1	2	3	4	5	6	7	8	9	10	11
1	Dehra Dun	1	Dehra	30,301	18,111	12,190	1,511	1,542	1,525	1,528
2	Saharanpur	1	Saharanpur	62,850	35,416	27,434	3,042	3,055	3,137	2,868
		2	Hardwar-Union	28,682	16,624	12,058	1,414	1,409	1,422	1,299
		3	Deoband	18,614	10,065	8,549	1,076	1,123	1,198	1,058
		4	Rurki	13,850	8,336	5,514	685	698	665	667
3	Muzaffarnagar	1	Muzaffarnagar	23,811	13,973	9,838	1,298	1,106	1,374	1,307
		2	Kairana	16,293	8,810	7,483	938	845	1,143	946
4	Meerut	1	Meerut	76,351	42,017	34,334	4,462	4,415	4,554	3,870
		2	Hapur	19,142	10,758	8,384	1,058	912	1,207	998
		3	Ghaziabad	11,304	6,346	4,958	979	673	543	487
5	Bulandshahr	1	Khurja	27,387	14,549	12,838	1,499	1,451	1,651	1,588
		2	Bulandshahr	19,383	10,679	8,704	1,051	917	1,160	1,166
		3	Sikandrabad	18,946	10,062	8,884	1,115	969	1,300	1,079
6	Aligarh	1	Koil	64,825	36,265	28,560	3,593	3,728	3,538	3,601
		2	Hathras	37,854	21,360	16,494	2,385	2,053	2,107	1,853
		3	Atrauli	15,730	8,150	7,580	965	951	1,190	893
		4	Sikandra Rao	10,109	5,308	4,801	576	578	779	630
7	Muttra	1	Muttra	54,332	29,624	24,708	2,826	2,698	3,025	2,857
		2	Brindaban	18,443	9,845	8,598	610	574	789	629
8	Agra	1	Agra	163,935	88,943	74,992	9,019	8,9[illegible]8	9 851	9,158
		2	Firozabad	13,571	7,184	6.387	769	709	756	794
9	Furrukhabad	1	Furrukhabad *cum* Fatehgarh	56,573	30,342	26,231	3,010	3,040	3,215	3,019
10	Mainpuri	1	Mainpuri	16,154	8,972	7,182	757	762	918	819
11	Etawah	1	Etawah	45,350	24.249	21,101	2,663	2,536	2,779	2,726
12	Etah	1	Kasganj	16,429	9,237	7.192	1,035	1,087	985	887
		2	Jalesar	13,283	6 960	6,323	764	733	876	824
		3	Soron	11,524	6,096	5,428	629	610	708	634
13	Bareilly	1	Bareilly	117,521	62,127	55,394	7,422	7,533	7,952	7,494
14	Bijnor	1	Nagina	19,625	10,072	9,553	1,280	1,224	1,125	995
		2	Najibabad	18,460	9,699	8,761	1,251	1,198	1,270	1,119
		3	Bijnor	17,439	9,209	8,230	1,224	1,190	1,151	1,042
		4	Chandpur	11,832	5,954	5,878	767	854	883	766
15	Budaun	1	Budaun	38,230	20,048	18,182	2,158	2,114	2,478	2,389
		2	Sahaswan	18,009	9,544	8,465	1,128	1,102	1,261	1,147
16	Moradabad	1	Moradabad	81,168	43,381	37,787	5,188	5,157	5,456	5,088
		2	Sambhal	45,276	23,234	22,042	3,206	3,128	3,[illegible]80	3,042
		3	Amroha	42,410	20,550	21,860	3,088	3,021	3,010	2,966
		4	Chandausi	22,255	12,367	9,888	1,358	1,369	1,416	1,264
17	Shahjahanpur	1	Shahjahanpur	71,778	36,789	34,989	4,208	4,306	4,271	4,388
		2	Tilhar	18,446	9,668	8,778	1,110	1,162	1,278	1,160
18	Pilibhit	1	Pilibhit	31,554	16,817	14,737	1,916	1,795	2,088	1,892
		2	Bisalpur	10,086	5,448	4,638	604	619	764	618
19	Cawnpore	1	Cawnpore	157,040	89,806	67,234	7,704	7,781	7,148	7,175
20	Fatehpur	1	Fatehpur (1)	16,939	8,720	8,219	827	991	1,454	996
21	Banda	1	Banda (2)	21,061	10,543	10,518	1,368	1,381	1,262	1,256
22	Allahabad	1	Allahabad	159,701	87,806	71,895	9 468	9,241	9,192	8,705
23	Jhansi	1	Jhansi	58,236	30,143	28,093	3,741	3,807	3,262	3,047
		2	Mau	12,927	6,487	6,440	876	837	770	605
		3	Lalitpur	12,449	6,347	6,102	889	942	755	681
24	Jalaun	1	Kunch	16,480	8,586	7,894	1,123	993	973	931
		2	Kalpi	10,568	5,275	5,293	667	680	668	650
25	Benares	1	Benares	199,868	103,126	96,742	11,261	11,799	10,964	11,002
26	Mirzapur	1	Mirzapur *cum* Bindhachal	32,332	16,861	15,471	2,076	2,288	1,607	1,008
27	Jaunpur	1	Jaunpur	30,473	15,888	14,585	1,635	1,757	1,742	1,698
28	Ghazipur	1	Ghazipur	22,165	12,005	10,160	1,165	1,339	1,327	1,198
29	Ballia	1	Ballia (3)	16,684	8,702	7,982	986	1,044	1,011	1,003
30	Gorakhpur	1	Gorakhpur	48,358	25,662	22,696	2,746	2,866	2,996	2,807
31	Azamgarh	1	Azamgarh	10,834	5,842	4,992	575	611	651	638

(1) Includes 127 males 78 females (Railway figures)
(2) Do. 95 do. 46 ditto
(3) Do. 202 do. 45 ditto

Municipalities with above 10,000 inhabitants. PROVINCIAL TABLE IV.

10—15.		15—20.		20—40.		40—60.		60 and over.		Unspecified.		Serial number of district.
Males.	Females.	Males.	Females.	Males.	Females.	Males.	Females.	Males.	Females.	Males.	Females.	
12	13	14	15	16	17	18	19	20	21	22	23	1
1,712	1,344	1,680	1,016	7,121	4,104	3,546	2,056	1,016	605	..	..	1
4,077	2,957	3,414	2,581	13,276	9,394	6,643	5,011	1,827	1,568	..	..	2
1,634	1,140	1,580	1,071	6,459	4,047	3,277	2,339	838	758	..	..	
1,359	1,052	913	722	3,152	2,688	1,781	1,462	586	444	..	..	
874	590	937	512	3,420	1,858	1,874	906	381	283	..	..	
1,689	1,069	1,508	870	4,969	3,115	2,461	1,894	674	477	..	..	3
1,197	911	885	718	2,739	2,410	1,398	1,237	510	416	..	..	
4,841	3,716	4,087	3,282	13,450	10,427	7,864	6,350	2,759	2,274	..	..	4
1,187	917	939	773	3,395	2,619	2,106	1,527	866	643	..	..	
729	483	533	426	1,995	1,651	1,120	939	447	299	..	..	
1,810	1,490	1,372	1,193	4,384	3,754	2,912	2,456	921	911	..	..	5
1,494	987	1,165	896	3,170	2,587	2,029	1,630	610	521	..	..	
1,376	1,122	1,056	752	2,707	2,464	1,940	1,834	568	664	..	..	
4,187	2,994	3,701	2,662	11,959	8,687	7,313	5,095	2,004	1,791	..	2	6
2,292	1,566	1,984	1,532	7,090	5,517	4,278	3,062	1,224	911	..	..	
1,132	698	762	936	2,223	2,300	1,424	1,371	454	431	..	..	
660	521	440	361	1,567	1,516	976	911	310	284	..	..	
3,429	2,509	2,932	2,429	9,871	8,025	5,916	4,792	1,619	1,392	6	6	7
995	657	908	833	3,452	2,730	2,448	2,310	703	865	..	..	
10,212	7,524	8,886	7,846	28,916	23,709	16,898	13,755	5,161	4,577	..	..	8
838	612	648	519	2,361	2,040	1,314	1,272	503	441	..	..	
3,285	2,459	2,578	2,209	9,974	8,292	6,358	5,317	1,977	1,895	..	..	9
1,251	738	921	677	3,002	2,283	1,739	1,498	389	405	..	..	10
2,955	2,169	2,446	1,901	7,951	6,954	4,273	3,632	1,182	1,183	..	..	11
1,058	671	816	564	3,087	2,218	1,674	1,286	582	479	..	..	12
922	718	651	579	2,110	1,974	1,328	1,178	309	317	..	..	
752	579	516	506	1,888	1,717	1,282	1,050	321	332	..	..	
6,917	5,518	5,435	4,662	19,017	16,411	11,338	9,797	4,051	3,979	..	..	13
1,320	1,067	975	760	2,984	3,089	1,809	1,706	579	712	..	..	14
1,446	924	689	665	2,864	2,840	1,579	1,459	600	556	..	..	
1,131	913	880	657	2,780	2,436	1,471	1,414	572	578	..	..	
845	617	431	501	1,541	1,759	1,040	954	447	427	..	..	
2,436	1,960	1,798	1,574	6,208	5,603	3,588	3,298	1,882	1,249	..	..	15
1,258	971	806	673	2,797	2,514	1,687	1,524	612	534	..	..	
5,131	4,129	3,966	3,277	13,693	11,388	7,445	6,510	2,502	2,288	..	..	16
2,858	2,336	1,920	1,790	6,578	6,622	3,922	3,611	1,470	1,518	..	..	
2,739	2,387	1,779	1,769	5,226	6,283	3,237	3,802	1,521	1,632	..	..	
1,241	894	1,101	787	4,046	3,058	2,423	1,850	782	646	..	..	
3,892	3,266	3,027	2,705	11,855	10,852	7,248	6,731	2,793	2,791	..	..	17
1,179	851	847	750	2,924	2,707	1,813	1,640	522	508	..	..	
1,704	1,828	1,413	1,205	5,796	4,851	3,057	2,703	898	963	..	..	18
658	442	519	373	1,712	1,455	929	826	262	305	..	..	
7,421	5,036	6,990	5,236	37,220	25,653	18,665	12,348	4,663	4,003	..	..	19
1,412	804	716	668	2,367	2,742	1,330	1,505	491	440	..	..	20
1,240	1,159	938	803	3,540	3,452	1,682	1,688	418	783	..	..	21
8,765	6,436	7,716	5,820	31,871	24,441	15,946	12,631	4,848	4,612	..	..	22
3,062	2,334	2,664	2,322	11,004	9,742	5,009	4,974	1,401	1,867	..	..	23
681	521	487	461	2,191	2,278	1,104	1,230	378	508	..	..	
674	468	570	506	2,249	2,184	939	963	271	358	..	..	
1,058	870	709	668	2,894	2,598	1,486	1,390	843	444	..	..	24
636	550	433	437	1,695	1,645	838	928	338	403	..	..	
10,842	8,141	8,492	7,069	33,084	29,473	20,410	19,516	8,073	9,742	..	..	25
1,571	847	1,242	861	6,006	4,200	3,368	3,451	991	2,816	..	..	26
1,698	1,207	1,207	1,022	5,261	4,994	3,109	2,852	1,176	1,055	..	..	27
1,238	930	922	660	4,290	3,354	2,317	1,888	746	791	..	..	28
933	682	667	510	2,949	2,744	1,512	1,361	442	593	..	..	29
2,707	1,924	2,180	1,688	9,131	7,883	4,468	4,010	1,434	1,518	..	..	30
639	499	431	310	2,045	1,725	1,173	892	328	322	..	..	31

for which details by age periods are not available.
ditto ditto ditto.
ditto ditto ditto.

PROVINCIAL TABLE IV. The ages of the population of

Serial number of district.	Name of district.	Serial number of Municipality.	Name of municipality.	Population.			0—5.		5—10.	
				Persons.	Males.	Females.	Males.	Females.	Males.	Females.
1	2	3	4	5	6	7	8	9	10	11
32	Naini Tal	1	Kashipur	12,773	6,560	6,213	853	1,100	886	598
33	Lucknow	1	Lucknow	240,016	131,502	108,514	12,433	12,578	12,577	11,809
34	Unao	1	Unao	11,809	6,911	4,898	616	613	609	363
35	Rae Bareli ..	1	Rae Bareli	17,329	9,527	7,802	872	890	909	902
36	Sitapur	1	Sitapur	21,578	12,359	9,219	1,024	1,038	1,202	1,208
		2	Khairabad	12,769	6,530	6,239	780	796	888	849
37	Hardoi	1	Hardoi	13,855	8,158	5,697	696	713	770	717
		2	Shahabad	19,545	10,171	9,374	1,290	1,355	1,351	1,246
		3	Sandila	15,241	7,697	7,544	871	922	964	963
38	Kheri	1	Lakhimpur	11,431	6,660	4,771	574	626	638	559
39	Fyzabad	1	Fyzabad *cum* Ajodhya ..	47,519	25,921	21,598	2,369	2,367	2,475	2,221
		2	Tanda	19,378	9,635	9,743	1,347	1,322	1,881	1,280
40	Gonda	1	Gonda	12,567	6,786	5,781	676	637	727	711
		2	Balrampur	13,937	7,191	6,746	653	702	858	821
41	Bahraich	1	Bahraich	26,907	14,227	12,680	1,450	1,548	1,705	1,756
42	Bara Banki ..	1	Nawabganj	14,127	7,894	6,233	767	707	846	690
43	Rampur	1	Rampur	72,208	36,817	35,391	5,120	5,152	5,067	4,563

Municipalities with above 10,000 inhabitants. PROVINCIAL TABLE IV.

10–15.		15–20.		20–40.		40–60.		60 and over.		Unspecified.		Serial number of district
Males.	Females.	Males.	Females.	Males.	Females.	Males.	Females.	Males.	Females.	Males.	Females.	
12	13	14	15	16	17	18	19	20	21	22	23	1
722	550	471	405	2,284	2,092	1,180	1,076	264	392	..	..	32
12,493	8,927	11,177	8,362	48,146	38,005	26,161	20,974	8,515	7,859	..	..	33
707	745	636	397	2,632	1,620	1,377	883	334	277	..	..	34
889	728	953	608	3,445	2,638	1,883	1,479	576	557	..	..	35
1,298	937	1,183	717	4,710	3,180	2,289	1,687	653	457	..	..	36
764	568	525	426	1,950	2,078	1,173	1,078	450	444	..	..	
773	509	771	518	3,239	1,932	1,506	995	403	313	..	..	37
1,115	859	820	681	3,176	2,818	1,709	1,711	710	704	..	..	
874	682	668	623	2,315	2,475	1,443	1,407	562	472	..	..	
664	426	569	385	2,589	1,658	1,303	829	323	288	..	..	38
2,232	1,560	2,060	1,488	9,503	7,661	5,446	4,605	1,836	1,696	..	..	39
1,110	934	717	685	2,876	3,179	1,615	1,664	589	679	..	..	
543	494	599	449	2,618	2,012	1,255	1,069	368	409	..	..	40
797	888	612	574	2,571	2,123	1,375	1,165	325	473	..	..	
1,605	1,185	1,187	992	5,047	4,387	2,498	2,105	735	707	..	..	41
795	602	715	470	2,679	2,191	1,608	1,170	484	403	..	..	42
4,187	3,312	2,457	2,310	10,536	10,925	6,920	6,431	2,530	2,493	..	203	43

APPENDIX.

NOTE.—On the 1st November 1911 a tenth division—that of Jhansi—was created; and on the 1st April 1911 certain portions of the Family Domains of the Maharaja of Benares were erected into a Native State. This appendix gives the figures of tables I, III, VI, VII, VIII, X, XI, XII, part II, XIII, XV-A, XVII and XVIII according to the arrangement resulting from these territorial changes. For tables I, III, VI, the information given is for all districts and divisions, as well as the State of Benares; in other tables, the new figures for British Territory, Agra Province, Benares division and district, Mirzapur district and the States are alone given.

Tables VII and XV-A according to the second census taken in June or July 1911 in certain cities (see paragraph 20 of the Report) are also appended.

TABLE I.—Showing the area, number of houses and population.

Serial number.	District or State.	Area in square miles.	Towns.	Villages.	Occupied houses.			Population.								
					Total.	In towns.	In villages.	Persons.			Males.			Females.		
								Total.	Urban.	Rural.	Total.	Urban.	Rural.	Total.	Urban.	Rural.
1	2	3	4	5	6	7	8	9	10	11	12	13	14	15	16	17
	British Territory ..	**106,402**	**417**	**104,549**	**10,123,520**	**1,056,094**	**9,067,426**	**46,835,108**	**4,807,210**	**42,027,898**	**24,469,373**	**2,596,147**	**21,873,226**	**22,365,735**	**2,211,063**	**20,154,672**
	Agra Province ..	**82,244**	**343**	**80,232**	**7,396,592**	**862,741**	**6,533,851**	**34,277,104**	**3,964,116**	**30,312,988**	**17,984,673**	**2,140,911**	**15,843,762**	**16,292,431**	**1,823,205**	**14,469,226**
	Meerut Division ..	*9,248*	*83*	*5,980*	*1,018,282*	*165,493*	*852,789*	*4,642,950*	*771,463*	*3,871,487*	*2,521,433*	*431,971*	*2,089,462*	*2,121,517*	*339,492*	*1,782,025*
1	Dehra Dun	1,190	7	423	46,632	15,001	31,631	205,075	55,654	149,421	120,908	37,265	83,643	84,167	18,389	65,778
2	Saharanpur	2,135	16	1,605	227,210	31,771	195,439	986,359	182,109	804,250	541,091	101,851	439,240	445,268	80,258	365,010
3	Muzaffarnagar ..	1,678	15	929	180,531	25,701	154,830	808,360	113,355	695,005	444,862	62,858	382,004	363,498	50,497	313,001
4	Meerut	2,844	24	1,502	328,020	56,232	271,788	1,519,364	253,678	1,265,686	822,305	141,637	680,668	697,059	112,041	585,018
5	Bulandshahr	1,906	21	1,521	235,889	36,788	199,101	1,123,792	166,667	957,125	592,267	88,360	503,907	531,525	78,307	453,218
	Agra Division ..	*8,654*	*66*	*6,712*	*987,969*	*159,400*	*828,569*	*4,513,458*	*696,902*	*3,816,556*	*2,461,847*	*380,051*	*2,081,796*	*2,051,611*	*316,851*	*1,734,760*
6	Aligarh	1,946	19	1,774	246,557	41,429	205,128	1,165,680	189,755	975,925	629,524	103,959	525,565	536,156	85,796	450,360
7	Muttra	1,450	14	832	152,633	30,920	121,713	656,310	122,198	534,112	361,507	66,933	294,574	294,803	55,265	239,538
8	Agra	1,855	9	1,205	227,775	50,732	177,043	1,021,847	229,550	792,297	557,320	125,012	432,308	464,527	104,538	359,989
9	Mainpuri	1,674	7	1,380	173,503	11,594	161,909	797,624	48,512	749,112	438,920	26,666	412,254	358,704	21,846	336,858
10	Etah	1,729	17	1,521	187,501	24,725	162,776	871,997	106,887	765,110	474,576	57,481	417,095	397,421	49,406	348,015
	Rohilkhand Division	*10,829*	*63*	*11,533*	*1,265,615*	*156,957*	*1,108,658*	*5,650,518*	*871,194*	*4,779,324*	*3,050,265*	*458,005*	*2,592,260*	*2,600,253*	*413,189*	*2,187,064*
11	Bareilly	1,579	11	1,938	246,817	34,037	212,780	1,094,663	180,604	914,059	593,836	97,782	496,054	500,827	82,822	418,005
12	Bijnor	1,879	16	2,139	186,624	33,795	152,829	806,202	163,060	643,142	427,153	83,565	343,588	379,049	79,495	299,554
13	Budaun	2,010	11	1,836	238,073	22,231	215,842	1,053,328	104,694	948,634	577,561	55,906	521,655	475,767	48,788	426,979
14	Moradabad	2,285	14	2,490	277,960	31,627	246,333	1,262,933	258,100	1,004,833	676,151	134,486	541,665	586,782	123,614	463,168
15	Shahjahanpur ..	1,726	6	2,062	208,582	24,360	184,222	945,775	113,450	832,325	513,562	58,965	454,597	432,213	54,485	377,728
16	Pilibhit	1,350	5	1,068	107,559	10,907	96,652	487,617	51,286	436,331	262,002	27,301	234,701	225,615	23,985	201,630
	Allahabad Division	*10,246*	*29*	*9,996*	*1,133,574*	*148,719*	*984,855*	*4,946,504*	*599,502*	*4,347,002*	*2,628,691*	*332,303*	*2,296,388*	*2,317,813*	*267,199*	*2,050,614*
17	Farrukhabad	1,688	8	1,669	201,970	27,590	174,380	900,022	115,727	784,295	494,017	61,844	432,173	406,005	53,883	352,122
18	Etawah	1,691	5	1,481	158,202	14,099	144,103	760,121	64,381	695,740	416,648	34,676	381,972	343,473	29,705	313,768
19	Cawnpore	2,372	4	1,978	276,765	55,707	221,058	1,142,286	190,458	951,833	623,437	109,678	513,759	518,849	80,775	438,074
20	Fatehpur	1,642	4	1,368	158,474	6,156	152,318	676,939	28,157	648,782	350,207	14,643	335,564	326,732	13,514	313,218
21	Allahabad	2,858	8	3,505	338,163	45,167	292,996	1,467,136	200,784	1,266,352	744,382	111,462	632,920	722,754	89,322	633,432
	Jhansi Division ..	*10,440*	*27*	*4,121*	*511,975*	*57,477*	*454,438*	*2,207,923*	*264,811*	*1,943,112*	*1,126,720*	*137,046*	*989,674*	*1,081,203*	*127,765*	*953,438*
22	Jhansi	3,634	11	1,321	157,424	28,667	128,757	680,688	133,190	547,498	350,192	70,307	279,885	330,496	62,883	267,613
23	Jalaun	1,549	5	836	89,929	10,801	79,128	404,775	47,793	356,982	209,525	24,683	184,842	195,250	23,110	172,140
24	Hamirpur	2,292	7	758	110,815	10,372	100,443	465,223	47,805	417,418	234,842	23,805	211,037	230,381	24,000	206,381
25	Banda	2,965	4	1,211	153,747	7,637	146,110	657,237	36,023	621,214	332,161	18,251	313,910	325,076	17,772	307,304
	Benares Division ..	*9,562*	*34*	*12,426*	*931,629*	*109,463*	*822,166*	*4,462,542*	*465,418*	*3,997,124*	*2,229,787*	*239,709*	*1,990,078*	*2,232,755*	*225,709*	*2,007,046*
26	Benares	1,007	8	1,990	187,460	53,992	133,468	896,344	217,012	679,332	451,545	112,926	338,619	444,799	104,086	340,713
27	Mirzapur	4,369	5	2,784	157,003	12,702	144,301	724,801	51,479	673,322	358,278	27,040	331,238	366,523	24,439	342,084
28	Jaunpur	1,550	7	3,169	244,851	12,629	232,222	1,156,254	52,889	1,103,365	576,070	27,260	548,810	580,184	25,629	554,555
29	Ghazipur	1,392	9	2,540	170,174	14,366	155,808	839,725	71,549	768,176	420,200	36,011	384,189	419,525	35,538	383,987
30	Ballia	1,244	10	1,943	172,141	15,774	156,367	845,418	72,489	772,929	423,694	36,472	387,222	421,724	36,017	385,707
	Native States ..	**5,944**	**6**	**3,659**	**243,199**	**22,830**	**220,369**	**1,178,972**	**93,061**	**1,085,911**	**603,898**	**48,476**	**555,422**	**575,074**	**44,585**	**530,489**
31	Rampur	899	5	998	125,082	22,112	102,970	531,217	89,657	441,560	282,978	46,774	236,204	248,239	42,883	205,356
32	Tehri-Garhwal ..	4,180	..	1,187	45,506	..	45,506	300,819	..	300,819	148,462	..	148,462	152,357	..	152,357
33	Benares Raj	865	1	1,474	72,611	718	71,893	346,936	3,404	343,532	172,458	1,702	170,756	174,478	1,702	172,776

TABLE III.—Towns and villages classified by population.

Serial number.	District or State.	Total number of inhabited towns and villages.	Population.	Under 500.		500—1,000.		1,000—2,000.		2,000—5,000.		5,000—10,000.		10,000—20,000.		20,000—50,000.		50,000—100,000.		100,000 and over.		Encampments, boats and railway population unclassed.
				No.	Population.	No.	Population.	No.	Population.	No.	Population.	No.	Population.	No.	Population.	No.	Population.	No.	Population.	No.	Population.	
1	2	3	4	5	6	7	8	9	10	11	12	13	14	15	16	17	18	19	20	21	22	23
	British Territory ..	**104,966**	**46,835,108**	**77,675**	**15,827,544**	**18,494**	**12,802,674**	**6,878**	**9,220,421**	**1,655**	**4,570,904**	**168**	**1,101,368**	**63**	**899,506**	**17**	**533,786**	**9**	**577,012**	**7**	**1,242,024**	**59,869**
	Agra Province ..	**80,575**	**34,277,104**	**61,554**	**11,961,758**	**12,749**	**8,801,611**	**4,831**	**6,494,577**	**1,231**	**3,417,188**	**133**	**870,352**	**48**	**685,814**	**15**	**485,559**	**8**	**522,815**	**6**	**983,060**	**54,370**
	Meerut Division ..	*6,063*	*4,642,950*	*3,318*	*782,089*	*1,544*	*1,098,485*	*832*	*1,138,158*	*312*	*899,959*	*41*	*267,754*	*10*	*154,806*	*4*	*118,144*	*1*	*62,232*	*1*	*118,034*	*3,294*
1	Dehra Dun ..	430	205,075	341	49,647	44	30,312	27	37,007	16	42,346	1	6,552	..	..	1	38,610	..	..	..	..	1
2	Saharanpur ..	1,621	986,359	1,029	236,360	393	272,933	153	199,967	38	113,108	3	24,602	3	46,048	1	28,544	1	62,232	..	..	2,565
3	Muzaffarnagar ..	944	808,360	463	106,754	244	176,312	156	216,138	68	197,971	11	69,489	1	17,699	1	23,603	..	..	..	..	394
4	Meerut ..	1,526	1,519,364	655	163,434	415	299,168	307	428,205	130	370.328	16	102,027	2	31,234	..	..	..	..	1	118,034	334
5	Bulandshahr ..	1,542	1,123,792	830	225,894	448	319,760	189	256,236	60	170,206	10	64,484	4	59,825	1	27,387	..	..	..	..	..
	Agra Division ..	*6,778*	*4,513,458*	*4,088*	*1,033,962*	*1,648*	*1,152,026*	*760*	*1,036,127*	*251*	*703,151*	*18*	*110,337*	*9*	*130,807*	*1*	*37,237*	*2*	*122,381*	*1*	*184,679*	*2,751*
6	Aligarh ..	1,793	1,165,680	1,080	277,143	443	303,934	210	288,984	54	153,762	2	13,234	2	25,944	1	37,237	1	64,825	..	..	617
7	Muttra	846	656,310	481	120,122	204	144,250	108	147,271	52	144,158	4	23,431	1	18,403	..	..	1	57,556	..	..	1,119
8	Agra	1,214	1,021,847	645	174,019	331	230,590	172	233,253	62	173.466	2	11,669	1	13,571	..	..	..	..	1	184,679	600
9	Mainpuri ..	1,387	797,624	889	218,579	317	223,655	127	172,377	48	128,770	4	23,950	2	30,086	..	..	..	..	..	..	207
10	Etah	1,588	871,997	993	244,099	353	249,597	148	194,242	36	102,995	6	38,033	3	42,803	..	..	..	..	..	..	208
	Rohilkhand Division	*11,596*	*5,650,518*	*8,357*	*1,907,763*	*2,358*	*1,607,903*	*702*	*930,224*	*131*	*377,040*	*28*	*184,522*	*12*	*178,619*	*5*	*179,189*	*2*	*152,186*	*1*	*128,628*	*4,444*
11	Bareilly	1,949	1,094,663	1,288	324,325	474	327,639	152	198,415	31	89,623	2	12,084	1	13,000	..	..	..	..	1	128,628	949
12	Bijnor	2,155	806,202	1,785	335,117	277	182,724	68	83,441	15	42,686	8	53,409	7	108,470	..	..	..	..	..	..	355
13	Budaun	1,847	1,053,328	1,151	289,908	475	327.937	182	244,413	30	87,786	7	46,946	1	17,993	1	38,190	..	..	..	..	155
14	Moradabad ..	2,504	1,262,953	1,834	430,535	501	336,588	132	173.609	26	77,421	6	42,816	1	10,682	3	109,747	1	80,472	..	..	1,063
15	Shahjahanpur ..	2,068	945,775	1,530	345,063	390	269,627	122	159,635	20	57,297	4	23,467	1	18,388	..	..	1	71,714	..	..	584
16	Pilibhit	1,073	487,617	769	182,815	241	163,388	51	70,711	9	22,227	1	5,800	1	10,086	1	31,252	..	..	..	..	1,338
	Allahabad Division	*10,025*	*4,946,504*	*7,201*	*1,631,102*	*1,884*	*1,310,305*	*758*	*1,009,352*	*167*	*447,358*	*9*	*54,415*	*2*	*34,786*	*1*	*45,781*	*1*	*59,447*	*2*	*348,297*	*5,661*
17	Farrukhabad ..	1,677	900,022	1,152	270,088	347	236,900	131	175,722	41	112,161	4	26,930	1	18,043	..	..	1	59,447	..	..	736
18	Etawah	1,486	760,121	1,020	248,645	315	219.993	121	157,363	26	71.131	3	16,852	..	..	1	45,781	..	..	..	..	356
19	Cawnpore ..	1,982	1,142,286	1,333	323,008	416	287,461	196	256,303	36	96,534	..	..	..	..	..	..	..	..	1	177,967	998
20	Fatehpur ..	1,367	676,939	956	222,167	250	179,404	124	165,609	35	87,363	1	5,614	1	16,743	..	..	..	..	..	..	39
21	Allahabad ...	3,513	1,467,136	2,740	567,199	556	386,547	186	254,355	29	80,149	1	5,019	..	..	..	..	..	..	1	170,330	3,587
	Jhansi Division ..	*4,148*	*2,207,923*	*2,790*	*597,568*	*850*	*592,291*	*396*	*539,914*	*94*	*259,597*	*11*	*73,829*	*5*	*63,226*	*1*	*20,980*	*1*	*70,208*	..	..	*310*
22	Jhansi	1,332	680,688	941	203,705	281	197,087	84	108,232	20	57,030	3	19,047	2	25,227	..	..	1	70,208	..	..	152
23	Jalaun	841	404,775	612	126,179	137	95,408	74	100 598	14	38,114	2	17,376	2	27,048	..	..	..	..	..	..	52
24	Hamirpur ..	760	465,223	456	99,674	175	120,930	97	129,242	26	72,535	5	31,815	1	10,951	..	..	..	..	..	..	76
25	Banda	1,215	657,237	781	168,010	257	178,866	141	191,842	34	91,918	1	5,591	..	..	1	20,980	..	..	..	..	30
	Benares Division ..	*12,460*	*4,462,542*	*10,025*	*1,781,936*	*1,707*	*1,169,597*	*588*	*789,124*	*121*	*308,452*	*13*	*93,888*	*2*	*26,770*	*3*	*84,228*	..	..	*1*	*203,422*	*5,125*
26	Benares	1,993	896,344	1,565	305,772	322	219,186	91	122,459	13	82,772	..	..	1	10,210	..	..	..	..	1	203,422	1,523
27	Mirzapur ..	2,789	724,801	2,470	397,582	243	170,249	62	79,723	12	34,592	1	8,609	..	..	1	32,168	..	..	..	..	1,878
28	Jaunpur ..	3,176	1,156,254	2,461	499,765	541	308,564	151	198,326	20	47,630	2	11,106	..	..	1	30,181	..	..	..	..	682
29	Ghazipur ..	2,549	839.725	2,092	341,591	306	210,436	121	164,728	25	67,840	4	32,678	..	..	1	21,879	..	..	..	..	578
30	Ballia	1,953	845,418	1,437	236,226	295	201,162	163	223,888	51	125,618	6	41,495	1	16,560	..	..	..	..	..	..	469
	Native States ..	**3,665**	**1,178,972**	**3,196**	**681,467**	**362**	**245,573**	**85**	**109,178**	**19**	**51,986**	**2**	**15,114**	..	..	..	..	**1**	**74,135**	..	..	**1,519**
31	Rampur ..	1,003	531,217	718	178,811	201	139,060	67	85,645	14	37,464	2	15,114	..	..	..	..	1	74,135	..	..	1,488
32	Tehri-Garhwal ..	1,187	300,819	1,161	285,982	26	14,837	..	..	..	..	..	..	..	..	..	..	..	..	..	..	..
33	Benares Raj ..	1,475	346,936	1,317	217,174	135	91,676	18	23,538	5	14,522	..	..	..	..	..	..	..	..	..	..	31

TABLE VI.—Population by Religion.

Serial number.	District or State.	Population.			Indo-Arya religions.											
					Hindu, Brahmanic.			Hindu, Arya.			Hindu, Brahmo.			Jain.		
		Persons.	Males.	Females.	Persons.	Males.	Females.	Persons.	Males.	Females.	Persons.	Males.	Females.	Persons.	Males.	Females.
1	2	3	4	5	6	7	8	9	10	11	12	13	14	15	16	17
	British Territory ..	**46,835,108**	**24,469,373**	**22,365,735**	**39,802,459**	**20,790,986**	**19,011,473**	**131,100**	**73,178**	**57,922**	**41**	**24**	**17**	**75,421**	**40,892**	**34,529**
	Agra Province ..	**34,277,104**	**17,984,673**	**16,292,431**	**28,969,975**	**15,191,154**	**13,778,841**	**125,653**	**69,976**	**55,677**	**29**	**15**	**14**	**73,704**	**39,947**	**33,757**
	Meerut Division ..	*4,642,950*	*2,521,433*	*2,121,517*	*3,377,847*	*1,835,542*	*1,542,305*	*43,377*	*24,441*	*18,936*	*8*	*8*	..	*31,220*	*17,089*	*14,131*
1	Dehra Dun	205,075	120,908	84,167	169,614	99,241	70,373	1,144	686	458	8	8	..	320	188	132
2	Saharanpur	986,359	541,091	445,268	638,354	350,151	288,203	6,841	4,042	2,799	..	..	..	4,451	2,388	2,063
3	Muzaffarnagar	808,360	444,862	363,498	558,793	308,607	250,186	6,224	3,551	2,673	..	..	..	8,163	4,469	3,694
4	Meerut	1,519,364	822,305	697,059	1,124,867	609,606	515,261	11,797	6,683	5,114	..	..	..	16,935	9,330	7,605
5	Bulandshahr	1,123,792	592,267	531,525	886,219	467,937	418,282	17,371	9,479	7,892	..	..	..	1,351	714	637
	Agra Division ..	*4,513,458*	*2,461,847*	*2,051,611*	*3,963,438*	*2,164,414*	*1,799,024*	*30,434*	*16,714*	*13,720*	*14*	*4*	*10*	*24,395*	*13,350*	*11,045*
6	Aligarh	1,165,680	629,524	536,156	991,634	535,646	455,988	15,874	8,559	7,315	7	2	5	2,831	1,564	1,267
7	Muttra	656,310	361,507	294,803	584,647	322,049	262,598	2,313	1,280	1,033	..	..	..	1,457	796	661
8	Agra	1,021,847	557,320	464,527	885,841	483,777	402,064	2,788	1,623	1,165	7	2	5	11,210	6,100	5,110
9	Mainpuri	797,624	438,920	358,704	741,028	408,225	332,803	4,923	2,770	2,153	..	..	..	4,605	2,569	2,036
10	Etah	871,997	474,576	397,421	760,288	414,717	345,571	4,536	2,482	2,054	..	..	..	4,292	2,321	1,971
	Rohilkhand Division	*5,650,518*	*3,050,265*	*2,600,253*	*4,153,593*	*2,260,282*	*1,893,311*	*31,608*	*17,512*	*14,096*	..	..	..	*1,940*	*1,028*	*912*
11	Bareilly	1,094,663	593,836	500,827	801,502	437,200	364,302	3,832	2,102	1,730	..	..	..	3	3	..
12	Bijnor	806,202	427,153	379,049	508,805	272,619	236,186	12,394	6,885	5,509	..	..	..	925	476	449
13	Budaun	1,053,328	577,561	475,767	859,688	473,457	386,231	5,631	3,146	2,485	..	..	..	197	121	76
14	Moradabad	1,262,933	676,151	586,782	784,550	424,397	360,153	6,985	3,855	3,130	..	..	..	785	410	375
15	Shahjahanpur	945,775	513,562	432,213	801,274	437,842	363,432	1,301	750	551	..	..	..	27	15	12
16	Pilibhit	487,617	262,002	225,615	397,774	214,767	183,007	1,465	774	691	..	..	..	3	3	..
	Allahabad Division ..	*4,946,504*	*2,628,691*	*2,317,813*	*4,383,598*	*2,334,308*	*2,049,290*	*12,075*	*6,839*	*5,236*	*2*	*1*	*1*	*3,574*	*1,958*	*1,616*
17	Farrukhabad	900,022	494,017	406,005	788,623	435,300	353,323	4,016	2,248	1,768	..	..	..	500	272	228
18	Etawah	760,121	416,648	343,473	707,354	388,388	318,966	4,474	2,563	1,911	..	..	..	1,933	1,064	869
19	Cawnpore	1,142,286	623,437	518,849	1,029,563	561,249	468,314	2,551	1,429	1,122	..	..	..	423	260	163
20	Fatehpur	676,939	350,207	326,732	597,966	310,830	287,136	442	231	211	..	..	..	81	41	40
21	Allahabad	1,467,136	744,382	722,754	1,260,092	638,541	621,551	592	368	224	2	1	1	637	321	316
	Jhansi Division ..	*2,207,923*	*1,126,720*	*1,081,203*	*2,059,745*	*1,050,588*	*1,009,157*	*971*	*555*	*416*	..	..	..	*12,020*	*6,206*	*5,814*
22	Jhansi	680,688	350,192	330,496	629,671	322,423	307,248	238	144	94	..	..	..	11,369	5,881	5,488
23	Jalaun	404,775	209,525	195,250	376,750	195,141	181,609	110	68	42	..	..	..	266	143	123
24	Hamirpur	465,223	234,842	230,381	434,024	219,756	214,268	266	151	115	..	..	..	85	41	44
25	Banda	657,237	332,161	325,076	619,300	313,268	306,032	357	192	165	..	..	..	300	141	159
	Benares Division ..	*4,462,542*	*2,229,787*	*2,232,755*	*4,085,141*	*2,043,095*	*2,042,046*	*3,212*	*1,737*	*1,475*	*5*	*2*	*3*	*439*	*245*	*194*
26	Benares	896,344	451,545	444,799	796,280	400,287	395,993	637	374	263	..	..	..	301	170	131
27	Mirzapur	724,801	358,278	366,523	681,888	336,762	345,126	468	241	227	5	2	3	125	67	58
28	Jaunpur	1,156,254	576,070	580,184	1,053,003	524,876	528,127	1,803	946	857	..	..	..	12	7	5
29	Ghazipur	839,725	420,200	419,525	762,435	383,730	378,705	155	92	63	..	..	..	1	1	..
30	Ballia	845,418	423,694	421,724	791,535	397,440	394,095	149	84	65	..	..	..	..	..	..
	Native States	*1,178,972*	*603,898*	*575,014*	*902,894*	*458,586*	*444,308*	**538**	**288**	**250**	..	..	..	**314**	**181**	**133**
31	Rampur	531,217	282,978	248,239	284,132	152,417	131,715	481	262	219	..	..	..	259	149	110
32	Tehri-Garhwal	300,819	148,462	152,357	298,983	147,514	151,469	3	2	1	..	..	..	49	29	20
33	Benares Raj	346,936	172,458	174,478	319,779	158,655	161,124	54	24	30	..	..	..	6	3	3

TABLE VI.—Population by Religion—(*concluded*).

Serial number.	District or State.	Indo-Aryan religions—(*concluded*) Sikh. Persons	Sikh. Males.	Sikh. Females.	Buddhist. Persons.	Buddhist. Males.	Buddhist. Females.	Muhammadan. Persons.	Muhammadan. Males.	Muhammadan. Females.	Christian. Persons.	Christian. Males	Christian. Females.	Parsi. Persons.	Parsi. Males.	Parsi. Females.	Jew. Persons.	Jew. Males.	Jew. Females.
1	2	18	19	20	21	22	23	24	25	26	27	28	29	30	31	32	33	34	35
	British Territory ..	**15,157**	**9,986**	**5,171**	**780**	**444**	**336**	**6,631,320**	**3,452,534**	**3,178,786**	**177,916**	**100,803**	**77,113**	**872**	**504**	**368**	**42**	**22**	**20**
	Agra Province ..	**12,615**	**8,265**	**4,350**	**749**	**429**	**320**	**4,930,633**	**2,583,205**	**2,347,428**	**163,036**	**91,296**	**71,740**	**689**	**394**	**295**	**21**	**12**	**9**
	Meerut Division ..	*1,007*	*4,228*	*2,779*	*6*	*6*	..	*1,142,016*	*616,488*	*525,528*	*41,420*	*23,599*	*17,821*	*49*	*32*	*17*	..	..	..
1	Dehra Dun	1,158	833	325	..	..	..	27,794	17,108	10,686	5,036	2,844	2,192	1	..	1	..	..	..
2	Saharanpur	2,055	1,316	739	6	6	..	329,094	179,846	149,248	5,548	3,333	2,215	10	9	1	..	..	..
3	Muzaffarnagar	720	410	310	..	..	..	231,873	125,338	105,535	2,583	1,485	1,098	4	2	2	..	..	..
4	Meerut	2,706	1,472	1,234	..	..	..	344,888	184,472	160,416	18,142	10,724	7,418	29	18	11	..	..	..
5	Bulandshahr	368	197	171	..	..	..	208,367	108,724	99,643	10,111	5,213	4,898	5	3	2	..	..	..
	Agra Division ..	*888*	*512*	*376*	..	..	..	*455,504*	*245,707*	*209,797*	*38,640*	*21,064*	*17,576*	*137*	*76*	*61*	*8*	*6*	*2*
6	Aligarh	59	45	14	..	..	..	143,314	77,507	65,807	11,947	6,193	5,754	14	8	6	..	..	..
7	Muttra	117	66	51	..	..	..	61,759	33,917	27,842	5,992	3,387	2,605	24	11	13	1	1	..
8	Agra	138	89	49	..	..	..	114,555	61,360	53,195	7,229	4,319	2,910	72	45	27	7	5	2
9	Mainpuri	171	98	73	..	..	..	44,477	23,977	20,500	2,395	1,271	1,124	25	10	15	..	..	..
10	Etah	403	214	189	..	..	..	91,399	48,946	42,453	11,077	5,894	5,183	2	2	..	..	..	..
	Rohilkhand Division ..	*1,243*	*762*	*481*	*3*	*3*	..	*1,411,809*	*742,773*	*669,036*	*50,266*	*27,866*	*22,400*	*56*	*39*	*17*	..	..	..
11	Bareilly	476	276	200	3	3	..	276,230	146,503	129,727	12,591	7,731	4,860	26	18	8	..	..	..
12	Bijnor	261	121	140	..	..	..	280,501	145,339	135,162	3,315	1,712	1,603	1	1	..	..	..	..
13	Budaun	138	76	62	..	..	..	176,376	94,727	81,649	11,298	6,034	5,264	..	..	..	..	..	..
14	Moradabad	296	248	48	..	..	..	453,269	238,140	215,129	17,023	9,084	7,939	25	17	8	..	..	..
15	Shahjahanpur	56	30	26	..	..	..	139,159	72,768	66,391	3,954	2,154	1,800	4	3	1	..	..	..
16	Pilibhit	16	11	5	..	..	..	86,274	45,296	40,978	2,085	1,151	934	..	..	..	..	..	..
	Allahabad Division ..	*1,545*	*1,271*	*274*	*25*	*16*	*9*	*529,851*	*274,993*	*254,858*	*15,662*	*9,192*	*6,470*	*165*	*110*	*55*	*7*	*3*	*4*
17	Farrukhabad	35	17	18	7	5	2	104,293	54,804	49,489	2,548	1,371	1,177	..	..	..	..	..	..
18	Etawah	29	17	12	1	..	1	45,628	24,227	21,401	693	383	310	7	5	2	2	1	1
19	Cawnpore	448	372	76	1	1	..	104,001	56,828	47,173	5,224	3,251	1,973	72	46	26	3	1	2
20	Fatehpur	..	..	..	..	..	..	78,308	39,052	39,256	142	53	89	..	..	..	..	..	..
21	Allahabad	1,033	865	168	16	10	6	197,621	100,082	97,539	7,055	4,134	2,921	86	59	27	2	1	1
	Jhansi Division ..	*1,094*	*920*	*174*	..	..	..	*129,100*	*65,418*	*63,682*	*4,726*	*2,905*	*1,821*	*267*	*128*	*139*	..	..	..
22	Jhansi	1,013	871	142	..	..	..	34,169	18,166	16,003	3,970	2,584	1,386	258	123	135	..	..	..
23	Jalaun	42	23	19	..	..	..	27,408	14,040	13,368	195	108	87	4	2	2	..	..	..
24	Hamirpur	30	20	10	..	..	..	30,455	14,777	15,678	363	97	266	..	..	..	..	..	..
25	Banda	9	6	3	..	..	..	37,068	18,435	18,633	198	116	82	5	3	2	..	..	..
	Benares Division ..	*568*	*407*	*161*	..	..	..	*368,845*	*182,229*	*186,616*	*4,317*	*2,063*	*2,254*	*7*	*4*	*3*	*8*	*5*	*3*
26	Benares	373	300	73	..	..	..	96,812	49,481	47,331	1,929	926	1,003	4	2	2	8	5	3
27	Mirzapur	118	67	51	..	..	..	41,499	20,823	20,676	695	314	381	3	2	1	..	..	..
28	Jaunpur	23	13	10	..	..	..	101,296	50,195	51,101	117	33	84	..	..	..	..	..	..
29	Ghazipur	5	3	2	..	..	..	76,561	36,090	40,471	568	284	284	..	..	..	..	..	..
30	Ballia	49	24	25	..	..	..	52,677	25,640	27,037	1,008	506	502	..	..	..	..	..	..
	Native States ..	**29**	**13**	**16**	..	..	..	**273,411**	**143,885**	**129,526**	**1,786**	**945**	**841**	..	..	..	..	..	..
31	Rampur	2	1	1	..	..	..	244,604	129,228	115,376	1,739	921	818	..	..	..	..	..	..
32	Tehri-Garhwal	24	10	14	..	..	..	1,754	904	850	6	3	3	..	..	..	..	..	..
33	Benares Raj	3	2	1	..	..	..	27,053	13,753	13,300	41	21	20	..	..	..	..	..	..

TABLE VII.—Age, sex and civil conditions

Serial number.	District or State.	Total.		0—5.		5—10.		10—15.	
		Males.	Females.	Males.	Females	Males.	Females.	Males.	Females.
1	2	3	4	5	6	7	8	9	10
								(1) All Reli	
	British Territory ..	**2,4469,373**	**2,2365,735**	**2,836,838**	**2,832,193**	**3,274,672**	**2,964,919**	**2,999,196**	**2,298,616**
	Benares Division ..	*2,229,787*	*2,232,755*	*277,182*	*289,651*	*321,874*	*296,527*	*270,516*	*215,048*
1	Benares	451,545	444,799	55,297	58,465	62,675	59,746	52,505	42,603
2	Mirzapur	358,278	366,523	47,202	50,673	52,597	50,874	42,607	35,600
	Native States	**603,898**	**575,074**	**76,546**	**78,504**	**82,671**	**76,679**	**70,241**	**57,632**
3	Rampur	282,978	248,239	36,577	36,520	37,712	33,426	30,848	23,384
4	Tehri-Garhwal	148,462	152,857	18,644	19,964	20,144	19,582	18,168	16,365
5	Benares Raj	172,458	174,478	21,325	22,020	24,815	23,671	21,225	17,883
								All Religions—	
	British Territory ..	**10,993,972**	**6,842,818**	**2,816,339**	**2,802,473**	**3,112,976**	**2,654,505**	**2,335,714**	**1,071,423**
	Benares Division ..	*969,104*	*644,973*	*272,351*	*281,980*	*292,930*	*249,857*	*192,473*	*84,201*
1	Benares	185,566	123,785	53,817	56,160	55,379	47,580	87,200	14,939
2	Mirzapur	159,191	114,172	46,507	49,710	49,322	43,891	31,250	15,395
	Native States	**272,989**	**176,187**	**75,950**	**77,298**	**78,279**	**66,590**	**53,550**	**25,449**
3	Rampur	129,963	80,524	36,513	36,317	36,693	30,204	24,699	10,689
4	Tehri-Garhwal	71,552	50,574	18,603	19,885	19,783	18,741	15,762	10,028
5	Benares Raj .. .	71,474	45,089	20,834	21,096	21,809	17,645	18,089	4,732
								All Religions—	
	British Territory ..	**11,562,768**	**11,684,116**	**19,578**	**27,482**	**154,591**	**296,007**	**639,879**	**1,195,586**
	Benares Division ..	*1,092,886*	*1,142,796*	*4,582*	*7,022*	*27,507*	*44,463*	*74,529*	*125,984*
1	Benares	238,171	231,812	1,418	2,175	7,088	11,652	14,833	26,791
2	Mirzapur	176,552	181,752	666	857	3,107	6,579	10,926	19,481
	Native States	**290,352**	**307,539**	**561**	**1,083**	**4,216**	**9,546**	**16,173**	**31,285**
3	Rampur	180,030	130,754	64	194	1,002	3,156	5,969	12,424
4	Tehri-Garhwal	72,313	83,056	40	76	361	817	2,884	6,273
5	Benares Raj	88,009	93,729	457	813	2,853	5,573	7,820	12,588
								All Religions—	
	British Territory ..	**1,912,633**	**3,838,801**	**921**	**2,238**	**7,105**	**14,407**	**23,603**	**31,607**
	Benares Division ..	*176,797*	*444,986*	*249*	*649*	*1,437*	*2,707*	*3,514*	*4,863*
1	Benares	82,808	89,202	62	130	258	514	472	875
2	Mirzapur	22,585	70,599	29	106	168	404	431	784
	Native States	**40,557**	**91,348**	**35**	**123**	**176**	**543**	**518**	**898**
3	Rampur	22,985	36,961		9	17	66	180	271
4	Tehri-Garhwal	4,597	18,727	1	8	..	24	22	64
5	Benares Raj	12,975	35,660	34	111	159	453	316	563
								Hindus—	
	British Territory ..	**20,790,986**	**19,011,473**	**2,395,331**	**2,386,647**	**2,776,397**	**2,508,312**	**2,542,862**	**1,943,930**
	Benares Division ..	*2,043,095*	*2,042,046*	*252,195*	*263,669*	*294,073*	*270,189*	*247,891*	*196,038*
1	Benares	400,287	395,993	48,720	51,533	55,908	52,743	46,360	37,410
2	Mirzapur	336,762	345,126	44,420	47,734	49,567	47,850	40,035	33,452
	Native States	**458,586**	**444,308**	**56,952**	**58,897**	**62,916**	**58,881**	**53,884**	**44,944**
3	Rampur	152,417	131,715	19,052	18,931	20,242	17,646	16,349	12,194
4	Tehri-Garhwal	147,514	151,469	18,516	19,821	20,017	19,481	18,051	16,257
5	Benares Raj	158,655	161,124	19,384	20,145	22,657	21,754	19,484	16,493
								Hindus—	
	British Territory ..	**9,278,850**	**5,694,730**	**2,377,262**	**2,360,620**	**2,630,393**	**2,233,972**	**1,952,912**	**867,521**
	Benares Division ..	*874,948*	*682,213*	*247,715*	*256,467*	*266,815*	*225,804*	*173,647*	*74,502*
1	Benares	162,565	106,677	47,318	49,336	48,876	41,224	31,975	12,086
2	Mirzapur	149,697	107,182	43,816	46,825	46,451	41,277	29,200	14,395
	Native States	**204,050**	**130,775**	**56,398**	**57,828**	**59,001**	**50,205**	**39,966**	**18,154**
3	Rampur	67,549	39,669	19,001	18,817	19,573	15,518	12,442	4,043
4	Tehri-Garhwal	71,089	50,240	18,475	19,742	19,656	18,641	15,660	9,958
5	Benares Raj	65,412	40,866	18,920	19,269	19,772	16,046	11,864	4,153

15—20.		20—40.		40—60.		60 and over.		Unspecified.		Serial number.
Males.	Females.	Males.	Females.	Males	Females.	Males.	Females.	Males	Females	
11	12	13	14	15	16	17	18	19	20	1
gions—Total.										
2,103,952	**1,692,493**	**7,859,194**	**7,409,043**	**4,212,412**	**3,884,976**	**1,182,839**	**1,283,358**	**270**	**137**	
173,528	*146,891*	*712,842*	*769,149*	*860,208*	*374,394*	*113,637*	*141,095*	..	..	
33,996	30,003	145,646	148,997	75,832	75,769	25,594	29,214	..	..	1
28,711	24,690	119,262	125,259	53,896	58,179	14,003	21,188	..	..	2
49,310	**41,441**	**195,422**	**190,546**	**101,127**	**97,223**	**28,581**	**32,844**	..	**205**	
21,653	17,374	93,175	81,327	49,903	42,411	13,110	13,592	..	205	3
!13,606	12,201	46,809	49,527	24,499	25,595	7,092	9,123	..	..	4
14,051	11,866	55,938	59,692	26,725	29,217	8,379	10,129	..	..	5
Unmarried.										
1,055,950	**137,624**	**1,322,150**	**122,248**	**283,946**	**40,645**	**66,744**	**13,834**	**153**	**66**	
77,473	*9,693*	*98,609*	*13,062*	*19,679*	*5,019*	*6,589*	*1,661*	..	..	
14,882	4,478	19,111	2,526	3,874	804	1,303	298	..	..	1
13,203	1,993	15,545	2,337	2,687	630	677	216	..	..	2
25,787	**2,913**	**33,335**	**2,754**	**4,951**	**822**	**1,137**	**281**	..	**80**	
11,920	1,818	17,176	1,414	2,491	403	471	99	..	80	3
8,866	1,242	8,247	523	680	115	111	40	..	..	4
|5,501	853	7,912	817	1,780	304	555	142	..	..	5
Married.										
998,574	**1,499,700**	**5,948,644**	**6,430,632**	**3,136,123**	**2,016,939**	**665,282**	**217,719**	**97**	**51**	
90,756	*130,882*	*555,783*	*639,920*	*273,693*	*171,961*	*66,036*	*22,564*	..	..	
18,353	27,414	116,986	125,210	59,338	34,493	15,205	4,077	..	..	1
14,745	21,691	95,475	103,760	42,774	25,628	8,859	3,756	..	..	2
22,536	**37,384**	**148,398**	**168,732**	**80,530**	**53,679**	**17,938**	**5,730**	..	**100**	
9,250	15,646	67,808	73,249	38,311	23,936	7,631	2,049	..	100	3
5,180	10,822	36 987	46,279	22,050	16,754	5,311	2,035	..	..	4
8,106	10,916	43,608	49,204	20,169	12,989	4,996	1,646	..	..	5
Widowed.										
49,428	**55,169**	**588,400**	**856,163**	**.792,343**	**1,827,392**	**450,813**	**1,051,805**	**20**	**20**	
5,299	*6,816*	*58,450*	*116,167*	*66,836*	*197,414*	*41,012*	*116,870*	..	..	
761	1,111	9,549	21,261	12,620	40,472	9,086	24,839	..	..	1
763	1,006	8,242	19,162	8,485	31,921	4,467	17,216	..	..	2
987	**1,144**	**13,689**	**19,060**	**15,646**	**42,722**	**9,506**	**26,833**	..	**25**	
483	410	8,196	6,664	9,101	18,072	5,008	11,444	..	25	3
60	137	1,075	2,725	1,769	8,726	1,670	7,048	..	..	4
444	597	4,418	9,671	4,776	15,924	2,828	8,341	..	..	5
Total.										
1,789,707	**1,428,728**	**6,711,756**	**6,330,567**	**3,596,525**	**3,326,424**	**978,147**	**1,086,733**	**261**	**132**	
159,598	*133,382*	*658,083*	*706,622*	*880,003*	*843,585*	*101,752*	*128,611*	..	..	
30,040	26,402	129,855	133,881	67,278	68,127	22,126	25,897	..	..	1
27,015	23,225	112,321	118,104	50,454	54,782	12,950	19,979	..	..	2
38,531	**32,574**	**146,943**	**148,076**	**76,059**	**75,339**	**21,301**	**25,595**	..	..	
11,990	9,476	51,085	43,576	27,062	22,753	6,637	7,139	..	..	3
13,525	12,116	46,025	49,244	24,332	25,475	7.048	9,075	..	..	4
13,016	10,982	51,838	55,258	24,665	27,111	7,616	9,881	..	..	5
Unmarried.										
873,824	**100,224**	**1,128,700**	**91,988**	**256,275**	**30,244**	**59,336**	**10,096**	**148**	**63**	
70,168	*8,065*	*91,914*	*11,427*	*18,872*	*4,484*	*6,317*	*1,464*	..	..	
12,592	1,073	16,939	2,057	3,649	654	1,216	247	..	..	1
12,320	1,848	14,697	2,128	2,569	537	644	177	..	..	2
19,343	**1,921**	**24,525**	**1,876**	**3,926**	**571**	**893**	**220**	..	..	
5,940	899	8,786	643	1,541	195	266	54	..	..	3
8,323	1,230	8,198	516	671	114	111	39	..	..	4
5,080	292	7,546	717	1,714	262	516	127	..	..	5

TABLE VII.—Age, sex and civil conditions

Serial number.	District or State.	Total.		0—5.		5—10.		10—15.	
		Males.	Females.	Males.	Females.	Males.	Females.	Males.	Females
1	2	3	4	5	6	7	8	9	10
								Hindus—	
	British Territory ..	**9,875,750**	**9,966,635**	**17,272**	**24,058**	**139,710**	**261,716**	**569,439**	**1,048,106**
	Benares Division ..	*1,005,541*	*1,047,023*	*4,251*	*6,604*	*26,876*	*41,863*	*70,449*	*116,983*
1	Benares	208,021	207,580	1,344	2,077	6,779	11,049	18 989	24,511
2	Mirzapur	165,931	171,080	580	809	2,958	6,226	10,435	18,323
	Native States	**224,295**	**241,441**	**524**	**962**	**3,752**	**8,169**	**13,494**	**25,992**
3	Rampur	71,266	72,112	51	109	655	2,090	3,789	7,962
4	Tehri-Garhwal	71,867	82,604	40	76	361	816	2,869	6,236
5	Benares Raj	81,162	86,725	433	777	2,736	5,263	7,336	11,794
								Hindus-	
	British Territory ..	**1,656,386**	**3,350,108**	**797**	**1,969**	**6,294**	**12,624**	**20,511**	**28,303**
	Benares Division ..	*162,606*	*412,810*	*229*	*598*	*1,382*	*2,522*	*3,295*	*4,553*
1	Benares	29,701	81,730	58	120	258	470	446	813
2	Mirzapur	21,114	66,864	24	100	158	347	400	734
	Native States	**30,241**	**72,092**	**32**	**107**	**163**	**507**	**424**	**798**
3	Rampur	13,602	19,934	..	5	14	38	118	189
4	Tehri-Garhwal	4,558	18,625	1	8	..	24	22	63
5	Benares Raj	12,081	33,538	31	99	149	445	284	546
								Muhamma	
	British Territory ..	**3,452,534**	**3,178,786**	**418,571**	**423,920**	**472,857**	**434,023**	**430,956**	**335,634**
	Benares Division ..	*182,229*	*186,616*	*24,509*	*25,490*	*27,287*	*25,767*	*22,681*	*18,624*
1	Benares	49,481	47,331	6,437	6,761	6,608	6,783	6,001	5,029
2	Mirzapur	20,823	20,676	2,671	2,863	2,941	2,929	2,503	2,146
	Native States	**143,885**	**129,526**	**19,427**	**19,402**	**19,561**	**17,624**	**16,198**	**12,587**
3	Rampur	129,228	115,376	17,373	17,400	17,285	15,624	14,348	11,096
4	Tehri-Garhwal	904	850	121	141	124	91	112	103
5	Benares Raj	13,753	13,800	1,938	1,861	2,152	1,909	1,738	1,388
								Muhamma	
	British Territory ..	**1,599,514**	**1,085,982**	**416,243**	**420,369**	**457,934**	**399,261**	**361,543**	**192,238**
	Benares Division ..	*82,951*	*61,001*	*24,165*	*25,027*	*26,119*	*23,025*	*18,457*	*9,440*
1	Benares	22,021	16,350	6,359	6,650	6,346	6,142	5,098	2,717
2	Mirzapur	9,165	6,711	2,585	2,811	2,788	2,529	1,994	956
	Native States	**68,319**	**44,975**	**19,387**	**19,266**	**19,087**	**16,222**	**13,459**	**7,260**
3	Rampur	61,835	40,460	17,360	17,312	16,988	14,539	12,140	6,614
4	Tehri-Garhwal	444	817	121	141	124	90	97	68
5	Benares Raj	6,040	4,198	1,906	1,813	2,025	1,593	1,222	578
								Muhamma	
	British Territory ..	**1,594,522**	**1,631,308**	**2,211**	**3,304**	**14,155**	**33,074**	**66,475**	**140,274**
	Benares Division ..	*85,398*	*93,977*	*327*	*418*	*1,115*	*2,561*	*4,007*	*8,874*
1	Benares	24,448	23,686	74	98	257	597	877	2,250
2	Mirzapur	10,289	10,352	84	46	144	345	479	1,140
	Native States	**65,370**	**65,461**	**37**	**120**	**461**	**1,366**	**2,646**	**5,229**
3	Rampur	58,120	58,040	18	84	344	1,057	2,147	4,401
4	Tehri-Garhwal	424	438	..	..	..	1	15	35
5	Benares Raj	6,826	6,983	24	36	117	308	484	793
								Muhamma	
	British Territory ..	**258,498**	**461,496**	**117**	**247**	**768**	**1,688**	**2,938**	**3,122**
	Benares Division ..	*13,880*	*31,548*	*17*	*50*	*53*	*181*	*217*	*310*
1	Benares	3,012	7,295	4	18	5	44	26	62
2	Mirzapur	1,369	3,613	2	6	9	55	30	50
	Native States	**10,196**	**19,090**	**3**	**16**	**13**	**36**	**93**	**98**
3	Rampur	9,273	16,876	..	4	3	28	61	81
4	Tehri-Garhwal	36	95	..	..	..	..	..	..
5	Benares Raj	887	2,119	3	12	10	8	32	17

15—20.		20—40.		40—60.		60 and over.		Unspecified.		Serial number.
Males.	Females.	Males.	Females.	Males.	Females.	Males.	Females.	Males.	Females.	
11	12	13	14	15	16	17	18	19	20	1
Married.										
873,282	**1,279,517**	**5,077,949**	**5,476,455**	**2,654,573**	**1,697,936**	**543,462**	**178,797**	**93**	**50**	
84,521	*119,371*	*511,929*	*585,911*	*249,383*	*155,936*	*58,632*	*20,355*	..	..	
16,746	24,295	104,220	111,925	52,094	30,205	12,899	3,524	..	..	1
13,993	20,441	89,880	97,713	39,940	24,005	8,165	3,563	..	..	2
18,406	**29,667**	**114,274**	**130,557**	**60,468**	**41,480**	**13,377**	**4,614**	..	..	
5,740	8,795	37,340	39,160	20,071	12,908	3,620	1,088	..	..	3
5,143	10,750	36,764	46,020	21,911	16,679	5,279	2,027	..	..	4
7,523	10,122	40,170	45,377	18,486	11,893	4,478	1,499	..	..	5
Widowed.										
42,631	**48,987**	**505,107**	**762,124**	**685,677**	**1,598,244**	**375,349**	**897,838**	**20**	**19**	
4,909	*5,896*	*54,240*	*109,284*	*61,748*	*183,165*	*36,803*	*106,792*	..	..	
702	1,034	8,696	19,899	11,535	37,268	8,011	22,126	..	..	1
702	936	7,744	18,268	7,945	30,240	4,141	16,239	..	..	2
782	**986**	**10,144**	**15,645**	**11,665**	**33,288**	**7,031**	**20,761**	..	..	
310	282	4,959	3,773	5,450	9,650	2,751	5,997	..	..	3
59	136	1,068	2,708	1,750	8,682	1,658	7,009	..	..	4
413	568	4,117	9,164	4,465	14,956	2,622	7,755	..	..	5
dans—Total.										
293,452	**247,268**	**1,061,197**	**1,020,584**	**580,588**	**529,761**	**194.904**	**187,591**	**9**	**5**	
13,531	*13,166*	*52,980*	*61,113*	*29,579*	*30,188*	*11,662*	*12,268*	..	..	
3,811	3,436	14,897	14,636	8,326	7,486	3,401	3,250	..	..	1
1,639	1,398	6,733	6,898	3,321	3,279	1,015	1,163	..	..	2
10,661	**8,767**	**45,977**	**42,052**	**24,842**	**21,688**	**7,219**	**7,201**	..	**205**	
9,550	7,805	41,621	37,861	22,637	19,479	6,414	6,406	..	205	3
80	82	270	273	154	112	43	48	..	..	4
1,031	880	4,086	4,418	2,051	2,097	762	747	..	..	5
dans—Unmarried.										
170,373	**53,876**	**162,412**	**26,988**	**24,320**	**9,689**	**6,684**	**3,558**	**5**	**3**	
7,074	*1,446*	*6,122*	*1,473*	*756*	*490*	*258*	*190*	..	..	
2,186	297	1,741	373	210	124	81	47	..	..	1
849	114	809	182	109	80	31	39	..	..	2
6,385	**985**	**8,745**	**854**	**1,015**	**247**	**241**	**61**	..	**80**	
5,924	913	8,330	751	941	206	202	45	..	80	3
43	12	51	5	8	..	..	1	..	..	4
418	60	364	98	66	41	39	15	..	..	5
dans—Married.										
116,770	**207,763**	**820,967**	**906,224**	**457,009**	**303,574**	**116,931**	**37,094**	**4**	**1**	
6,077	*11,305*	*42,736*	*52,926*	*28,853*	*15,722*	*7,283*	*2,176*	..	..	
1,566	8,063	12,338	12,950	7,067	4,182	2,269	546	..	..	1
731	1,216	5,439	5,855	2,741	1,566	671	184	..	..	2
4,076	**7,624**	**33,733**	**37,819**	**19,888**	**12,093**	**4,529**	**1,110**	..	**100**	
3,458	6,764	30,097	33,749	18,082	10,930	3,979	955	..	100	3
36	69	213	254	128	71	32	8	..	..	4
582	791	3,423	3,816	1,678	1,092	518	147	..	..	5
dans— Widowed.										
6 309	**5,629**	**77,818**	**87,572**	**99,259**	**216,498**	**71,289**	**146,939**	..	**1**	
360	*415*	*4,122*	*6,714*	*4,970*	*13,976*	*4,121*	*9,902*	..	..	
59	76	818	1,813	1,049	8,130	1,051	2,657	..	..	1
59	68	485	861	471	1,633	313	940	..	..	2
200	**158**	**3,499**	**3,379**	**3,939**	**9,348**	**2,449**	**6,030**	..	**25**	
168	128	3,194	2,861	3,614	8,343	2,283	5,406	..	25	3
1	1	6	14	18	41	11	39	..	..	4
31	29	299	504	307	964	205	585	..	..	5

Serial number.	District or State.	Age.	Total liter					
			Urdu only.		Hindi only.		Urdu and Hindi, knowing Urdu better.	
			Males.	Females.	Males.	Females.	Males.	Females.
1	2	3	4	5	6	7	8	9
							B.—District	
	British Territory	*Total*	*286,442*	*22,479*	*1,008,216*	*69,361*	*84,668*	*3,002*
		0—10	13,381	2,004	33,370	5,865	1,096	206
		10—15	42,811	3,424	121,175	10,442	6,939	476
		15—20	38,370	3,248	110,693	9,702	12,144	559
		20 and over	192,380	13,803	742,978	43,352	64,489	1,761
	Benares division	*Total*	*15,662*	*1,813*	*124,710*	*7,934*	*7,181*	*336*
		0—10	841	180	5,191	659	145	23
		10—15	2,294	261	15,679	1,025	787	88
		15—20	1,910	255	13,497	913	942	92
		20 and over	10,617	1,117	90,343	5,337	5,357	133
1	Benares	*Total*	*4,101*	*637*	*39,232*	*3,898*	*2,283*	*215*
		0—10	219	69	2,010	303	42	16
		10—15	528	98	5,136	441	246	66
		15—20	474	99	4,279	477	334	71
		20 and over	2,880	371	27,807	2,672	1,661	62
2	Mirzapur	*Total*	*1,452*	*133*	*18,170*	*834*	*963*	*53*
		0—10	75	17	651	95	43	3
		10—15	196	18	2,018	120	102	11
		15—20	218	25	2,017	108	95	15
		20 and over	963	73	13,484	511	723	24
	Native States	*Total*	*4,989*	*313*	*21,211*	*688*	*511*	*9*
		0—10	115	17	611	59	9	..
		10—15	389	29	2,282	131	55	1
		15—20	448	23	2,333	88	76	2
		20 and over	4,037	244	15,985	410	371	6
1	Rampur	*Total*	*4,748*	*285*	*1,109*	*98*	*117*	*7*
		0—10	105	17	18	4	2	..
		10—15	355	28	66	9	6	1
		15—20	432	23	73	11	13	2
		20 and over	3,856	217	952	74	96	4
2	Tehri-Garhwal	*Total*	*32*	..	*10,756*	*206*	*78*	..
		0—10	..	..	321	25	..	..
		10—15	3	..	1,129	32	10	..
		15—20	3	..	1,265	27	21	..
		20 and over	26	..	8,041	122	47	..
3	Benares Raj	*Total*	*209*	*28*	*9,346*	*384*	*316*	*2*
		0—10	10	..	272	30	7	..
		10—15	31	1	1,087	90	39	..
		15—20	18	..	995	50	42	..
		20 and over	155	27	6,992	214	228	2
								All ages
	British Territory	*Total*	*111,869*	*2,595*	*952,614*	*59,213*	*66,537*	*1,089*
		0—10	6,285	272	30,884	4,095	841	68
		10—15	20,529	297	115,013	8,663	5,595	152
		15—20	16,538	329	105,102	8,098	9,864	186
		20 and over	68,510	1,697	701,615	37,757	50,237	683
	Benares division	*Total*	*4,117*	*220*	*119,758*	*7,335*	*5,630*	*128*
		0—10	326	43	4,983	570	132	14
		10—15	840	31	15,140	940	622	27
		15—20	600	25	13,052	855	786	23
		20 and over	2,851	121	86,583	4,970	4,090	64
1	Benares	*Total*	*859*	*53*	*38,067*	*3,691*	*1,797*	*59*
		0—10	81	14	1,939	273	39	9
		10—15	156	3	4,998	411	204	9
		15—20	126	8	4,185	453	276	13
		20 and over	496	28	26,945	2,554	1,278	28
2	Mirzapur	*Total*	*478*	*51*	*17,472*	*728*	*745*	*40*
		0—10	45	9	629	72	42	2
		10—15	76	12	1,932	111	95	10
		15—20	88	13	1,942	96	85	9
		20 and over	274	17	12,969	449	523	19

ate in—										
Hindi and Urdu, knowing Hindi better.		Other languages than English.		Total literate.			Literate in English.			Serial number.
Males.	Females.	Males.	Females.	Persons.	Males.	Females.	Persons.	Males.	Females.	
10	11	12	13	14	15	16	17	18	19	1
Totals.										
66,401	*1,643*	*50,007*	*15,615*	*1,607,834*	*1,495,734*	*112,100*	*136,409*	*121,327*	*15,082*	
1,044	95	2,098	1,496	60,655	50,989	9,666	4,069	2,716	1,853	
6,206	244	3,066	1,728	196,011	179,697	16,314	12,641	10,816	1,825	
10,466	278	3,908	1,558	190,926	175,581	15,345	20,011	18,064	1,947	
48,685	1,026	40,935	10,833	1,160,242	1,089,467	70,775	99,688	89,731	9,957	
7,527	*196*	*6,832*	*2,614*	*174,805*	*161,912*	*12,898*	*12,810*	*11,960*	*850*	
175	20	360	212	7,806	6,712	1,094	349	281	68	
798	42	586	234	21,744	20,094	1,650	1,455	1,379	76	
1,140	29	686	247	19 717	18,181	1,536	2,123	2,011	112	
5,408	105	5,200	1,921	125,538	116,925	8,613	8,883	8,289	594	
2,645	*86*	*5,965*	*2,321*	*61,378*	*54,226*	*7,152*	*7,834*	*7,270*	*564*	
63	6	309	192	3,229	2,643	586	230	179	51	
291	19	509	215	7,549	6,710	839	921	862	59	
417	9	572	206	6,938	6,076	862	1,265	1,199	66	
1,874	52	4,575	1,708	43,662	38,797	4,865	5,418	5,030	388	
1,043	*56*	*403*	*160*	*23,267*	*22,031*	*1,236*	*1,264*	*1,107*	*157*	
53	8	43	14	1,002	865	187	81	70	11	
104	14	82	9	2,624	2,452	172	126	115	11	
135	17	44	13	2,687	2,509	178	174	158	16	
751	17	284	124	16,954	16,205	749	1,883	764	119	
394	*5*	*74*	*24*	*28,218*	*27,179*	*1,039*	*983*	*951*	*32*	
7	..	5	..	823	747	76	13	13	..	
30	1	7	..	2,925	2,763	162	93	91	2	
61	1	4	2	3,038	2,922	116	161	156	5	
296	8	58	22	21,432	20,747	685	716	691	25	
24	*3*	*47*	*16*	*6,454*	*6,045*	*409*	*494*	*473*	*21*	
..	..	2	..	148	127	21	6	6	..	
..	..	5	..	470	482	38	37	35	2	
3	1	3	2	563	524	39	70	67	3	
21	2	37	14	5,273	4,962	311	381	365	16	
45	*1*	*12*	*3*	*11,133*	*10,923*	*210*	*282*	*276*	*6*	
1	..	2	..	349	324	25	4	4	..	
7	..	2	..	1,183	1,151	32	39	39	..	
3	..	1	..	1,320	1,293	27	54	52	2	
34	1	7	3	8,281	8,155	126	185	181	4	
325	*1*	*15*	*5*	*10,631*	*10,211*	*420*	*207*	*202*	*5*	
6	..	1	..	326	296	30	3	3	..	
23	1	..	..	1,272	1,180	92	17	17	..	
55	..	..	..	1,155	1,105	50	37	37	..	
241	..	14	5	7,878	7,630	248	150	145	5	
—Hindus.										
57,180	*894*	*15,895*	*3,635*	*1,271,514*	*1,204,088*	*67,426*	*64,695*	*63,600*	*1,095*	
842	47	712	312	44,958	39,564	5,394	1,058	986	72	
5,373	132	1,333	340	157,427	147,843	9,584	6,600	6,429	171	
9,278	148	1,729	392	151,664	142,511	9,153	11,274	11,078	196	
41,687	567	12,121	2,591	917,465	874,170	43,295	45,763	45,107	656	
6,588	*130*	*5,964*	*2,123*	*151,993*	*142,057*	*9,936*	*9,538*	*9,262*	*276*	
158	16	818	168	6,728	5,917	811	237	215	22	
725	27	557	201	19,110	17,884	1,226	1,170	1,130	40	
1,044	22	644	207	17,258	16,126	1,132	1,684	1,634	50	
4,661	65	4,445	1,547	108,897	102,130	6,767	6,447	6,283	164	
2,395	*55*	*5,351*	*2,049*	*54,376*	*48,469*	*5,907*	*6,233*	*5,994*	*239*	
58	3	286	163	2,865	2,403	462	161	141	20	
264	10	494	196	6,745	6,116	629	785	750	35	
385	9	553	193	6,201	5,525	676	1,090	1,052	38	
1,688	33	4,018	1,497	38,565	34,425	4,140	4,197	4,051	146	
930	*41*	*256*	*24*	*20,765*	*19,881*	*884*	*833*	*816*	*17*	
48	5	25	3	883	789	94	52	52	..	
101	9	20	1	2,367	2,224	143	101	98	3	
124	12	34	2	2,400	2,268	132	130	127	3	
657	12	177	18	15,115	14,600	515	550	539	11	

Serial number.	District or State.	Age.	Total liter Urdu only. Males.	Urdu only. Females.	Hindi only. Males.	Hindi only. Females.	Urdu and Hindi, knowing Urdu better. Males.	Urdu and Hindi, knowing Urdu better. Females.
1	2	3	4	5	6	7	8	9
	B.—District							
	Native States ..	*Total* ..	*1,424*	*49*	*20,970*	*651*	*459*	*5*
		0—10 ..	56	2	604	56	9	
		10—15 ..	151	3	2,265	126	52	
		15—20 ..	141	1	2,309	81	65	1
		20 and over ..	1,076	43	15,792	388	333	4
1	Rampur ..	*Total* ..	*1,329*	*35*	*1,037*	*80*	*97*	*5*
		0—10 ..	43	2	18	4	2	..
		10—15 ..	138	3	60	5	6	..
		15—20 ..	136	1	65	3	9	1
		20 and over ..	1,012	29	894	68	80	4
2	Tehri-Garhwal ..	*Total* ..	*11*	..	*10,713*	*206*	*71*	..
		0—10 ..	..	..	319	25	..	..
		10—15 ..	1	..	1,127	32	10	..
		15—20 ..	1	..	1,263	27	21	..
		20 and over ..	9	..	8,004	122	40	..
3	Benares Raj ..	*Total* ..	*84*	*14*	*9,220*	*365*	*291*	..
		0—10 ..	8	..	267	27	7	..
		10—15 ..	17	..	1,078	89	36	..
		15—20 ..	4	..	981	46	35	..
		20 and over ..	55	14	6,894	203	213	..
	All ages—							
	British territory ..	*Total* ..	*161,431*	*16,257*	*23,752*	*1,443*	*11,299*	*393*
		0—10 ..	6,263	1,129	663	146	134	23
		10—15 ..	19,891	2,336	2,025	210	703	46
		15—20 ..	19,875	2,257	1,814	154	1,370	53
		20 and over ..	115,402	10,535	19,250	933	9,092	271
	Benares division ..	*Total* ..	*11,423*	*1,475*	*4,064*	*228*	*1,394*	*45*
		0—10 ..	510	122	117	19	11	3
		10—15 ..	1,434	215	415	32	92	2
		15—20 ..	1,288	201	347	17	135	6
		20 and over ..	8,191	937	3,185	160	1,156	34
1	Benares ..	*Total* ..	*3,176*	*484*	*877*	*51*	*430*	*14*
		0—10 ..	134	42	40	5	3	1
		10—15 ..	362	81	107	6	29	
		15—20 ..	337	68	57	8	50	1
		20 and over ..	2,343	293	673	32	348	12
2	Mirzapur ..	*Total* ..	*963*	*75*	*507*	*6*	*186*	*1*
		0—10 ..	29	8	6	..	..	1
		10—15 ..	118	6	56	..	6	..
		15—20 ..	134	10	51	..	9	..
		20 and over ..	682	51	394	6	171	..
	Native States ..	*Total* ..	*3,488*	*259*	*150*	*1*	*31*	*2*
		0—10 ..	59	14	3	..	..	..
		10—15 ..	227	25	10	1	3	..
		15—20 ..	294	22	15	..	7	..
		20 and over ..	2,908	198	122	..	21	2
1	Rampur ..	*Total* ..	*3,344*	*245*	*17*	*1*	*6*	..
		0—10 ..	57	14	..	..	..	..
		10—15 ..	211	24	1	1	..	..
		15—20 ..	283	22	3	..	..	..
		20 and over ..	2,793	185	13	..	6	..
2	Tehri-Garhwal ..	*Total* ..	*21*	..	*34*	..	..	..
		0—10 ..	..	..	1	..	..	..
		10—15 ..	2	..	2	..	..	..
		15—20 ..	2	..	2	..	..	..
		20 and over ..	17	..	29	..	..	..
3	Benares Raj ..	*Total* ..	*123*	*14*	*99*	..	*25*	*2*
		0—10 ..	2	..	2	..	..	..
		10—15 ..	14	1	7	..	3	..
		15—20 ..	9	..	10	..	7	..
		20 and over ..	98	13	80	..	15	2

ate in—										
Hindi and Urdu, knowing Hindi better.		Other languages than English.		Total literate.			Literate in English.			Serial number.
Males.	Females.	Males.	Females.	Persons.	Males.	Females.	Persons.	Males.	Females.	
10	11	12	13	14	15	16	17	18	19	1
Total.										
367	*2*	*27*	*1*	*23,955*	*23,247*	*708*	*651*	*645*	*6*	
6	..	1	..	734	676	58	8	8	..	
£0	1	4	..	2,632	2,502	130	66	65	1	
57	1	3	..	2,659	2,575	84	108	106	2	
2:4	..	19	1	17,930	17,494	436	469	466	3	
21	*1*	*16*	*1*	*2,622*	*2,500*	*122*	*196*	*193*	*3*	
..	..	..	..	74	68	6	2	2	..	
..	..	4	..	211	203	8	15	14	1	1
3	1	2	..	226	215	11	20	20	..	
18	..	10	1	2,111	2,014	97	159	157	2	
42	..	*1*	..	*11,044*	*10,838*	*206*	*273*	*270*	*3*	
1	..	..	..	345	320	25	3	3	..	
7	..	..	..	1,177	1,145	32	38	38	..	2
3	..	1	..	1,316	1,289	27	54	52	2	
31	..	..	..	8,206	8,084	122	178	177	1	
304	*1*	*10*	..	*10,289*	*9,909*	*380*	*182*	*182*	..	
5	..	1	..	315	288	27	3	3	..	
23	1	..	..	1,244	1,154	90	13	13	..	3
51	..	..	..	1,117	1,071	46	34	34	..	
225	..	9	..	7,613	7,396	217	132	132	..	
Muhammadans.										
4,333	*165*	*4,129*	*802*	*224,004*	*204,944*	*19,060*	*21,506*	*20,951*	*555*	
95	16	101	67	8,637	7,256	1,381	334	316	18	
809	23	289	205	26,037	23,217	2,820	2,229	2,137	92	
535	33	566	85	26,742	24,160	2,582	4,105	4,022	83	
3,894	93	3,173	445	162,588	150,311	12,277	14,838	14,476	362	
736	*20*	*88*	*5*	*19,478*	*17,705*	*1,773*	*1,735*	*1,716*	*19*	
10	1	2	..	795	650	145	17	17	..	
48	1	3	1	2,243	1,992	251	188	186	2	
ᵃ70	2	16	3	2,085	1,856	229	318	315	3	
608	16	67	1	14,355	13,207	1,148	1,212	1,198	14	
168	*2*	*26*	*2*	*5,225*	*4,672*	*553*	*638*	*633*	*5*	
1	..	..	..	226	178	48	8	8	..	
12	..	1	..	598	511	87	80	78	2	1
18	..	5	1	545	467	78	114	113	1	
184	2	£0	1	3,856	3,516	340	436	434	2	
77	*2*	*23*	..	*1,842*	*1,756*	*86*	*149*	*145*	*4*	
2	..	1	..	47	38	9	..	..	..	
1	..	1	..	188	182	6	6	6	..	2
7	1	2	..	214	203	11	21	19	2	
67	1	19	..	1,393	1,333	60	122	120	2	
21	..	*31*	*1*	*3,924*	*3,721*	*263*	*264*	*263*	*1*	
1	..	2	..	79	65	14	2	2	..	
..	..	1	..	267	241	26	20	20	..	
4	..	1	..	343	321	\22	46	46	..	
16	..	27	1	3,295	3,094	201	196	195	1	
..	..	*22*	*1*	*3,636*	*3,389*	*247*	*249*	*248*	*1*	
..	..	..	..	71	57	14	2	2	..	
..	..	..	..	237	212	25	16	16	..	1
..	..	1	..	309	287	22	43	43	..	
..	..	21	1	3,019	2,833	186	188	187	1	
..	..	*9*	..	*64*	*64*	..	..	..	..	
..	..	2	..	3	3	..	..	..	..	
..	..	1	..	5	5	..	..	..	..	2
..	..	..	..	4	4	..	..	..	..	
..	..	6	..	52	52	..	..	..	..	
21	..	..	..	*284*	*268*	*16*	*15*	*15*	..	
1	..	..	..	5	- 5	..	..	..	..	
..	..	..	..	25	24	1	4	4	..	3
4	..	..	..	30	30	..	3	3	..	
16	..	..	..	224	209	15	8	8	..	

TABLE X.—Language—Part A.—Vernaculars of the U. P. of Agra and

Serial number.	District or State.	Population			Vernaculars of the — Hindi.		
		Persons.	Males.	Females.	Persons.	Males.	Females.
1	2	3	4	5	6	7	8
	British Territory	**46,835,108**	**24,469,373**	**22,365,735**	**43,121,481**	**22,495,892**	**20,625,589**
	Agra Province	**34,277,104**	**17,984,673**	**16,292,431**	**31,069,681**	**16,281,214**	**14,788,467**
	Benares Division	*4,462,542*	*2,229,787*	*2,232,755*	*4,307,305*	*2,151,346*	*2,155,959*
1	Benares	**896,344**	**451,545**	**444,799**	**811,224**	408,595	402,629
2	Mirzapur	**724,801**	**358,278**	**366,523**	**717,570**	354,379	363,191
	Native States	**178,972**	**603,898**	**575,074**	**648,178**	**321,110**	**327,068**
3	Rampur	**531,217**	**282,978**	**248,239**	**1,761**	1,025	736
4	Tehri-Garhwal	**300,819**	**148,462**	**152,357**	**300,378**	148,113	152,265
5	Benares Raj	**346,936**	**172,458**	**174,478**	**346,039**	171,972	174,037

Serial number.	District or State.	Indo-Euro — Aryan Sub- — Eranian Branch. — Western Group. — Persian.			Eastern Group. — Baloch and Pashto.			Indian Branch non-Sanskritic Sub-Branch. — Kashmiri.		
		Persons.	Males.	Females.	Persons.	Males.	Females.	Persons.	Males.	Females.
1	2	21	22	23	24	25	26	27	28	29
	British Territory	**4,841**	**2,672**	**2,169**	**2,003**	**1,804**	**199**	**87**	**66**	**21**
	Agra Province	**4,790**	**2,633**	**2,157**	**1.800**	**1,605**	**195**	**52**	**44**	**8**
	Benares Division	*8*	*8*	..	*201*	*192*	*9*	*17*	*9*	*8*
1	Benares	..	..	..	**177**	169	8	..	..	..
2	Mirzapur	..	..	..	**17**	16	1	..	..	..
	Native States	..	..	..	**47**	**46**	**1**	**1**	**1**	..
3	Rampur	..	..	..	**43**	42	1	**1**	1	..
4	Tehri-Garhwal	..	..	..	**4**	4	..	..	..	..
5	Benares Raj	..	..	..	..	..	..	..	..	..

Serial number.	District or State.	Indo-Euro — Aryan Sub- — Indian Branch — Western Group. — Rajasthani (4).			Gujrati.			Punjabi (5).		
		Persons.	Males.	Females.	Persons.	Males.	Females.	Persons.	Males.	Females.
1	2	42	43	44	45	46	47	48	49	50
	British Territory	**4,402**	**2,319**	**2,083**	**4,043**	**2,352**	**1,697**	**26,946**	**19,461**	**7,485**
	Agra Province	**4,069**	**2,119**	**1,950**	**3,506**	**1,980**	**1,526**	**23,768**	**16,929**	**6,839**
	Benares Division	*410*	*184*	*226*	*1,605*	*838*	*767*	*681*	*557*	*124*
1	Benares	**364**	161	203	**1,543**	799	744	**646**	523	123
2	Mirzapur	**2**	**2**	..	**42**	26	16	**29**	28	1
	Native States	**1**	**1**	..	**19**	**17**	**2**	**358**	**300**	**58**
3	Rampur	..	..	..	**19**	17	2	**36**	23	13
4	Tehri-Garhwal	**1**	1	..	..	..	..	**322**	277	45
5	Benares Raj	..	..	..	..	..	..	..	..	..

Serial number.	District or State.	Semetic Family. — Arabic.			Hebrew.			Turkish.		
		Persons.	Males.	Females.	Persons.	Males.	Females	Persons.	Males.	Females.
1	2	63	64	65	66	67	68	69	70	71
	British Territory	**435**	**407**	**28**	**19**	**13**	**6**	**12**	**1**	**11**
	Agra Province	**427**	**400**	**27**	**14**	**11**	**3**	..	..	..
	Benares division	*1*	..	*1*	*8*	*5*	*3*	..	..	..
1	Benares	1	..	1	**8**	**5**	**3**	..	..	..
2	Mirzapur	..	..	..	..	..	..	..	..	..
	Native States	**7**	**7**	..	..	..	..	**11**	**7**	**4**
3	Rampur	**4**	4	..	..	..	..	..	..	..
4	Tehri-Garhwal	**3**	3	..	..	..	..	**11**	7	4
5	Benares Raj	..	..	..	..	..	..	..	..	..

(1) Includes Tibetan, Ladakhi, Balti and Bhotani.
(2) Includes Newari, Manipuri and Burmese.
(8) Includes Tamil, Malayalam, Kanarese, Coorgi and Telugu.
(7) Includes Kanjari, Banjari, Haburi, Sansya,

Oudh, selected vernaculars of other parts of India, and also English by districts. APPENDIX.

United Provinces.			Tibeto-Chinese Family. Tibeto-Burman Sub-Family. Tibeto-Himalayan Branch.						Dravidian Languages (8).			Serial number.
Urdu or Hindostani.			Tibetan Languages (1).			Other Languages (2).						
Persons.	Males.	Females.	Persons.	Males.	Females.	Persons.	Males.	Females.	Persons.	Males.	Females.	
9	10	11	12	13	14	15	16	17	18	19	20	1
3,565,560	**1,879,172**	**1,686,388**	**5,225**	**2,598**	**2,627**	**137**	**78**	**59**	**1,406**	**749**	**657**	
3,080,941	**1,623,774**	**1,457,167**	**5,217**	**2,590**	**2,627**	**137**	**78**	**59**	**1,330**	**714**	**616**	
133,373	*68,029*	*65,344*	..	..	..	*6*	*6*	..	*1,000*	*547*	*453*	
64,378	33,190	31,188	..	..	..	**6**	6	..	**998**	545	453	1
6,609	3,536	3,073	..	..	..	..	..	..	**2**	2	..	2
530,168	**282,268**	**247,900**	**2**	**2**	..	**1**	**1**	..	**2**	..	**2**	
529,225	281,753	247,472	..	..	..	**1**	1	..	**1**	..	1	3
60	37	23	**2**	2	..	..	..	..	**1**	..	1	4
883	478	405	..	..	..	..	..	..	..	..	..	5

pean Family.

Family.

Indian Branch Sanskritic Sub-Branch.												
North-Western Group.			Southern Group.			Eastern Group.						Serial number.
Lahnda, Sindhi and Kachchhi.			Marathi and Konkani.			Bengali.			Oriya and Assamese.			
Persons.	Males.	Females.	Persons.	Males.	Females.	Persons.	Males.	Females.	Persons.	Males.	Females.	
30	31	32	33	34	35	36	37	38	39	40	41	1
363	**218**	**145**	**6,028**	**3,477**	**2,551**	**22,498**	**10,595**	**11,903**	**103**	**84**	**19**	
363	**218**	**145**	**5,907**	**3,415**	**2,494**	**19,555**	**8,968**	**10,587**	**97**	**79**	**18**	
13	*11*	*2*	*2,624*	*1,356*	*1,268*	*13 090*	*5,551*	*7,539*	*22*	*18*	*4*	
13	11	2	**2,600**	1,351	1,249	**12,607**	5,233	7,374	**21**	17	4	1
..	..	..	**13**	5	8	**209**	148	61	..	..	..	2
..	..	..	**1**	**1**	..	**114**	**106**	**8**	**1**	**1**	..	
..	..	..	..	..	..	**103**	101	2	..	..	..	3
..	..	..	..	..	..	**9**	3	6	**1**	1	..	4
..	..	..	**1**	1	..	**2**	2	..	..	..	..	5

peon Family—(*concluded.*)

Family—(*concluded.*)

Sanskritic Sub-Branch—(*concluded.*)						European Sub-Family.						Serial number.
			Northern-Group.									
Western Pahari (Kangri)			Eastern Pahari or Naipali.			English.			Other languages (6).			
Persons.	Males.	Females.	Persons.	Males.	Females.	Persons.	Males.	Females	Persons.	Males.	Females.	
51	52	53	54	55	56	57	58	59	60	61	62	1
33	**23**	**10**	**18,266**	**13,512**	**4,754**	**41,609**	**28,456**	**13,153**	**679**	**579**	**100**	
33	**23**	**10**	**17,497**	**12,856**	**4,641**	**32,659**	**21,922**	**10,737**	**568**	**508**	**60**	
1	*1*	..	*959*	*440*	*519*	*1,210*	*688*	*522*	*5*	*3*	*2*	
1	1	..	**956**	439	517	**788**	494	294	**5**	3	2	1
..	..	..	..	..	..	**308**	186	172	..	..	..	2
..	..	..	**23**	**12**	**11**	**37**	**18**	**19**	**1**	..	**1**	
..	..	..	..	..	..	**22**	11	11	**1**	..	1	3
..	..	..	**23**	12	11	**4**	2	2	..	..	..	4
..	..	..	..	..	.	**11**	5	6	..	..	..	5

Mongolian family.						Malya Polynesian Family.			Gipsy dialects (7).			Serial number.
Chinese.			Japanese.			Malya.						
Persons.	Males.	Females.	Persons.	Males.	Females	Persons.	Males.	Females.	Persons.	Males.	Females.	
72	73	74	75	76	77	78	79	80	81	82	83	1
77	**51**	**26**	**31**	**6**	**25**	**20**	**2**	**18**	**8,804**	**4,786**	**4,018**	
73	**47**	**26**	**12**	**3**	**9**	**20**	**2**	**18**	**4,588**	**2,543**	**2,045**	
..	..	..	*3*	*3*	..	..	..	..	*5*	..	*5*	
..	..	.	**3**	3	..	..	..	..	**5**	..	5	1
..	..	..	..	..	..	..	..	..	..	..	..	2
..	..	..	..	..	..	..	..	..	..	..	..	
..	..	..	..	..	..	..	..	..	..	..	..	3
..	..	..	..	..	..	..	..	..	..	..	..	4
..	..	..	..	..	..	..	..	..	..	..	..	5

(4) Includes Rajasthani Marwari, Bagri, Malvi and Rangri.
(5) Includes Punjabi and Dogri.
(6) Includes German, Italian, French, Portuguese, Russian, Norwegian, Danish, Dutches, Bohemian, Armenian and Greek.
Natki, Pachwi, Kurchbandhi, Kanphati and Meithei.

TABLE XI.—Part I. A—Born in Districts within

Serial number.	District or State.	Total A. Persons.	Total A. Males.	Total A. Females.	Dehra Dun. Persons.	Dehra Dun. Males.	Dehra Dun. Females.
1	2	3	4	5	6	7	8
	British Territory	46,179,021	24,177,660	22,001,361	155,154	84,949	70,205
	Agra Province	33,667,046	17,722,062	15,944,984	154,786	84,763	70,023
	Benares Division	*4,389,934*	*2,205,184*	*2,184,750*	*17*	*10*	*7*
1	Benares	865,814	438,416	427,398	13	8	5
2	Mirzapur	706,302	350,649	355,653	2	1	1
	Native States	1,174,968	602,126	572,842	150	71	79
3	Rampur	530,311	282,351	247,960	13	10	3
4	Tehri-Garhwal	300,181	147,953	152,228	137	61	76
5	Benares Raj	344,476	171,822	172,654	..	..	..

Serial number.	District or State.	Bulandshahr. Persons.	Bulandshahr. Males.	Bulandshahr. Females.	Aligarh. Persons.	Aligarh. Males.	Aligarh. Females.
		18	19	20	21	22	23
	British Territory	1,097,639	587,057	510,582	1,158,179	628,930	529,249
	Agra Province	1,096,956	586,565	510,391	1,157,203	628,275	528,928
	Benares Division	*125*	*88*	*37*	*189*	*121*	*68*
1	Benares	64	40	24	100	60	40
2	Mirzapur	22	18	4	40	31	9
	Native States	165	92	73	204	111	93
3	Rampur	153	85	68	200	109	91
4	Tehri-Garhwal	11	6	5	..	..	..
5	Benares Raj	1	1	..	4	2	2

Serial number.	District or State.	Mainpuri. Persons.	Mainpuri. Males.	Mainpuri. Females.	Etawah. Persons.	Etawah. Males.	Etawah. Females.
		33	34	35	36	37	38
	British Territory	779,433	435,559	343,874	736,326	404,214	332,112
	Agra Province	778,373	434,932	343,441	735,065	403,584	331,481
	Benares Division	*84*	*51*	*33*	*108*	*70*	*38*
1	Benares	43	24	19	66	42	24
2	Mirzapur	13	12	1	23	16	7
	Native States	30	17	13	12	4	8
3	Rampur	30	17	13	7	4	3
4	Tehri-Garhwal	..	..	..	..	..	..
5	Benares Raj	..	..	..	5	..	5

Serial number.	District or State.	Budaun. Persons.	Budaun. Males.	Budaun. Females.	Moradabad. Persons.	Moradabad. Males.	Moradabad. Females.
		48	49	50	51	52	53
	British Territory	1,066,813	582,917	483,896	1,278,319	685,359	592,960
	Agra Province	1,065,341	581,986	483,355	1,276,281	684,050	592,231
	Benares Division	*102*	*70*	*32*	*307*	*203*	*104*
1	Benares	48	32	16	184	121	63
2	Mirzapur	26	18	8	48	36	12
	Native States	3,700	1,437	2,263	28,865	12,430	16,435
3	Rampur	3,689	1,430	2,259	28,863	12,428	16,435
4	Tehri-Garhwal	1	1	..	1	1	..
5	Benares Raj	10	6	4	1	1	..

Serial number.	District or State.	Fatehpur. Persons.	Fatehpur. Males.	Fatehpur. Females.	Banda. Persons.	Banda. Males.	Banda. Females.
		63	64	65	66	67	68
	British Territory	676,637	351,482	325,155	655,428	326,142	329,286
	Agra Province	669,226	349,291	319,935	654,166	325,672	328,494
	Benares Division	*549*	*364*	*185*	*389*	*163*	*226*
1	Benares	359	251	108	173	93	80
2	Mirzapur	115	42	73	180	51	129
	Native States	43	20	23	39	8	31
3	Rampur	7	6	1	5	3	2
4	Tehri-Garhwal	..	..	..	1	1	..
5	Benares Raj	36	14	22	33	4	29

Saharanpur.			Muzaffarnagar.			Meerut.			Serial number.
Persons.	Males.	Females.	Persons.	Males.	Females.	Persons.	Males.	Females.	
9	10	11	12	13	14	15	16	17	1
952,674	**524,041**	**428,633**	**770,970**	**433,965**	**337,005**	**1,457,900**	**798,476**	**659,424**	
952,120	**523,695**	**428,425**	**770,412**	**433,610**	**336,802**	**1,456,268**	**797,517**	**658,751**	
127	*82*	*45*	*54*	*36*	*18*	*246*	*159*	*87*	
97	61	36	30	19	11	166	107	59	1
11	11	..	9	9	..	24	17	7	2
100	**70**	**34**	**50**	**37**	**1**	**194**	**115**	**79**	
69	41	28	34	24	10	134	77	57	3
33	28	5	12	9	3	59	38	21	4
2	1	1	4	4	..	1	..	1	5

Muttra.			Agra.			Farrukhabad.			Serial number.
24	25	26	27	28	29	30	31	32	
612,484	**347,967**	**264,517**	**971,870**	**540,813**	**431,057**	**894,216**	**488,322**	**405,894**	
611,603	**347,432**	**264,171**	**969,575**	**539,499**	**430,076**	**878,310**	**481,480**	**396,830**	
288	*191*	*97*	*634*	*363*	*271*	*256*	*158*	*98*	
213	139	74	415	229	186	150	83	67	1
27	18	9	101	67	34	36	23	13	2
26	**13**	**13**	**88**	**53**	**35**	**51**	**19**	**32**	
23	10	13	69	40	29	48	16	32	3
1	1	..	..	..	..	1	1	..	4
2	2	..	19	13	6	2	2	..	5

Etah.			Bareilly.			Bijnor.			Serial number.
39	40	41	42	43	44	45	46	47	
847,712	**464,111**	**383,601**	**1,091,101**	**593,114**	**497,987**	**834,554**	**444,558**	**389,996**	
847,143	**463,750**	**383,393**	**1,084,518**	**589,727**	**494,791**	**833,614**	**443,964**	**389,650**	
61	*37*	*24*	*408*	*225*	*183*	*134*	*84*	*50*	
25	15	10	236	142	94	59	41	18	1
7	6	1	80	36	44	19	10	9	2
102	**36**	**66**	**19,867**	**6,860**	**13,007**	**706**	**392**	**314**	
101	36	65	19,859	6,854	13,005	671	369	302	3
..	..	..	6	4	2	33	21	12	4
1	..	1	2	2	..	2	2	..	5

Shahjahanpur.			Pilibhit.			Cawnpore.			Serial number.
54	55	56	57	58	59	60	61	62	
978,552	**525,483**	**453,069**	**483,479**	**256,860**	**226,619**	**1,079,772**	**583,472**	**496,300**	
932,331	**504,724**	**427,607**	**480,408**	**255,181**	**225,227**	**1,063,483**	**576,954**	**486,529**	
207	*123*	*84*	*32*	*25*	*7*	*912*	*469*	*443*	
113	60	47	9	5	4	557	252	305	1
36	23	13	7	7	..	148	100	48	2
257	**117**	**140**	**334**	**107**	**227**	**71**	**34**	**37**	
248	115	133	331	106	225	47	26	21	3
..	..	..	..	..	..	..	..	..	4
9	2	7	3	1	2	24	8	16	5

Hamirpur.			Allahabad.			Jhansi.			Serial number.
69	70	71	72	73	74	75	76	77	
447,314	**230,539**	**216,775**	**1,437,327**	**727,163**	**710,164**	**590,107**	**314,222**	**275,885**	
446,850	**230,321**	**216,529**	**1,412,254**	**720,966**	**691,288**	**589,426**	**313,906**	**275,520**	
98	*56*	*42*	*15,007*	*3,692*	*11,315*	*248*	*144*	*104*	
34	16	18	1,614	732	882	191	108	83	1
51	31	20	6,281	1,621	4,660	31	21	10	2
9	**2**	**7**	**4,437**	**644**	**3,793**	**19**	**9**	**10**	
2	..	2	83	49	34	9	4	5	3
..	..	..	..	..	..	..	..	..	4
7	2	5	4,354	595	3,759	10	5	5	5

TABLE XI.—Part I. A.—Born in District within

Serial number.	District or State.	Jalaun. Persons.	Jalaun. Males.	Jalaun. Females.	Benares. Persons.	Benares. Males.	Benares. Females.
1	2	78	79	80	81	82	83
	British Territory	**380,979**	**201,812**	**179,167**	**839,151**	**424,853**	**414,298**
	Agra Province	**380,482**	**201,539**	**178,943**	**836,406**	**423,471**	**412,935**
	Benares Division	*53*	*29*	*24*	*829,612*	*420,537*	*409,075*
1	Benares	47	23	24	796,901	414,235	382,606
2	Mirzapur	5	5	..	12,923	3,045	9,878
	Native States	..	..	..	**9,555**	**2,571**	**6,984**
3	Rampur	..	..	..	18	8	10
4	Tehri-Garwal	..	..	..	1	1	..
5	Benares Raj	..	..	..	9,536	2,562	6,974

Serial number.	District or State.	Ballia. Persons.	Ballia. Males.	Ballia. Females.	Gorakhpur. Persons.	Gorakhpur. Males.	Gorakhpur. Females.
		93	94	95	96	97	98
	British Territory	**840,232**	**424,630**	**415,602**	**3,102,653**	**1,556,798**	**1,545,855**
	Agra Province	**839,290**	**424,137**	**415,153**	**3,094,891**	**1,553,768**	**1,541,123**
	Benares Division	*822,749*	*419,131*	*403,618*	*4,155*	*1,831*	*2,324*
1	Benares	646	420	226	1,184	815	369
2	Mirzapur	163	123	40	118	85	33
	Native States	**24**	**14**	**10**	**78**	**33**	**45**
3	Rampur	..	..	..	7	5	2
4	Tehri-Garhwal	..	..	..	1	1	..
5	Benares Raj	24	14	10	70	27	43

Serial number.	District or State.	Almora. Persons.	Almora. Males.	Almora. Females.	Garhwal. Persons.	Garhwal. Males.	Garhwal. Females.
		108	109	110	111	112	113
	British Territory	**563,004**	**286,788**	**276,216**	**483,288**	**239,069**	**244,219**
	Agra Province	**562,458**	**286,456**	**276,002**	**482,896**	**238,724**	**244,172**
	Benares Division	*126*	*117*	*9*	*78*	*74*	*4*
1	Benares	113	108	5	57	54	3
2	Mirzapur	7	4	3	13	13	..
	Native States	**50**	**31**	**19**	**3,773**	**1,654**	**2,119**
3	Rampur	32	21	11	73	66	7
4	Tehri-Garhwal	17	10	7	3,700	1,588	2,112
5	Benares Raj	1	..	1	..	..	..

Serial number.	District or State.	Sitapur. Persons.	Sitapur. Males.	Sitapur. Females.	Hardoi. Persons.	Hardoi. Males.	Hardoi. Females.
		123	124	125	126	127	128
	British Territory	**1,153,174**	**614,975**	**538,199**	**1,157,341**	**624,869**	**532,472**
	Agra Province	**5,930**	**3,239**	**2,691**	**48,941**	**16,200**	**32,741**
	Benares Division	*206*	*134*	*72*	*178*	*113*	*65*
1	Benares	124	82	42	103	65	38
2	Mirzapur	11	9	2	14	11	3
	Native States	**59**	**26**	**33**	**86**	**34**	**52**
3	Rampur	50	22	28	81	32	49
4	Tehri-Garhwal	1	1	..	3	1	2
5	Benares Raj	8	3	5	2	1	1

Serial number.	District or State.	Bahraich. Persons.	Bahraich. Males.	Bahraich. Females.	Sultanpur. Persons.	Sultanpur. Males.	Sultanpur. Females.	Partabgarh. Persons.	Partabgarh. Males.	Partabgarh. Females.
1	2	138	139	140	141	142	143	144	145	146
	British Territory	**1,003,472**	**521,672**	**481,800**	**1,048,301**	**522,919**	**525,382**	**906,050**	**445,889**	**460,161**
	Agra Province	**2,089**	**1,148**	**941**	**20,392**	**8,404**	**11,988**	**38,458**	**14,248**	**24,210**
	Benares Division	*285*	*225*	*60*	*6,752*	*2,006*	*4,746*	*6,209*	*1,889*	*4,320*
1	Benares	241	209	32	490	340	150	422	299	123
2	Mirzapur	13	8	5	113	84	29	234	111	123
	Native States	**17**	**13**	**4**	**48**	**26**	**22**	**185**	**108**	**77**
3	Rampur	3	1	2	8	6	2	98	74	24
4	Tehri-Garhwal	11	11	..	..	..	..	..	..	..
5	Benares Raj	3	1	2	40	20	20	87	34	53

Mirzapur.			Jaunpur.			Ghazipur.			Serial number.
Persons.	Males.	Females.	Persons.	Males.	Females.	Persons.	Males.	Females.	
84	85	83	87	88	89	90	91	92	1
734,190	**356,451**	**377,739**	**1,185,189**	**586,557**	**598,632**	**847,495**	**423,838**	**423,657**	
732,255	**355,796**	**376,459**	**1,134,222**	**577,968**	**556,254**	**845,727**	**422,866**	**422,861**	
714,734	*350,286*	*364,448*	*1,101,593*	*568,018*	*533,575*	*827,943*	*418,491*	*409,452*	
21,210	5,211	15,999	**14,772**	4,668	10,104	**15,508**	4,157	11,351	1
682,839	343,674	339,165	**1,288**	**517**	771	**452**	215	237	2
297,422	**153,781**	**143,641**	**6,150**	**1,010**	**5,140**	**102**	**83**	**19**	
..	..	..	**29**	17	12	**13**	**7**	**6**	3
..	..	..	**4**	1	3	..	..	..	4
297,422	153,781	143,641	**6,117**	992	5,125	**89**	76	18	5

Basti.			Azamgarh.			Naini Tal.			Serial number.
99	100	101	102	103	104	105	106	107	
1,866 724	**953,161**	**913,563**	**1,528,553**	**765,540**	**763,013**	**204,230**	**109,290**	**94,940**	
1,803,894	**926,656**	**877,238**	**1,495,841**	**757,748**	**738,093**	**202,907**	**108,642**	**94,265**	
603	*415*	*188*	*47,931*	*11,450*	*36,481*	*54*	*32*	*22*	
331	267	64	**5,629**	2 820	2,809	**44**	29	15	1
41	27	14	**289**	188	101	**8**	2	6	2
11	**6**	**5**	**157**	**83**	**74**	**3,821**	**1,444**	**2,377**	
5	3	2	**26**	16	10	**3,807**	1,432	2,375	3
..	..	..	..	..	..	**14**	12	2	4
6	3	3	**131**	67	64	..	..	..	5

Lucknow.			Unao.			Rae Bareli.			Serial number.
114	115	116	117	118	119	120	121	122	
694,434	**369,497**	**324,937**	**935,983**	**491,488**	**444,495**	**1,014,953**	**515,575**	**499,378**	
17,791	**10,028**	**7,763**	**29,600**	**14,287**	**15,313**	**15,968**	**8,344**	**7,624**	
1,243	*713*	*530*	*321*	*199*	*122*	*687*	*412*	*275*	
761	424	337	**216**	131	85	**417**	253	161	1
133	92	41	**42**	27	15	**122**	65	57	2
252	**153**	**99**	**29**	**15**	**14**	**46**	**40**	**6**	
234	141	93	**13**	8	5	**9**	8	6	3
3	3	..	..	..	..	**1**	1	..	4
15	9	6	**16**	7	9	**36**	36	..	5

Kheri.			Fyzabad.			Gonda.			Serial number.
129	130	131	132	133	134	135	136	137	
904,187	**479,131**	**425,056**	**1,143,949**	**573,070**	**575,879**	**1,404,987**	**719,782**	**685,205**	
21,647	**8,788**	**12,859**	**37,780**	**13,133**	**24,647**	**28,410**	**12,388**	**16,022**	
57	*33*	*22*	*2,796*	*1,351*	*1,445*	*411*	*323*	*88*	
29	18	11	**948**	608	340	**302**	253	4	1
11	9	2	**87**	61	26	**23**	15		2
11	**4**	**7**	**63**	**36**	**27**	**98**	**66**	**32**	
10	4	6	**30**	18	12	**95**	64	31	3
..	..		..	..	..	**2**	1	1	4
1	..	1	**33**	18	15	**1**	1	..	5

Bara Banki.			Rampur.			Tehri-Garhwal.			Benares Raj.			United Provinces. Unspecified			Serial number
Persons.	Males.	Females.	Persons.	Males.	Females	Persons.	Males.	Females.	Persons.	Males.	Females.	Persons.	Males.	Females	
147	148	149	150	151	152	153	154	155	156	157	158	159	160	161	1
1,111,659	**582,841**	**528,818**	**59,710**	**23,954**	**35,756**	**6,081**	**3,446**	**2,635**	**26,291**	**13,497**	**12,794**	**92**	**48**	**44**	
7,598	**5,057**	**2,541**	**59,315**	**23,713**	**35,602**	**6,074**	**3,440**	**2,634**	..	..	..	**92**	**48**	**44**	
422	*313*	*109*	*71*	*32*	*39*	..	..	..	..	..	..	*83*	*44*	*39*	
224	171	53	**55**	23	32	..	..	..	..	..	..	**81**	**44**	37	1
20	16	4	**8**	7	1	..	..	..	..	..	..	..	..	..	2
41	**25**	**16**	**470,743**	**258,526**	**212,217**	**296,125**	**146,148**	**149,977**	**26,291**	**13,497**	**12,794**	**208**	**1**	**207**	
26	19	7	**470,741**	258,524	212,217	..	..	..	..	..	..	**208**	1	207	3
..	..	..	**2**	2	..	**296,125**	146,148	149,977	..	..	..	..	..	..	4
15	6	9	..	..	..	..	..	..	**26,291**	13,497	12,794	..	..	..	5

Serial number.	District or State.	Total other Provinces.			Assam.			Ajmer-Merwara.		
		Persons.	Males.	Females.	Persons.	Males.	Females.	Persons.	Males.	Females.
1	2	3	4	5	6	7	8	9	10	11
	British Territory	**276,278**	**120,723**	**155,555**	**994**	**543**	**451**	**2,415**	**1,336**	**1,079**
	Agra Province	**252,711**	**105,804**	**146,907**	**688**	**385**	**303**	**1,930**	**1,015**	**915**
	Benares Division	*59,085*	*18,459*	*40,626*	*13*	*9*	*4*	*73*	*39*	*34*
1	Benares	25,875	10,528	15,347	4	4	..	26	11	15
2	Mirzapur	10,063	4,320	5,743	1	1	..	7	7	..
	Native States	**3,329**	**1,359**	**1,970**	**58**	**56**	**2**	**2**	..	**2**
3	Rampur	593	447	146	58	56	2	2	..	2
4	Tehri-Garhwal	406	319	87	..	..	..	..	..	..
5	Benares Raj	2,330	593	1,737	..	..	..	..	..	..

Serial number.	District or State.	Burma.			Central Provinces and Berar.			Coorg.		
		Persons.	Males.	Females.	Persons.	Males.	Females.	Persons.	Males.	Females.
1	2	27	28	29	30	31	32	33	34	35
	British Territory	**722**	**403**	**319**	**14,528**	**6,416**	**8,112**	**1**	**1**	..
	Agra Province	**364**	**211**	**153**	**12,804**	**5,459**	**7,345**	**1**	**1**	..
	Benares Division	*30*	*14*	*16*	*3,223*	*1,585*	*1,638*	..	..	..
1	Benares	16	8	8	504	270	234	..	..	..
2	Mirzapur	2	..	2	2,641	1,275	1,366	..	..	..
	Native States	**10**	**5**	**5**	**55**	**26**	**29**	..	..	..
3	Rampur	..	..	..	24	18	6	..	..	..
4	Tehri-Garhwal	10	5	5	1	1	..	..	..	..
5	Benares Raj	..	..	..	30	7	23	..	..	..

Serial numbers.	District or State.	Assam States.			Baroda.			Bengal States.		
		Persons.	Males.	Females.	Persons.	Males.	Females.	Persons.	Males.	Females.
1	2	48	49	50	51	52	53	54	55	56
	British Territory	**170**	**113**	**57**	**298**	**171**	**127**	**81**	**30**	**51**
	Agra Province	**164**	**110**	**54**	**227**	**131**	**96**	**81**	**3**	**51**
	Benares Division	*3*	*1*	*2*	*62*	*32*	*30*	*61*	*19*	*42*
1	Benares	3	1	2	59	29	30	61	19	42
2	Mirzapur	..	..	..	1	1	..	..	..	..
	Native States	..	..	..	*4*	*1*	*3*	..	..	..
3	Rampur	..	..	..	..	..	..	..	..	..
4	Tehari-Garhwal	..	..	..	4	1	3	..	..	..
5	Benares Raj	..	..	..	..	..	..	..	..	..

Serial number.	District or State.	Kashmir.			Madras States (including Cochin and Travancore).			Mysore.			North-West Frontier Provinces (Agencies and Tribal areas).		
		Persons.	Males.	Females.	Persons.	Male.	Females.	Persons.	Males.	Females.	Persons.	Males.	Females.
1	2	72	73	74	75	76	77	78	79	80	81	82	83
	British Territory ..	**1,937**	**1,480**	**457**	**98**	**54**	**44**	**414**	**231**	**183**	1	..	1
	Agra Province ..	**1,765**	**1,336**	**429**	**86**	**44**	**42**	**377**	**209**	**168**	1	..	1
	Benares Division ..	*41*	*18*	*23*	*48*	*19*	*29*	*196*	*95*	*101*	..	..	..
1	Benares	22	7	15	48	19	29	196	95	101	..	..	..
2	Mirzapur	..	..	..	..	..	..	..	..	..	..	..	..
	Native States ..	**19**	**14**	**5**	..	..	..	**2**	**2**	..	..	..	..
3	Rampur	6	3	3	..	..	..	2	2	..	..	..	..
4	Tehri-Garhwal	13	11	2	..	..	..	..	..	..	..	..	..
5	Benares Raj	..	..	..	..	..	..	..	..	..	..	..	..

Andamans and Nicobars			Baluchistan (districts and administered territories).			Bengal.			Bihar and Orissa.			Bombay (including Aden).			Serial number.
Persons.	Males.	Females.	Persons.	Males.	Females.	Persons.	Males.	Females.	Persons.	Males.	Females.	Persons.	Males.	Females	
12	13	14	15	16	17	18	19	20	21	22	23	24	25	26	1
154	**78**	**76**	**566**	**428**	**138**	**25,575**	**11,851**	**13,724**	**102,725**	**34,062**	**68,663**	**8,771**	**5,195**	**3,576**	
39	**21**	**18**	**181**	**129**	**52**	**21,567**	**9,892**	**11,675**	**98,642**	**31,615**	**67,027**	**6,997**	**4,183**	**2,814**	
21	*9*	*12*	*4*	*2*	*2*	*11,762*	*4,758*	*7,024*	*39,386*	*8,988*	*30,398*	*1,003*	*581*	*422*	
11	4	7	3	2	1	10,396	4,275	6,121	10,779	3,159	7,620	919	539	380	1
..	..	..	..	..	..	660	116	544	6,587	2,819	3,768	19	10	9	2
..	..	..	1	1	..	163	131	32	2,288	581	1,707	41	28	13	
..	..	..	1	1	..	144	115	29	19	14	5	25	14	11	3
..	..	..	..	..	..	16	13	3	1	1	..	11	11	..	4
..	..	..	..	..	..	3	3	..	2,268	566	1,702	5	3	2	5

Madras (including Laccadive).			North-West Frontier Provinces (Districts and Administered Territories).			Punjab.			Total States in India.			Serial number.
Persons.	Males.	Females.	Persons.	Males.	Females.	Persons.	Males.	Females.	Persons	Males.	Females.	
36	37	38	39	40	41	42	43	44	45	46	47	1
2,254	**1,294**	**960**	**1,895**	**1,575**	**320**	**115,678**	**57,541**	**58,137**	**310,246**	**123,362**	**186,884**	
1,859	**1,075**	**784**	**1,658**	**1,417**	**241**	**105,981**	**50,401**	**55,580**	**303,134**	**118,967**	**184,167**	
752	*446*	*306*	*272*	*257*	*15*	*2,526*	*1,771*	*755*	*11,759*	*5,130*	*6,629*	
736	439	297	271	256	15	2,210	1,561	649	3,081	1,708	1,373	1
11	5	6	..	..	..	135	87	48	8,372	3,273	5,099	2
2	2	2	53	51	2	654	478	176	561	330	231	
2	..	2	46	45	1	272	184	88	252	134	118	3
2	2	..	7	6	1	358	280	78	190	160	30	4
..	..	..	..	..	..	24	14	10	119	86	33	5

Bihar and Orissa States.			Bombay States.			Central India Agency.			Central Provinces States.			Hyderabad.			Serial number.
Persons.	Males.	Females.	Persons.	Males.	Females.	Persons.	Males.	Females.	Persons	Males.	Females.	Persons.	Males.	Females.	
57	58	59	60	61	62	63	64	65	66	67	68	69	70	71	1
68	**48**	**20**	**497**	**300**	**197**	**195,733**	**71,501**	**124,232**	**240**	**140**	**100**	**1,341**	**865**	**476**	
61	**42**	**19**	**426**	**243**	**183**	**192,931**	**70,130**	**122,801**	**240**	**140**	**100**	**977**	**689**	**288**	
22	*12*	*10*	*62*	*27*	*35*	*9,128*	*3,657*	*5,471*	..	..	..	*245*	*138*	*107*	
22	12	10	42	8	34	834	453	381	..	..	..	217	123	94	1
..	..	..	16	16	..	8,223	3,178	5,045	..	..	..	..	..	..	2
..	..	..	17	17	..	209	70	139	..	..	..	8	2	6	
..	..	..	..	..	..	123	61	62	..	..	..	7	2	5	3
..	..	..	8	8	..	4	4	..	..	..	..	..	..	..	4
..	..	..	9	9	..	82	5	77	..	..	..	1	..	1	5

Punjab States.			Rajputana Agency.			Sikkim.			India unspecified.			French and Portuguese Settlements.			Serial number.
Persons.	Males.	Females.	Persons.	Males.	Females.	Persons.	Males.	Females.	Persons.	Males.	Females.	Persons.	Males.	Females.	
84	85	83	87	88	89	90	91	92	93	94	95	96	97	98	1
5,803	**4,061**	**1,742**	**102,907**	**43,974**	**58,933**	**7**	**4**	**3**	**315**	**111**	**204**	**336**	**279**	**57**	
4,752	**3,207**	**1,545**	**100,529**	**42,358**	**58,171**	**2**	..	**2**	**274**	**91**	**183**	**241**	**207**	**34**	
174	*158*	*16*	*1,640*	*954*	*686*	..	..	..	*77*	..	*77*	..	..	..	
167	153	14	1,338	789	549	..	..	..	72	..	72	..	..	..	1
2	2	..	125	76	49	..	..	..	5	..	5	..	..	..	2
177	145	32	117	74	43	..	..	..	8	5	3	..	..	..	
34	28	11	77	43	34	..	..	..	3	..	3	..	..	..	3
143	122	21	18	14	4	..	..	..	..	..	..	..	..	..	4
..	..	..	22	17	5	..	..	..	5	5	..	..	..	..	5

TABLE XI.—Part I. C.—Born

Serial number.	District or State.	Total countries in Asia. Persons.	Males.	Females.	Afghanistan. Persons.	Males.	Females.
1	2	3	4	5	6	7	8
	British Territory	**46,018**	**27,848**	**18,170**	**1,571**	**1,407**	**164**
	Agra Province	**36,106**	**22,668**	**13,438**	**1,230**	**1,089**	**141**
	Benares Division	*1,209*	*669*	*540*	*92*	*87*	*5*
1	Benares	1,119	599	520	61	58	3
2	Mirzapur	27	25	2	15	14	
	Native States	**99**	**75**	**24**	**34**	**33**	**1**
3	Rampur	57	44	13	27	26	1
4	Tehri-Garhwal	40	29	11	7	7	..
5	Benares Raj	2	2		..	..	..

Serial number.	District or State.	Chinese Turkestan.			French Indo-China.		
		21	22	23	24	25	26
	British Territory	**6**	**3**	**3**	**3**	**3**	..
	Agra Province	**2**	**2**	..	..	..	..
	Benares Division	..	..	..	..	..	..
1	Benares	..	..	..	..	..	..
2	Mirzapur	..	..	..	..	..	..
	Native States	..	..	..	..	..	..
3	Rampur	..	..	..	..	..	..
4	Tehr.-Garhwal	..	..	..	..	..	..
5	Benares Raj	..	..	..	..	..	..

Serial number.	District or State.	Russian Turkestan.			Siam.		
		39	40	41	42	43	44
	British Territory	**24**	**18**	**6**	**4**	**1**	**3**
	Agra Province	**11**	**10**	**1**	**2**	..	**2**
	Benares Division	..	..	..		..	*1*
1	Benares	..	..	..	..	..	..
2	Mirzapur	..	..	..	..	..	..
	Native States	..	..	..	..	..	..
3	Rampur	..	..	..	..	..	..
4	Tehri-Garhwal	..	..	..	..	..	..
5	Benares Raj	..	..	..	..	..	..

TABLE XI.—Part I. D.—Born in

Serial number.	District or State.	Total Europe. Persons.	Males.	Females.	United Kingdom. Persons.	Males.	Females.	Austria Hungary. Persons.	Males.	Females.
1	2	3	4	5	6	7	8	9	10	11
	British Territory	**22,460**	**19,172**	**3,288**	**21,996**	**18,841**	**3,155**	**1**	..	**1**
	Agra Province	**17,429**	**14,769**	**2,660**	**17,072**	**14,510**	**2,562**	**1**	..	**1**
	Benares Division	*517*	*324*	*193*	*505*	*317*	*188*	..	..	..
1	Benares	435	284	151	425	278	147	..	..	..
2	Mirzapur	32	9	23	31	8	23	..	..	..
	Native States	**13**	**6**	**7**	**10**	**5**	**5**	..	..	..
3	Rampur	4	2	2	1	1	..	..	..	..
4	Tehr.-Garhwal	2	1	1	2	1	1	..	..	..
5	Benares Raj	7	3	4	7	3	4	..	..	..

Arabia.			Bhotan.			Ceylon.			China.			Serial number.
Persons.	Males	Females.	Persons.	Males.	Females.	Persons.	Males.	Females.	Persons.	Males.	Females.	
9	10	11	12	13	14	15	16	17	18	19	20	1
158	116	42	12	9	3	97	65	32	151	93	58	
82	63	19	7	6	1	54	33	21	128	79	49	
17	*15*	*2*	*1*	*1*	..	*6*	*5*	*1*	*6*	*3*	*3*	
3	2	1	1	1	..	5	5	..	2	2	..	1
10	20	..	..	..	..	1	..	1	..	..	..	2
15	8	7	..	..	..	..	..	..	1	..	1	
15	8	7	..	..	..	..	..	..	..	..	..	3
..	..	..	..	..	..	..	..	..	1	..	1	4
..	..	..	..	..	..	..	..	..	..	..	..	5

Hong Kong.			Japan.			Nepal.			Persia.			Serial number.
27	28	29	30	31	32	33	34	35	36	37	38	
5	2	3	44	19	25	43,319	25,721	17,598	42	24	18	
2	1	1	21	13	8	33,972	21,005	12,967	36	20	16	
..	..	..	*3*	*3*	..	*1,074*	*550*	*524*	*1*	*1*	..	
..	..	..	3	3	..	1,036	524	512	1	1	..	1
..	..	..	..	..	..	1	1	..	..	..	..	2
..	..	..	..	..	..	28	17	11	8	6	2	
..	..	..	..	..	..	8	5	3	7	5	2	3
..	..	..	..	..	..	19	11	8	..	..	..	4
..	..	..	..	..	..	1	1	..	1	1	..	5

Straits Settlements and Malaya.			Tibet.			Turkey in Asia.			Asia unspecified.			Serial number.
45	46	47	48	49	50	51	52	53	54	55	56	
2	2	..	525	323	202	34	30	4	21	12	9	
..	..	..	517	315	202	22	20	2	20	12	8	
..	..	..	..	..	..	*2*	*2*	..	*6*	*2*	*4*	
..	..	..	..	..	..	2	2	..	5	1	4	1
..	..	..	..	..	..	..	..	..	..	..	..	2
..	..	..	13	11	2	..	..	..	..	..	..	
..	..	..	..	..	..	..	..	..	..	..	..	3
..	..	..	13	11	2	..	..	..	..	..	..	4
..	..	..	..	..	..	..	..	..	..	..	..	5

countries in Europe.

Belgium.			Denmark.			France.			Germany.			Gibralter.			Greece.			Holland.			Serial number.
Persons.	Males.	Females.	Persons.	Males.	Females.	Persons.	Males.	Females.	Persons.	Males.	Females.	Persons.	Males.	Females.	Persons.	Males.	Females.	Persons.	Males.	Females.	
12	13	14	15	16	17	18	19	20	21	22	23	24	25	26	27	28	29	30	31	32	1
18	10	8	14	13	1	35	26	9	130	87	43	18	16	2	9	9	..	7	6	1	
18	10	8	12	11	1	20	16	4	111	74	37	15	15	..	9	9	..	5	5	..	
1	*1*	..	*1*	*1*	..	..	..	..	*3*	*1*	*2*	..	..	..	*2*	*2*	..	..	..	..	
..	..	..	1	1	..	..	..	..	3	1	2	..	..	..	2	2	..	..	..	..	1
1	1	..	..	..	..	..	..	..	..	..	..	..	..	..	..	..	..	..	..	..	2
..	..	..	..	..	..	1	..	1	2	1	1	..	..	..	..	..	..	..	..	..	
..	..	..	..	..	..	1	..	1	2	1	1	..	..	..	..	..	..	..	..	..	3
..	..	..	..	..	..	..	..	..	..	..	..	..	..	..	..	..	..	..	..	..	4
..	..	..	..	..	..	..	..	..	..	..	..	..	..	..	..	..	..	..	..	..	5

TABLE XI.—Part I. D.—Born

Serial number	District or State.	Italy. Persons.	Italy. Males.	Italy. Females	Malta. Persons.	Malta. Males.	Malta. Females.	Norway. Persons	Norway. Males.	Norway. Females.	Sweden. Persons.	Sweden. Males	Sweden. Females.	Portugal. Persons.	Portugal. Males.	Portugal. Females.
1	2	38	34	35	36	37	38	39	40	41	42	43	44	45	46	47
	British Territory ..	**125**	**98**	**27**	**31**	**22**	**9**	**5**	**2**	**3**	**1**	..	**1**	**7**	**4**	**3**
	Agra Province ..	**103**	**81**	**22**	**20**	**14**	**6**	**2**	**1**	**1**	**1**	..	**1**	**1**	**1**	..
	Benares Division ..	*3*	*1*	*2*	*2*	*1*	*1*	..	..	..	..	..	..	..	..	..
1	Benares	3	1	2	1	1	..	..	..	..	..	..	..	..	..	..
2	Mirzapur	..	..	..	..	..	..	..	..	..	..	..	..	..	..	..
	Native States ..	..	..	..	..	..	..	..	..	..	..	..	..	..	..	..
3	Rampur	..	..	..	..	..	..	..	..	..	..	..	..	..	..	..
4	Tehri-Garhwal	..	..	..	..	..	..	..	..	..	..	..	..	..	..	..
5	Benares Raj	..	..	..	..	..	..	..	..	..	..	..	..	..	..	..

TABLE XI.—Part I. E.—Born

Serial number.	District or State.	Total Africa. Persons.	Total Africa. Males.	Total Africa. Females.	East Africa (British). Persons.	East Africa (British). Males.	East Africa (British). Females.	Egypt. Persons.	Egypt. Males.	Egypt. Females.	Mauritius. Persons.	Mauritius. Males.	Mauritius. Females.
1	2	3	4	5	6	7	8	9	10	11	12	13	14
	British Territory	**275**	**167**	**108**	**4**	**1**	**3**	**38**	**15**	**23**	**27**	**13**	**14**
	Agra Province	**211**	**131**	**80**	**2**	**1**	**1**	**33**	**13**	**20**	**24**	**10**	**14**
	Benares Division	*7*	*2*	*5*	..	..	..	..	..	..	*1*	*1*	..
1	Benares	4	1	3	..	..	..	..	..	..	..	..	..
2	Mirzapur	1	1	..	..	..	..	..	..	..	1	1	..
	Native States	**2**	**2**	..	..	..	..	..	..	..	**2**	**2**	..
3	Rampur	..	..	..	..	..	..	..	..	..	..	..	..
4	Tehri-Garhwal	..	..	..	..	..	..	..	..	..	..	..	..
5	Benares Raj	2	2	..	..	..	..	..	..	..	2	2	..

TABLE XII.—Part II.—Infirmities—

Serial number.	District or State.	Total afflicted. Total.	Total afflicted. Males.	Total afflicted. Females.	Insane. Total.	Insane. Males.	Insane. Females.
1	2	3	4	5	6	7	8
	British Territory	**152,929**	**84,797**	**68,132**	**8,282**	**5,626**	**2,656**
	Agra Province	**106,614**	**59,825**	**46,789**	**5,971**	**4,070**	**1,901**
	Benares Division	*10,375*	*6,007*	*4,368*	*801*	*569*	*232*
1	Benares	2,184	1,311	873	412	306	106
2	Mirzapur	1,460	776	684	68	38	30
	Native States	**2,874**	**1,694**	**1,180**	**154**	**103**	**51**
3	Rampur	964	601	363	48	37	11
4	Tehri-Garhwal	1,244	725	519	64	38	26
5	Benares Raj	666	368	298	42	28	14

Rumania.			Russia.			Spain.			Switzerland.			Turkey in Europe.			Europe, unspecified.			Serial number.
Persons.	Males.	Females.	Persons.	Males.	Females.	Persons.	Males.	Females.	Persons.	Males.	Females.	Persons.	Males.	Females.	Persons.	Males.	Females.	
48	49	50	51	52	53	54	55	56	57	58	59	60	61	62	63	64	65	1
1	..	1	26	20	6	11	9	2	14	3	11	6	4	2	5	2	3	
1	..	1	13	11	2	9	8	1	11	1	10	2	2	..	5	2	3	
..	..	..	..	..	..	..	..	..	..	..	..	..	..	..	..	..	..	
..	..	..	..	..	..	..	..	..	..	..	..	..	..	..	..	..	..	1
..	..	..	..	..	..	..	..	..	..	..	..	..	..	..	..	..	..	2
..	..	..	..	..	..	..	..	..	..	..	..	..	..	..	..	..	..	
..	..	..	..	..	..	..	..	..	..	..	..	..	..	..	..	..	..	3
..	..	..	..	..	..	..	..	..	..	..	..	..	..	..	..	..	..	4
..	..	..	..	..	..	..	..	..	..	..	..	..	..	..	..	..	..	5

in Countries in Africa.

Natal.			Seychelles.			St. Helena.			Transvaal.			Africa unspecfied.			Serial number.
Persons.	Males.	Females.	Persons.	Males.	Females.	Persons.	Males.	Females.	Persons.	Males.	Females.	Persons.	Males.	Females.	
15	16	17	18	19	20	21	22	23	24	25	26	27	28	29	1
57	30	27	1	..	1	1	..	1	2	2	..	145	106	39	
37	19	18	1	..	1	..	..	..	2	2	..	112	86	26	
1	..	*1*	..	..	..	..	..	..	..	..	..	*5*	*1*	*4*	
1	..	1	..	..	..	..	..	..	..	..	..	3	1	2	1
..	..	..	..	..	..	..	..	..	..	..	..	..	..	..	2
..	..	..	..	..	..	..	..	..	..	..	..	..	..	..	
..	..	..	..	..	..	..	..	..	..	..	..	..	..	..	3
..	..	..	..	..	..	..	..	..	..	..	..	..	..	..	4
..	..	..	..	..	..	..	..	..	..	..	..	..	..	..	5

Distribution by districts.

Deaf-mute.			Blind.			Leper.			Serial number
Total.	Males.	Females.	Total.	Males.	Females.	Total.	Males.	Females.	
9	10	11	12	13	14	15	16	17	1
26,440	**16,351**	**10,089**	**104,126**	**51,236**	**52,890**	**14,081**	**11,584**	**2,497**	
19,955	**12,444**	**7,511**	**71,325**	**35,780**	**35,545**	**9,363**	**7,531**	**1,832**	
1,905	*1,202*	*703*	*6,508*	*3,300*	*3,208*	*1,161*	*936*	*225*	
441	268	173	1,108	566	542	223	171	52	1
243	154	89	987	462	525	162	122	40	2
685	**412**	**273**	**1,596**	**845**	**751**	**439**	**334**	**105**	
146	88	58	713	428	285	57	48	9	3
417	249	168	443	202	241	320	236	84	4
122	75	47	440	215	225	62	50	12	5

Serial number.	District or State.	Population.		Ahar.		Aheriya.		Ahir.	
		Males.	Females.	Males.	Females.	Males.	Females.	Males.	Females.
1	2	3	4	5	6	7	8	9	10
	British Territory ..	**20,790,986**	**19,011,473**	**149,993**	**119,456**	**10,441**	**10,119**	**2,001,640**	**1,820,612**
	Agra Province ..	**15,191,134**	**13,778,841**	**149,992**	**119,438**	**10,441**	**10,119**	**1,328,666**	**1,199,273**
	Benares Division ..	*2,043,095*	*2,042,046*	*75*	*67*	..	..	*291,800*	*277,284*
1	Benares ..	400,287	395,993	21	..	..	..	41,672	39,614
2	Mirzapur ..	336,762	345,126	..	..	..	..	28,244	29,567
	Native States ..	**458,586**	**444,308**	..	..	..	..	**31,663**	**30,403**
3	Rampur ..	152,417	131,715	..	..	..	..	7,975	6,674
4	Tehri-Garhwal ..	147,514	151,469	..	..	..	..	..	1
5	Benares Raj ..	158,655	161,124	..	..	..	..	23,688	23,728

Serial number.	District or State.	Agarwal.		Agrahari.		Barasenī.		Baranwal.	
		Males.	Females.	Males.	Females.	Males.	Females.	Males.	Females.
	2	23	24	25	26	27	28	29	30
	British Territory ..	**142,070**	**113,209**	**39,488**	**37,061**	**15,519**	**12,959**	**5,547**	**4,267**
	Agra Province ..	**136,805**	**109,553**	**23,420**	**21,656**	**15,456**	**12,953**	**5,450**	**4,194**
	Benares Division ..	*3,137*	*2,975*	*4,156*	*3,475*	..	..	*63*	*68*
1	Benares ..	1,507	1,423	1,162	1,103	..	..	..	..
2	Mirzapur ..	350	389	1,560	1,378	..	..	..	..
	Native States ..	**1,172**	**932**	**286**	**348**	**53**	**48**	**115**	**67**
3	Rampur ..	1,020	816	..	..	53	48	73	67
4	Tehri-Garhwal ..	87	48	..	..	..	..	..	..
5	Benares Raj ..	65	68	286	348	..	..	42	..

Bania—(*concluded*).

Serial number.	District or State.	Mahesri.		Rauniar.		Rustogi.		Umar.	
		Males.	Females.	Males.	Females.	Males.	Females.	Males.	Females.
	2	41	42	43	44	45	46	47	48
	British Territory ..	**5,078**	**4,443**	**4,023**	**3,744**	**5,979**	**5,569**	**15,504**	**13,821**
	Agra Province ..	**5,012**	**4,407**	**4,011**	**3,738**	**4,689**	**4,428**	**10,397**	**9,278**
	Benares Division ..	*90*	*56*	*950*	*917*	*714*	*528*	*2,425*	*2,428*
1	Benares ..	90	56	..	..	364	342	198	199
2	Mirzapur ..	..	..	714	711	28	40	452	424
	Native States ..	**50**	**25**	..	..	**62**	**62**	**304**	**352**
3	Rampur ..	49	25	..	..	4	4	..	..
4	Tehri-Garhwal ..	..	..	..	..	..	..	..	..
5	Benares Raj ..	1	..	..	..	58	58	304	352

Serial number.	District or State.	Bari.		Barwar.		Basor.		Bayar.	
	2	61	62	63	64	65	66	67	68
	British Territory ..	**31,410**	**30,723**	**1,945**	**2,336**	**7,798**	**7,562**	**7,622**	**8,419**
	Agra Province ..	**18,137**	**17,276**	**475**	**531**	**7,798**	**7,562**	**7,622**	**8,419**
	Benares Division ..	*3,570*	*3,791*	..	..	..	..	*7,408*	*8,226*
1	Benares ..	934	927	..	..	..	..	1,414	1,621
2	Mirzapur ..	544	583	..	..	..	..	5,957	6,605
	Native States ..	**253**	**256**	**277**	**285**	..	..	**575**	**655**
3	Rampur ..	69	58	277	285	..	..	..	..
4	Tehri-Garhwal ..	..	..	..	..	..	..	..	..
5	Benares Raj ..	184	198	..	..	..	..	575	655

Bhangi—(*concluded*).

Serial number.	District or State.	Dhanuk.		Hari.		Hela.		Lal Begi.	
	2	81	82	83	84	85	86	87	88
	British Territory ..	**6,360**	**6,171**	**9**	**97**	**6,740**	**6,845**	**119,655**	**105,787**
	Agra Province ..	**2,926**	**2,977**	**3**	**1**	**4,118**	**4,166**	**110,135**	**97,766**
	Benares Division ..	..	..	..	..	*230*	*235*	*137*	*92*
1	Benares ..	..	..	..	..	168	155	71	62
2	Mirzapur ..	..	..	..	..	..	..	66	30
	Native States ..	**6**	**5**	..	..	..	..	**3,594**	**3,221**
3	Rampur ..	6	5	..	..	..	..	3,588	3,210
4	Tehri-Garhwal ..	..	..	..	..	..	..	6	11
5	Benares Raj ..	..	..	..	..	..	..	..	..

Arakh.		Atit.		Badhik.		Baghban.		Bahelia.		Bania. Total.		Serial number.
Males.	Females.	Males.	Females.	Males.	Females.	Males	Females.	Males.	Females.	Males.	Females.	
11	12	13	14	15	16	17	18	19	20	21	22	1
43,648	**40,941**	**15,180**	**14,518**	**43**	**11**	**60,626**	**53,153**	**18,115**	**15,850**	**588,885**	**515,725**	
18,728	**18,626**	**13,652**	**12,851**	**43**	**11**	**60,626**	**53,153**	**12,049**	**10,037**	**476,811**	**414,428**	
1	..	*4,592*	*4,275*	..	..	..	..	*1,008*	*908*	*55,768*	*53,739*	
1	..	64	33	..	..	..	..	260	250	**9,693**	**9,196**	**1**
..	..	..	..	..	..	..	..	457	407	**6,988**	**6,681**	**2**
1	**1**	**2**	**3**	..	..	**11,460**	**10,167**	**131**	**115**	**4,909**	**4,510**	
..	..	..	..	..	..	11,460	10,167	6	4	**2,975**	**2,451**	**3**
..	..	..	..	..	..	..	..	..	..	**142**	**71**	**4**
1	1	2	3	..	..	..	..	125	111	**1,792**	**1,988**	**5**

Bania—(*continued*).

Gahoi.		Kandu.		Kasarwani.		Kasaundhan.		Khandelwal.		Serial number.
Males.	Females.	Males.	Females.	Males.	Females.	Males.	Females.	Males.	Females.	
31	32	33	34	35	36	37	38	39	40	
11,408	**10,697**	**74,679**	**71,821**	**22,419**	**22,984**	**43,041**	**39,501**	**2,544**	**2,091**	
10,933	**10,213**	**66,212**	**63,903**	**22,034**	**22,163**	**19,599**	**18,329**	**2,516**	**2,056**	
..	..	*23,537*	*23,789*	*6,766*	*6,088*	*910*	*861*	*121*	*82*	
..	..	1,809	1,622	2,067	2,156	489	455	10	19	**1**
..	..	621	546	2,119	2,234	31	14	38	37	**2**
90	**65**	**187**	**204**	**432**	**530**	..	..	..	..	
90	65	..	..	2	..	..	..	..	..	**3**
..	..	..	..	..	..	..	..	..	..	**4**
..	..	187	204	430	530	..	..	..	..	**5**

Uswal.		Others.		Banjara.		Bansphor.		Barai.		Barhai.		Serial number.
Males.	Females.	Males.	Females.	Males.	Females.	Males.	Females.	Males.	Females.	Males.	Females.	
49	50	51	52	53	54	55	56	57	58	59	60	
162	**142**	**201,424**	**173,416**	**25,803**	**20,046**	**3,645**	**3,647**	**70,559**	**67,529**	**266,381**	**233,271**	
145	**142**	**150,132**	**127,415**	**22,477**	**17,356**	**844**	**861**	**48,607**	**46,737**	**191,159**	**166,138**	
..	..	*12,899*	*12,472*	..	*8*	..	*87*	*11,028*	*10,915*	*3,670*	*4,017*	
..	..	1,997	1,821	..	..	..	..	1,986	2,102	519	403	**1**
..	..	1,075	908	..	8	..	..	1,372	1,834	155	97	**2**
..	..	**2,158**	**1,877**	**61**	**15**	..	..	**507**	**436**	**1,851**	**1,244**	
..	..	1,684	1,426	2	4	..	..	..	..	1.478	1,201	**3**
..	..	55	23	59	11	..	..	..	..	2	..	**4**
..	..	419	428	..	..	..	..	507	436	378	43	**5**

Beldar.		Belwar.		Beria.		Bhangi. Total.		Bhangi. Balmiki.		Bhangi. Bansphor.		Serial number.
69	70	71	72	73	74	75	76	77	78	79	80	
19,667	**19,001**	**913**	**713**	**6,318**	**7,333**	**204,093**	**185,130**	**10,343**	**8,498**	**14,052**	**13,213**	
18,590	**17,950**	**95**	**13**	**3,706**	**4,092**	**180,241**	**162,855**	**10,035**	**8,256**	**10,192**	**9,711**	
..	..	..	..	*40*	*64*	*2,301*	*2,479*	..	*6*	*311*	*271*	
..	..	..	..	..	..	**666**	**586**	..	6	8	4	**1**
..	..	..	..	5	4	**296**	**326**	..	..	..	..	**2**
127	**129**	..	..	**1**	..	**4,560**	**4,078**	**23**	**32**	**1**	**3**	
127	129	..	..	..	..	**4,535**	**4,056**	23	32	1	3	**3**
..	..	..	..	..	..	**20**	**21**	..	..	..	..	**4**
..	..	..	..	1	..	**5**	**1**	..	..	..	..	**5**

Rawat.		Shaikh.		Others.		Bhar.		Bharbhunja.		Bhat.		Serial number.
89	90	91	92	93	94	95	96	97	98	99	100	
639	**657**	..	**14**	**48,295**	**43,848**	**192,796**	**199,593**	**150,852**	**134,414**	**58,978**	**55,949**	
599	**610**	..	**4**	**42,233**	**39,364**	**171,279**	**177,652**	**80,561**	**71,614**	**36,813**	**34,407**	
308	*415*	..	..	*1,315*	*1,460*	*83,820*	*85,341*	*7,011*	*7,010*	*3,825*	*4 025*	
37	41	..	..	387	318	20,420	21,288	944	970	796	642	**1**
35	31	..	..	195	265	1,588	1,259	764	872	564	611	**2**
1	..	..	..	**935**	**817**	**636**	**493**	**2,782**	**2,631**	**403**	**682**	
..	..	..	..	917	806	..	..	1,759	1,534	82	78	**3**
..	..	..	..	14	10	..	..	..	..	..	..	**4**
1	..	..	..	4	1	636	498	1,023	1,097	321	600	**5**

Serial number.	District or State.	Bhoksa. Males.	Bhoksa. Females.	Bhotiya. Males.	Bhotiya. Females.	Bhuinhar. Males.	Bhuinhar. Females.	Bind. Males.	Bind. Females.
1	2	101	102	103	104	105	106	107	108
	British Territory ..	**3,536**	**3,101**	**5,669**	**7,388**	**66,767**	**65,928**	**35,424**	**36,389**
	Agra Province ..	**3,536**	**3,101**	**5,597**	**7,318**	**66,584**	**65,759**	**35,263**	**36,185**
	Benares Division ..	..	..	..	..	*29,847*	*29,045*	*26,665*	*27,475*
1	Benares ..	..	..	..	..	10,038	10 105	5 990	6,048
2	Mirzapur ..	..	..	..	..	4,592	4,147	4,131	4,221
	Native States ..	..	..	..	..	**788**	**854**	**787**	**907**
3	Rampur ..	..	..	..	..	38	36	..	..
4	Tehri-Garhwal	..	..	..	..	..	..	..	..
5	Benares Raj	..	..	..	..	750	818	787	907

Serial number.	District or State.	Panchgaur—(concluded). Utkala.		Panchgaur—(concluded). Total.		Panch Dravid.		Sapadh.	
1	2	121	122	123	124	125	126	127	128
	British Territory ..	**77**	**35**	**841,947**	**717,605**	**13,320**	**11,286**	**245,226**	**199,114**
	Agra Province ..	**27**	**10**	**530,662**	**456,855**	**13,077**	**11,386**	**236,338**	**190,854**
	Benares Division ..	*13*	*7*	*48,715*	*49,615*	*1,768*	*2,198*	*1,140*	*432*
1	Benares ..	13	7	5,620	4,950	1,630	2,079	241	149
2	Mirzapur ..	..	..	2,300	2,366	15	54	43	24
	Native States ..	..	..	**5,011**	**3,992**	**111**	**146**	**3,033**	**2,365**
3	Rampur ..	..	..	2,816	2,205	4	5	3,028	2,365
4	Tehri-Garhwal	..	..	1,890	1,539	..	..	..	..
5	Benares Raj	..	..	305	248	107	141	5	..

Serial number.	District or State.	Chai or Chain		Chamar.		Chhippi.		Chik.	
1	2	141	142	143	144	145	146	147	148
	British Territory ..	**15,438**	**14,966**	**3,051,396**	**2,931,202**	**10,307**	**8,870**	**5,546**	**4,932**
	Agra Province ..	**10,685**	**10,629**	**2,342,559**	**2,237,852**	**9,940**	**8,497**	**5,541**	**4,923**
	Benares Division ..	..	..	*259,098*	*278,312*	*3*	*36*	*15*	*9*
1	Benares ..	..	..	49 104	52,053	..	36	..	..
2	Mirzapur ..	..	..	46,020	47,369	3	..	15	9
	Native States ..	..	..	**46,821**	**46,662**	**259**	**230**	**25**	**31**
3	Rampur ..	..	..	23,115	20,840	258	229	..	..
4	Tehri-Garhwal	..	..	1,545	1,400	..	..	..	..
5	Benares Raj	..	..	22,161	24,422	1	1	25	31

Serial number.	District or State.	Dhusar Bhargava		Dom.		Dusadh.		Faqir.	
1	2	161	162	163	164	165	166	167	168
	British Territory ..	**1,237**	**1,045**	**143,853**	**134,527**	**33,134**	**35,862**	**79,914**	**63,387**
	Agra Province ..	**1,233**	**1,035**	**139,519**	**130,503**	**33,075**	**35,798**	**75,568**	**61,471**
	Benares Division ..	..	..	*1,918*	*1,791*	*16,740*	*18,660*	*1,800*	*765*
1	Benares ..	..	..	344	820	2,099	2 203	557	148
2	Mirzapur ..	..	..	280	385	2,585	2,865	78	157
	Native States ..	..	..	**25,837**	**24,937**	**1,005**	**917**	**599**	**516**
3	Rampur ..	..	..	..	..	18	18	436	372
4	Tehri-Garhwal	..	..	25,759	24,832	..	..	151	133
5	Benares Raj	..	..	78	105	987	899	12	11

Serial number.	District or State.	Gujar.		Habura.		Halwai.		Jat.	
1	2	181	182	183	184	185	186	187	188
	British Territory ..	**166,100**	**125,174**	**1,027**	**791**	**28,835**	**25,566**	**401,069**	**307,165**
	Agra Province ..	**165,895**	**125,015**	**969**	**717**	**17,219**	**15,472**	**399,838**	**306.391**
	Benares Division ..	*136*	*146*	..	..	*6,741*	*6.438*	*52*	*34*
1	Benares ..	29	21	..	..	2,045	1.978	23	6
2	Mirzapur ..	105	125	..	..	1,707	1,792	5	..
	Native States ..	**410**	**384**	..	..	**1.431**	**1,397**	**1,120**	**841**
3	Rampur ..	410	384	..	..	6	5	1,119	841
4	Tehri-Garhwal	..	..	..	..	..	..	..	..
5	Benares Raj	..	..	..	..	1,425	1,392	1	..

Boriya.		Brahmin.												
		Total.		Panchgaur.										
				Gaur.		Kanaujia.		Saraswati.		Maithila.				
Males.	Females.	Males.	Females.	Males.	Females.	Males.	Females.	Males.	Females.	Males.	Females.	Serial number.
109	110	111	112	113	114	115	116	117	118	119	120	1
9,256	**8,630**	**2,381,540**	**2,137,197**	**223,209**	**181,859**	**591,588**	**512,757**	**24,349**	**20,153**	**2,724**	**2,801**	
8,546	**8,058**	**1,691,271**	**1,495,536**	**217,400**	**177,489**	**297,747**	**253,841**	**22,880**	**18,778**	**2,608**	**2,741**	
..	..	*257,328*	*252,408*	*2,885*	*2,535*	*44,557*	*45,466*	*1,517*	*1,425*	*248*	*182*	
..	..	51,930	48,650	1,864	2,031	2,747	1,989	911	884	85	39	1
..	..	40,482	41,519	206	96	2,029	2,237	65	33	..	..	2
..	..	**70,582**	**70,419**	**2,422**	**1,795**	**1,096**	**740**	**1,486**	**1,456**	**7**	**1**	
..	..	7,139	5,553	2,080	1,616	636	497	93	91	7	1	3
..	..	30,304	31,329	329	176	189	85	1,372	1,328	..	..	4
..	..	33,139	33,537	18	8	271	208	21	37	..	..	5

Brahmin—*(concluded)*.

Sarwarja.		Sakaldweep.		Mathuria Chaube.		Kashmiri.		Jhinjhotia.		Others.		
129	130	131	132	133	134	135	136	137	138	139	140	
857,935	**803,905**	**32,031**	**30,562**	**4,938**	**4,543**	**1,353**	**971**	**34,332**	**31,943**	**350,458**	**337,268**	
520,447	**475,065**	**13,419**	**13,271**	**4,632**	**4,178**	**783**	**511**	**34,324**	**31,936**	**327,589**	**315,776**	
151,907	*146,414*	*3,658*	*3,892*	*68*	*13*	*321*	*219*	*106*	*64*	*49,745*	*49,561*	
31,888	29,062	529	511	44	7	26	24	..	3	12,452	11,865	1
32,237	32,418	219	36	..	..	35	..	..	..	5,633	6,621	2
31,292	**31,994**	**48**	**32**	**20**	**22**	**3**	**29**	..	**14**	**31,064**	**31,825**	
25	18	..	..	20	22	..	..	..	14	1,246	924	3
..	..	..	..	..	..	..	..	..	..	28,414	29,790	4
31,267	31,976	48	32	..	..	3	29	..	..	1,404	1,111	5

Darzi.		Dhanuk.		Dharkar.		Dhimar.		Dhobi.		Dhunia.		
149	150	151	152	153	154	155	156	157	158	159	160	
43,052	**37,533**	**69,070**	**60,206**	**19,090**	**18,521**	**1,801**	**2,252**	**316,916**	**297,631**	**14,175**	**12,984**	
37,566	**32,487**	**56,555**	**49,457**	**14,831**	**14,024**	**1,703**	**2,162**	**217,982**	**203,018**	**14,143**	**12,959**	
497	*588*	*5*	..	*5,882*	*5,919*	*37*	*21*	*20,372*	*20,480*	*3*	*13*	
278	713	5	..	919	884	31	21	3,631	3,775	3	13	1
76	122	..	..	2,793	2,782	6	..	3,415	3,505	..	..	2
731	**659**	**1**	**3**	**566**	**535**	**35**	**23**	**4,405**	**4,097**	**584**	**499**	
657	591	1	3	..	..	..	..	2,864	2,476	577	490	3
..	..	..	..	..	..	35	23	1	2	..	..	4
74	68	..	..	566	535	..	..	1,540	1,619	7	9	5

Gadariya.		Gharuk.		Gond.		Goriya.		Goshain.		Gorkha.		
169	170	171	172	173	174	175	176	177	178	179	180	
507,200	**459,591**	**524**	**494**	**52,854**	**56,365**	**40,994**	**41,821**	**48,735**	**42,497**	**4,145**	**1,925**	
370,702	**332,709**	**33**	**16**	**52,851**	**56,360**	**2,770**	**3,448**	**23,768**	**20,475**	**4,121**	**1,917**	
32,216	*31,500*	..	..	*27,211*	*29,253*	*806*	*703*	*5,128*	*4,385*	*49*	*29*	
6,504	6,454	..	..	5,430	6,795	373	284	2,104	1,757	49	29	1
7,184	7,172	..	..	2,862	3,244	..	..	1,388	1,999	..	..	2
7,835	**7,383**	..	..	**378**	**629**	..	..	**1,405**	**1,231**	**6**	..	
3,558	3,233	..	..	..	..	..	..	628	504	2	..	3
..	..	..	..	..	..	..	..	111	81	4	..	4
4,282	4,150	..	..	376	629	..	..	666	646	..	..	5

Julaha.		Kachhi.		Kadhera.		Kahar.		Kalwar.		Kamboh.		
189	190	191	192	193	194	195	196	197	198	199	200	
17,886	**15,545**	**385,008**	**338,212**	**12,627**	**10,828**	**561,124**	**522,688**	**144,564**	**136,039**	**2,157**	**1,703**	
17,886	**15,545**	**332,753**	**293,562**	**4,965**	**4,256**	**429,928**	**395,151**	**91,142**	**86,695**	**2,157**	**1,703**	
..	..	*200*	*187*	..	..	*29,929*	*32,405*	*26,707*	*27,102*	..	..	
..	..	2	3	..	..	6,444	7,115	7,645	7,732	..	..	1
..	..	19	10	..	..	5,292	5,392	4,021	4,072	..	..	2
1,994	**1,806**	**2,770**	**2,516**	..	..	**10,628**	**10,201**	**2,716**	**2,671**	..	..	
1,991	1,802	2,762	2,509	..	..	8,341	7,624	294	271	..	..	3
3	4	..	..	..	..	..	..	..	..	..	..	4
..	..	8	7	..	..	2,287	2,577	2,422	2,400	..	..	5

Serial number.	District or State.	Kamkar. Males.	Kamkar. Females.	Kanjar. Males.	Kanjar. Females.	Kayastha. Males.	Kayastha. Females.	Kewat. Males.	Kewat. Females.
1	2	201	202	203	204	205	206	207	208
	British Territory ..	**17,045**	**19,672**	**8,863**	**8,817**	**244,283**	**217,724**	**214,654**	**212,954**
	Agra Province ..	**17,030**	**19,661**	**7,184**	**7,110**	**169,587**	**150,351**	**178,699**	**176,830**
	Benares Division ..	*7,779*	*9,519*	*65*	*30*	*30,298*	*30,598*	*26,847*	*26,825*
1	Benares	..	..	47	14	8,224	8,460	896	914
2	Mirzapur	4	..	18	16	3,450	3,572	11,949	11,824
	Native States	..	..	**131**	**146**	**5,138**	**4,396**	**8,754**	**8,742**
3	Rampur	..	..	131	146	3,009	2,471	..	..
4	Tehri-Garhwal	..	..	..	..	4	..	..	..
5	Benares Raj	..	..	..	..	2,125	1,925	8,754	8,742

Serial number.	District or State.	Kisan.		Koeri.		Kol.		Kori.	
	2	221	222	223	224	225	226	227	228
	British Territory ..	**188,568**	**160,512**	**219,430**	**211,241**	**31,807**	**32,792**	**437,490**	**418,006**
	Agra Province	**166,400**	**141,554**	**215,628**	**207,485**	**31,781**	**32,769**	**242,814**	**223,011**
	Benares Division ..	..	..	*101,604*	*96,047*	*15,297*	*15,457*	*6,524*	*7,117*
1	Benares	..	..	19,498	18,610	..	..	1,252	1,155
2	Mirzapur	..	..	12,831	12,627	15,283	15,448	697	1,078
	Native States	**2,526**	**2,086**	**6,816**	**6,651**	**484**	**564**	**2,375**	**2,011**
3	Rampur	2,526	2,086	..	..	..	..	2,041	1,665
4	Tehri-Garhwal	..	..	..	..	..	..	..	..
5	Benares Raj	..	..	6,816	6,651	484	564	334	346

Serial number.	District or State.	Maha Brahmin.		Mahajan.		Mali.		Mallah.	
	2	241	242	243	244	245	246	247	248
	British Territory ..	**11,960**	**10,956**	**17,299**	**14,280**	**94,998**	**84,324**	**114,359**	**128,823**
	Agra Province	**9,043**	**8,151**	**17,297**	**14,276**	**77,596**	**68,347**	**102,134**	**116,215**
	Benares Division ..	*1,602*	*1,711*	..	..	*3,022*	*3,051*	*20,759*	*32,068*
1	Benares	320	283	..	..	795	852	3,643	4,926
2	Mirzapur	149	172	..	..	424	366	3,313	6,410
	Native States	**139**	**101**	**308**	**267**	**48**	**767**	**767**	**1,294**
3	Rampur	40	34	308	267	622	541	..	..
4	Tehri-Garhwal	..	..	..	..	..	..	..	..
5	Benares Raj	99	67	..	..	226	226	767	1,294

Serial number.	District or State.	Nat.		Orh.		Pasi.		Patwa.	
	2	261	262	263	264	265	266	267	268
	British Territory ..	**21,209**	**21,046**	**4,502**	**4,569**	**665,038**	**635,127**	**13,460**	**13,173**
	Agra Province	**14,344**	**13,789**	**4,502**	**4,569**	**169,012**	**165,758**	**8,591**	**8,671**
	Benares Division ..	*1,118*	*1,163*	..	..	*21,631*	*22,536*	*1,140*	*1,313*
1	Benares	383	454	..	..	2,358	2,217	877	343
2	Mirzapur	154	208	..	..	4,258	4,125	..	..
	Native States	**628**	**544**	..	..	**5,389**	**5,666**	**158**	**135**
3	Rampur	517	457	..	..	45	1	158	135
4	Tehri-Garhwal	..	..	..	..	..	..	..	..
5	Benares Raj	111	87	..	..	5,344	5,665	..	..

Serial number.	District or State.	Rajput, Bargujar.		Rajput, Bandhalgoti.		Rajput, Bhadauria.		Rajput, Bhale Sultan.	
	2	281	282	283	284	285	286	287	288
	British Territory ..	**17,232**	**14,911**	**5,440**	**5,125**	**19,189**	**15,702**	**7,397**	**6,693**
	Agra Province	**17,111**	**14,796**	**484**	**303**	**14,409**	**11,428**	**2,649**	**2,426**
	Benares Division ..	*6*	..	*192*	*66*	*1,433*	*982*	*88*	*118*
1	Benares	6	..	..	..	2	2	61	55
2	Mirzapur	..	..	4	..	121	136	7	3
	Native States	**46**	**98**	..	..	**35**	**27**	**1**	..
3	Rampur	46	98	..	..	85	27	..	..
4	Tehri-Garhwal	..	..	..	..	..	..	1	..
5	Benares Raj	..	..	..	..	..	..		..

Khagi.		Khangar.		Kharwar.		Khatik.		Khattri.		Kirar.		Serial number.
Males.	Females.	Males.	Females	Males.	Females.	Males.	Females.	Males.	Females.	Males.	Females.	
209	210	211	212	213	214	215	216	217	218	219	220	1
25,233	**22,385**	**14,412**	**14,275**	**7,370**	**7,568**	**94,128**	**86,884**	**21,668**	**19,728**	**1,240**	**693**	
25,233	**22,369**	**14,412**	**14,275**	**7,370**	**7,568**	**81,149**	**74,595**	**16,712**	**14,639**	**1,240**	**693**	
..	..	*207*	*14*	*7,867*	*7,568*	*7,077*	*6,919*	*2,221*	*1,986*	..	..	
..	..	..	..	..	..	3,075	3,238	1,775	1,717	..	..	1
..	..	207	14	7,867	7,568	1,615	1,451	132	47	..	..	2
874	**757**	..	..	..	**520**	**418**	**443**	**201**	**167**	..	..	
874	757	..	..	..	..	55	40	180	155	..	..	3
..	..	..	..	..	..	..	..	1	..	..	..	4
..	..	..	..	..	520	363	403	20	12	..	..	5

Kumhar.		Kunjra.		Kurmi.		Lodha.		Lohar.		Luniya.		
229	230	231	232	233	234	235	236	237	238	239	240	
362,719	**341,215**	**409**	**262**	**965,004**	**892,914**	**565,669**	**506,668**	**257,636**	**236,175**	**203,306**	**200,108**	
285,445	**267,541**	**242**	**86**	**532,794**	**495,497**	**370,356**	**326,712**	**192,881**	**177,268**	**133,026**	**132,223**	
37,150	*38,147*	*85*	*34*	*105,773*	*105,836*	*72*	..	*49,597*	*48,385*	*39,821*	*39,530*	
7,958	8,007	10	..	43,383	43,296	10	..	10,847	10,673	7,811	7,541	1
5,466	5,792	..	..	30,427	30,348	.	..	7,605	7,595	2,828	2,812	2
5,936	**5,645**	..	..	**15,907**	**13,739**	**20,767**	**18,074**	**4,377**	**4,234**	**2,812**	**2,784**	
2,811	2,427	..	..	12,801	10,833	20,767	18,074	259	215	..	..	3
85	67	..	..	..	..	..	..	..	..	..	..	4
3,040	3,151	..	..	3,106	2,906	..	..	4,118	4,019	2,812	2,784	5

Meo.		Mochi.		Murao.		Musahar.		Nai.		Naik.		
249	250	251	252	253	254	255	256	257	258	259	260	
5,816	**5,013**	**2,909**	**2,291**	**348,086**	**312,281**	**21,100**	**20,770**	**348,423**	**317,584**	**2,258**	**2,779**	
5,816	**5,013**	**2,078**	**1,773**	**169,005**	**147,383**	**17,460**	**17,227**	**256,198**	**231,158**	**2,257**	**2,779**	
..	..	*143*	*110*	*646*	*664*	*7,900*	*7,735*	*26,464*	*26,634*	..	..	
..	..	86	74	164	143	1,895	1,943	5,312	5,303	..	..	1
..	..	29	28	345	360	1,827	1,791	4,659	4,855	..	..	2
305	**282**	**54**	**30**	**7,257**	**6,251**	**2,081**	**1,892**	**4,374**	**4,203**	**248**	**29**	
305	282	13	..	7,257	6,251	..	..	2,002	1,769	..	..	3
..	..	17	17	..	..	..	..	46	32	248	29	4
..	..	24	13	..	..	2,081	1,892	2,826	2,402	..	..	5

Radha.		Rajput, Thakur or Kshattriya. Total.		Amethia.		Bachhal.		Bachhgoti.		Bais.		
269	270	271	272	273	274	275	276	277	278	279	280	
1,427	**1,503**	**1,734,407**	**1,485,380**	**5,242**	**5,116**	**11,104**	**10,177**	**17,997**	**15,789**	**130,404**	**112,185**	
249	**258**	**1,408,232**	**1,200,615**	**1,554**	**1,438**	**7,301**	**7,137**	**3,686**	**2,126**	**72,162**	**59,789**	
1	..	*195,108*	*179,728*	*28*	*60*	*56*	*265*	*2,701*	*1,519*	*20,476*	*18,627*	
..	..	26,096	23,826	1	..	..	..	114	93	1,286	1,426	1
1	..	1 ,849	12,331	..	..	..	..	129	11	1,842	2,127	2
12	**14**	**103,552**	**105,492**	..	..	**20**	**26**	..	..	**76**	**1,504**	
12	14	5,816	4,292	..	..	20	26	..	..	76	118	3
..	..	88,299	92,493	..	..	..	..	..	..	..	..	4
..	..	9,437	8,707	..	..	..	..	..	..	..	1,886	5

Thakur, or Kshattriya—*(continued)*.

Bhatti.		Bisen.		Bundela.		Chamargaur.		Chandel.		Chandrabansi.		
289	290	291	292	293	294	295	296	297	298	299	300	
3,767	**2,815**	**33,374**	**36,204**	**4,534**	**4,198**	**1,261**	**887**	**34,672**	**30,514**	**3,091**	**1,834**	
3,764	**2,772**	**23,347**	**23,030**	**4,442**	**4,091**	**1,058**	**812**	**27,989**	**25,398**	**2,921**	**1,697**	
110	*234*	*'7,429*	*5,860*	*17*	*64*	*26*	*6*	*8,138*	*9,381*	*1,185*	*708*	
..	..	748	394	..	..	..	6	171	766	58	44	1
..	..	575	431	17	64	26	..	853	1,221	28	51	2
..	..	**1,323**	**337**	**5**	**3**	..	..	**309**	**318**	**3**	**2**	
..	..	..	..	5	3	..	..	..	5	3	2	3
..	..	..	..	..	..	..	..	..	..	..	..	4
..	..	1,328	337	..	..	..	..	309	318	..	..	5

Rajput,

Serial number.	District or State.	Chauhan. Males.	Chauhan. Females.	Dhakra. Males.	Dhakra. Females.	Dikhit. Males.	Dikhit. Females.	Gahlot. Males.	Gahlot. Females.
1	2	301	302	303	304	305	306	307	308
	British Territory	**204,116**	**165,644**	**6,534**	**5,459**	**25,835**	**19,449**	**18,069**	**12,257**
	Agra Province	**170,312**	**136,191**	**5,796**	**4,932**	**19,135**	**14,100**	**17,432**	**11,787**
	Benares Division ..	*6,448*	*6,117*	..	..	*6,760*	*4,586*	*256*	*126*
1	Benares	450	366	..	..	212	276	126	19
2	Mirzapur	710	632	..	..	156	185	26	29
	Native States	**2,071**	**1,559**	..	..	**64**	**49**	**1**	..
3	Rampur	1,979	1,496	..	..	4	..	1	..
4	Tehri-Garhwal	15	20	..	..	..	..	..	..
5	Benares Raj	77	43	..	..	60	49	..	..

Rajput,

Serial number.	District or State.	Janwar.		Kachwaha.		Kalhans.		Kanpuria.	
	2	321	322	323	324	325	326	327	328
	British Territory ..	**9,560**	**7,834**	**29,992**	**23,095**	**11,990**	**10,909**	**8,847**	**9,236**
	Agra Province	**1,150**	**1,034**	**25,365**	**19,236**	**2,720**	**1,924**	**532**	**433**
	Benares Division ..	..	*82*	*853*	*758*	*25*	*19*	*249*	*225*
1	Benares	..	..	13	4	17	9	1	..
2	Mirzapur	..	..	9	25	..	..	..	..
	Native States	..	..	**79**	**43**	..	..	..	..
3	Rampur	..	..	60	35	..	..	..	..
4	Tehri-Garhwal	..	..	..	..	..	..	..	..
5	Benares Raj	..	..	19	8	..	..	..	..

Rajput,

Serial number.	District or State.	Raikwar.		Rajkumar.		Rathor.		Sengar.	
	2	341	342	343	344	345	346	347	348
	British Territory ..	**11,961**	**8,573**	**12,362**	**12,585**	**32,908**	**25,626**	**29,701**	**24,477**
	Agra Province	**2,716**	**2,586**	**3,203**	**3,649**	**26,737**	**20,236**	**28,188**	**23,082**
	Benares Division ..	*126*	*448*	*2,622*	*2,804*	*1,709*	*1,281*	*9,923*	*8,003*
1	Benares	53	379	65	118	247	198	92	10
2	Mirzapur	1	8	82	46	46	34	25	22
	Native States	..	..	**325**	**188**	**291**	**147**	..	**27**
3	Rampur	..	..	..	3	291	147	..	..
4	Tehri-Garhwal	..	..	..	..	..	..	..	..
5	Benares Raj	..	..	325	185	..	..	..	27

Serial number.	District or State.	Rawa. Males.	Rawa. Females.	Saini. Males.	Saini. Females.	Santhwar. Males.	Santhwar. Females.	Sonar. Males.	Sonar. Females.	Sunkar. Males.	Sunkar. Females.	Taga. Males.	Taga. Females.
	2	361	362	363	364	365	366	367	368	369	370	371	372
	British Territory ..	**7,346**	**6,022**	**36,784**	**29,454**	**60,412**	**58,674**	**137,735**	**113,616**	**5,257**	**4,149**	**58,434**	**44,789**
	Agra Province ..	**7,346**	**6,022**	**36,768**	**29,441**	**60,409**	**58,674**	**108,801**	**94,099**	**5,257**	**4,149**	**58,432**	**44,782**
	Benares Division ..	..	..	..	..	..	..	*18,865*	*17,113*	..	*1*	..	..
1	Benares	..	..	..	..	..	..	4,127	3,993	..	..	..	..
2	Mirzapur	..	..	..	..	..	..	1,875	1,707	..	..	..	..
	Native States ..	..	..	..	..	..	..	**2,857**	**2,823**	..	..	**2**	**1**
3	Rampur ..	..	..	..	..	..	..	1,396	1,223	..	..	2	1
4	Tehri-Garhwal ..	..	..	..	..	..	..	667	916	..	..	..	..
5	Benares Raj ..	..	..	..	..	..	..	794	684	..	..	..	..

Thakur or Kshattriya—*(continued).*

Gaharwar.		Gaur.		Gautam.		Jadon.		Jadubansi.		Jaiswar.		Serial number.
Males.	Females.	Males.	Females.	Males.	Females.	Males.	Females.	Males.	Females.	Males.	Females.	
309	310	311	312	313	314	315	316	317	318	319	320	1
20,345	**17,397**	**40,857**	**30,192**	**34,922**	**27,874**	**39,256**	**31,509**	**4,894**	**3,967**	**4,594**	**3,610**	
16,105	**13,833**	**28,934**	**20,968**	**28,885**	**22,650**	**39,179**	**31,426**	**4,654**	**3,833**	**4,134**	**3,514**	
9,044	*7,348*	*343*	*76*	*5,726*	*5,321*	..	..	*96*	*92*	*286*	*247*	
438	..	83	..	603	..	..	..	..	12	..	55	1
2,984	2,378	7	5	119	101	..	..	..	..	..	..	2
854	**765**	**121**	**121**	**151**	**135**	..	..	**2**	..	**1**	..	
4	2	100	89	40	45	..	..	2	..	1	..	3
..	..	..	..	..	..	..	..	..	..	..	..	4
850	763	21	32	111	90	..	..	..	..	..	..	5

Thakur or Kshattriya—*(continued).*

Katheria.		Nikumbh.		Panwar.		Parihar.		Pundir.		Raghubansi.		
329	330	331	332	333	334	335	336	337	338	339	340	
15,960	**12,423**	**8,028**	**5,722**	**36,893**	**26,114**	**17,373**	**15,114**	**16,596**	**10,599**	**28,192**	**24,792**	
14,161	**10,970**	**5,386**	**3,700**	**24,159**	**17,628**	**15,700**	**13,608**	**16,591**	**10,599**	**22,640**	**19,722**	
..	..	*2,001*	*1,215*	*2,377*	*2,543*	*2,910*	*3,162*	..	..	*16,818*	*15,527*	
..	..	18	1	296	494	..	..	..	..	7,261	5,587	1
..	..	22	19	149	260	242	329	..	..	373	333	2
1,266	**831**	..	..	**54**	**57**	**24**	**44**	..	..	**234**	**233**	
1,266	831	..	..	6	3	..	..	..	..	7	9	3
..	..	..	..	48	54	..	..	..	..	..	..	4
..	..	..	..	..	..	24	44	..	..	227	224	5

Thakur or Kshattriya—*(concluded).*

Sikarwar.		Solankhi.		Sombansi.		Surajbansi.		Tomar.		Others.		
349	350	351	352	353	354	355	356	357	358	359	360	
17,843	**12,335**	**7,443**	**6,417**	**29,350**	**23,189**	**22,248**	**17,360**	**21,145**	**17,783**	**669,889**	**613,689**	
15,103	**10,229**	**7,360**	**6,387**	**12,651**	**9,222**	**15,808**	**11,719**	**18,401**	**15,440**	**632,218**	**578,733**	
4,163	*3,110*	*173*	*868*	*2,340*	*2,103*	*4,580*	*3,579*	*141*	*97*	*73,254*	*77,151*	
333	435	..	18	678	507	509	438	..	..	12,284	12,124	1
61	31	37	10	72	89	1,271	1,124	..	..	2,855	2,227	2
99	**60**	**2**	..	**95**	**73**	**124**	**97**	**58**	**58**	**95,818**	**96,690**	
50	14	2	..	36	13	10	8	58	58	1,714	1,260	3
..	..	..	..	..	..	..	..	..	..	88,236	92,419	4
49	46	..	..	59	60	114	89	..	..	5,868	5,011	5

Tamboli.		Tawaif.		Teli.		Tharu.		Thathera.		Turha.		Minor castes or others.		
Males.	Females	Males.	Females	Males.	Females.	Males.	Females.	Males.	Females.	Males.	Females.	Males.	Females.	
373	374	375	376	377	378	379	380	381	382	383	384	385	386	
35,103	**32,442**	**1,926**	**3,003**	**374,718**	**350,181**	**14,932**	**12,787**	**10,539**	**9,444**	**3,328**	**4,589**	**136,966**	**131,895**	
13,014	**12,752**	**1,387**	**2,250**	**260,059**	**244,082**	**11,671**	**9,832**	**6,786**	**6,027**	**3,328**	**4,589**	**115,972**	**112,394**	
333	*382*	*446*	*877*	*46,250*	*46,303*	..	..	*1,035*	*919*	*1,126*	*1,965*	*32,930*	*33,871*	
325	368	129	289	9,794	9,945	..	..	815	286	..	..	4,850	2,792	1
..	..	10	21	7,531	7,533	..	..	85	13	..	..	25,936	26,688	2
112	**100**	**23**	**24**	**4,754**	**4,681**	..	..	**77**	**73**	..	..	**3,210**	**2,229**	
109	100	..	..	1,275	1,161	..	..	3	1	..	..	2,136	1,900	3
..	..	..	..	..	..	..	..	..	..	..	..	11	7	4
3	..	23	24	3,479	3,520	..	..	74	72	..	..	1,063	322	5

Serial number.	District or State.	Population.		Ahar.		Ahir.		Arakh.	
		Males.	Females.	Males.	Females.	Males.	Females.	Males.	Females.
1	2	3	4	5	6	7	8	9	10
	British Territory ..	**3,452,534**	**3,178,786**	**1**	**4**	**6,322**	**6,244**	**61**	**4**
	Agra Province ..	**2,583,205**	**2,347,428**	**1**	**4**	**4,007**	**3,947**	**58**	**4**
	Benares Division ..	*182,229*	*186,616*	..	..	*293*	*323*	..	..
1	Benares	49,481	47,331	..	..	48	38	..	..
2	Mirzapur	20,823	20,676	..	..	18	12	..	..
	Native States	**143,865**	**129,526**	..	..	..	..	..	..
3	Rampur	129,228	115,376	..	..	..	..	..	..
4	Tehri-Garhwal	904	850	..	..	..	..	..	..
5	Benares Raj	13,753	13,300	..	..	..	..	..	..

Serial number.	District or State.	Bari.		Barwar		Beldar.		Beria.	
	2	23	24	25	26	27	28	29	30
	British Territory ..	**285**	**128**	**70**	**94**	**69**	**41**	**154**	**248**
	Agra Province	**285**	**128**	**70**	**94**	**51**	**32**	**45**	**62**
	Benares Division ..	..	*2*	*66*	*94*	..	..	..	..
1	Benares	..	2	..	..	..	..	..	..
2	Mirzapur	..	..	..	..	..	..	..	..
	Native States	..	..	..	..	**1**	..	..	..
3	Rampur	..	..	..	..	1	..	..	..
4	Tehri-Garhwal	..	..	..	..	..	..	..	..
5	Benares Raj	..	..	..	..	..	..	..	..

Serial number.	District or State.	Bhangi—*(concluded)*.							
		Lalbogi.		Rawat.		Shaikh		Others.	
	2	43	44	45	43	47	48	49	50
	British Territory ..	**2,342**	**2,142**	**827**	**633**	**2,097**	**1,929**	**3,895**	**3,868**
	Agra Province	**455**	**406**	**824**	**630**	**1,659**	**1,531**	**2,936**	**2,939**
	Benares Division ..	*80*	*44*	*15*	*15*	*302*	*245*	*1,021*	*1,080*
1	Benares	34	20	..	..	90	54	260	295
2	Mirzapur	8	5	..	..	78	72	100	80
	Native States	..	..	..	..	**60**	**54**	**62**	**51**
3	Rampur	..	..	..	..	..	..	2	2
4	Tehri-Garhwal	..	..	..	..	..	..	..	..
5	Benares Raj	..	..	..	..	60	54	60	49

Serial number.	District or State.	Chamar.		Chhipi.		Chik.		Churihar.	
	2	63	64	65	66	67	68	69	70
	British Territory ..	**2,740**	**2,883**	**7,259**	**6,079**	**2,304**	**2,325**	**15,506**	**14,917**
	Agra Province	**2,672**	**2,834**	**7,152**	**5,974**	**871**	**757**	**12,120**	**11,373**
	Benares Division ..	*3*	*8*	*41*	*20*	*46*	*58*	*3,128*	*2,462*
1	Benares	..	..	..	..	..	25	441	476
2	Mirzapur	..	..	2	3	..	..	1,204	448
	Native States	**19**	**9**	**24**	**35**	..	..	**321**	**353**
3	Rampur	19	9	24	35	..	..	..	..
4	Tehri-Garhwal	..	..	..	..	..	..	..	..
5	Benares Raj	..	..	..	..	..	..	321	353

Serial number.	District or State.	Dhusar		Dom.		Dusadh.		Faqir.	
	2	83	84	85	86	87	88	89	90
	British Territory ..	..	**1**	**2,227**	**2,234**	**26**	..	**191,264**	**176,186**
	Agra Province	..	**1**	**2,224**	**2,219**	**26**	..	**130,964**	**118,255**
	Benares Division ..	..	..	..	..	..	..	*6,052*	*6,089*
1	Benares	..	..	..	..	..	..	1,168	1,097
2	Mirzapur	..	..	..	..	..	..	496	528
	Native States	..	..	**51**	**64**	..	..	**8 264**	**7,285**
3	Rampur	..	..	51	64	..	..	7,420	6,510
4	Tehri-Garhwal	..	..	..	..	..	..	..	..
5	Benares Raj	..	..	..	..	..	..	844	775

Baheliya. Males.	Baheliya. Females.	Bania. Males.	Bania. Females.	Banjara. Males.	Banjara. Females.	Bansphor. Males.	Bansphor. Females.	Barai. Males.	Barai. Females.	Barhai. Males.	Barhai. Females.	Serial number
11	12	13	14	15	16	17	18	19	20	21	22	1
2,325	**2,105**	**206**	**11**	**19,337**	**17,879**	**222**	**221**	**2**	**4**	**46,541**	**41,244**	
1,470	**1,435**	**205**	**9**	**17,355**	**16,298**	**222**	**221**	**2**	**3**	**43,365**	**38,308**	
49	*50*	*56*	..	*45*	*17*	..	..	..	..	*22*	..	
47	50	1	..	..	..	..	..	..	..	22	..	1
2	..	55	..	18	..	..	..	..	..	..	..	2
80	**74**	..	..	**4,870**	**4,788**	..	..	..	..	**4,146**	**5,713**	
80	74	..	..	4,870	4,788	..	..	..	..	4,146	3,713	3
..	..	..	..	..	..	..	..	..	..	..	..	4
..	..	..	..	..	..	..	..	..	..	..	..	5

Bhangi. Total.		Bhangi. Balmiki.		Bhangi. Bansphor.		Bhangi. Dhanuk.		Bhangi. Hari.		Bhangi. Hela.		Serial number
31	32	33	34	35	36	37	38	39	40	41	42	
10,102	**9,463**	**5**	..	**22**	**16**	**9**	**11**	**5**	**12**	**900**	**852**	
6,565	**6,170**	**2**	..	..	..	..	..	**5**	**12**	**684**	**652**	
1,647	*1,606*	..	..	..	..	..	..	..	..	*229*	*222*	
384	370	..	..	..	..	..	..	..	..	..	1	1
248	220	..	..	..	..	..	..	..	..	62	63	2
197	**169**	..	..	..	..	..	..	..	..	**75**	**84**	
2	2	..	..	..	..	..	..	..	..	..	..	3
..	..	..	..	..	..	..	..	..	..	..	..	4
195	167	..	..	..	..	..	..	..	..	75	64	5

Bharbhunja.		Bhat.		Bhathiyara.		Bhishti.		Bhuinhar.		Brahmin.		Serial number
51	52	53	54	55	56	57	58	59	60	61	62	
5,403	**4,814**	**14,308**	**14,199**	**18,012**	**15,131**	**50,422**	**45,018**	**6**	..	**53**	**26**	
4,315	**3,794**	**7,067**	**7.359**	**16,751**	**13,882**	**49,182**	**43,813**	**6**	..	**51**	**24**	
..	..	*1,786*	*1,945*	*838*	*765*	*18*	*20*	*6*	..	..	..	
..	..	214	241	447	369	6	9	6	..	..	..	1
..	..	133	186	145	99	..	..	..	..	..	..	2
372	**305**	**247**	**112**	**556**	**514**	**1,501**	**1,312**	..	..	..	..	
372	305	49	49	556	514	1,501	1,312	..	..	..	..	3
..	..	..	..	..	..	..	..	..	..	..	..	4
..	..	198	63	..	..	..	..	..	..	..	..	5

Dafali.		Darzi		Dhanuk.		Dharkar.		Dhobi.		Dhunia.		Serial number
71	72	73	74	75	76	77	78	79	80	81	82	
16,267	**15,870**	**86,178**	**80,834**	**21**	**13**	**5**	**12**	**50,218**	**46,137**	**187,571**	**182,117**	
8,685	**8,547**	**49,209**	**45,658**	**21**	**12**	**4**	**3**	**40,537**	**37,088**	**122,135**	**117,908**	
3,507	*3,494*	*6,487*	*6,575*	..	..	..	*2*	*1,732*	*1,790*	*9,774*	*10,926*	
1,191	1,152	1,137	1,092	..	..	..	..	428	406	2,030	2,021	1
486	584	885	885	..	..	..	..	265	285	996	1,588	2
537	**521**	**1,947**	**1,780**	..	..	..	..	**3,305**	**3,004**	**3,537**	**3,271**	
..	..	1,233	1,080	..	..	..	..	3,123	2,815	2,537	2,287	3
..	..	..	..	..	..	..	..	..	..	..	..	4
537	521	714	700	..	..	..	..	182	189	1,000	984	5

Gadariya.		Gaddi.		Gara.		Ghosi.		Gond.		Goriya.		Serial number
91	92	93	94	95	96	97	98	99	100	101	102	
340	**219**	**29,358**	**24,990**	**26,981**	**22,062**	**14,811**	**13,951**	**2**	**6**	**2,162**	**2,085**	
183	**80**	**10,086**	**8,278**	**26,981**	**22,062**	**8,343**	**7,546**	**2**	**6**	**1,283**	**1,129**	
23	*18*	*4*	*7*	..	..	*77*	*74*	..	..	*340*	*390*	
6	..	4	..	..	..	48	33	..	..	85	122	1
..	..	..	7	..	..	..	..	..	..	22	59	2
..	..	**363**	**311**	..	..	**3,753**	**3,310**	..	..	**72**	**104**	
..	..	363	311	..	..	3,753	3,810	..	..	..	..	3
..	..	..	..	..	..	..	..	..	..	..	..	4
..	..	..	..	..	..	..	..	..	..	72	104	5

Serial number.	District or State.	Gujar. Males.	Gujar. Females.	Halwai. Males.	Halwai. Females.	Iraqi. Males	Iraqi. Females	Jat. Males.	Jat. Females
1	2	103	104	105	106	107	108	109	110
	British Territory ..	**38,555**	**33,719**	**17,689**	**16,142**	**4,070**	**4,681**	**9,828**	**7,761**
	Agra Province	**24,133**	**19,799**	**4,723**	**4,343**	**3,014**	**3,675**	**9,768**	**7,706**
	Benares Division ..	*113*	*97*	*91*	*85*	*1,806*	*2,221*	..	..
1	Benares	8	2	6	5	44	45	..	..
2	Mirzapur	..	..	3	..	42	35	..	..
	Native States	**6**	**12**	**130**	**101**	..	..	**1**	..
3	Rampur	2	4	130	101	..	..	1	..
4	Tehri-Garhwal	4	8	..	..	..	..	..	..
5	Benares Raj	..	..	..	..	..	..	..	..

Serial number.	District or State.	Kamboh. Males.	Kamboh. Females.	Kamkar Males.	Kamkar Females.	Kanjar Males.	Kanjar Females.	Kayastha Males.	Kayastha Females.
	2	123	124	125	126	127	128	129	130
	British Territory ..	**1,204**	**1,106**	**71**	**57**	**138**	**126**	**529**	**698**
	Agra Province	**1,181**	**1,103**	**3**	**3**	**103**	**100**	**431**	**586**
	Benares Division ..	..	*1*	..	..	..	..	..	..
1	Benares	..	..	..	..	..	..	..	..
2	Mirzapur	..	..	..	..	..	..	..	..
	Native States	**4**	..	..	..	**124**	..	**4**	..
3	Rampur	4	..	..	..	124	..	4	..
4	Tehri-Garhwal	..	..	..	..	..	..	..	..
5	Benares Raj	..	..	..	..	..	..	..	..

Serial number.	District or State.	Koeri. Males.	Koeri. Females.	Kori. Males.	Kori. Females.	Kumhar. Males.	Kumhar. Females.	Kungra. Males	Kungra. Females.
	2	143	144	145	146	147	148	149	150
	British Territory ..	**16**	**710**	**279**	**273**	**5,597**	**4,780**	**57,206**	**54,943**
	Agra Province	**16**	**8**	**256**	**257**	**4,638**	**3,923**	**22,543**	**21,646**
	Benares Division ..	..	..	*31*	*19*	..	..	*3,666*	*3,757*
1	Benares	..	..	..	..	..	..	491	519
2	Mirzapur	..	..	6	..	..	..	209	203
	Native States	..	..	..	..	**158**	**154**	**369**	**417**
3	Rampur	..	..	..	..	158	154	139	220
4	Tehri-Garhwal	..	..	..	..	..	..	..	..
5	Benares Raj	..	..	..	..	..	..	230	197

Serial number.	District or State.	Meo. Males.	Meo. Females	Mochi. Males.	Mochi. Females.	Mughal. Males	Mughal. Females.	Murao Males.	Murao Females.
	2	165	166	167	168	169	170	171	172
	British Territory ..	**30,646**	**26,605**	**1,843**	**1,599**	**30,732**	**28,156**	**257**	**38**
	Agra Province	**28,833**	**24,804**	**1,094**	**908**	**18,706**	**16,423**	**248**	**27**
	Benares Division ..	..	..	*158*	*129*	*1,351*	*916*	*2*	*5*
1	Benares	..	..	28	20	437	458	..	..
2	Mirzapur	..	..	..	..	53	75	..	..
	Native States	**2,786**	**2,513**	**114**	**29**	**830**	**644**	..	..
3	Rampur	2,786	2,513	..	..	780	599	..	..
4	Tehri-Garhwal	..	..	..	..	16	12	..	..
5	Benares Raj	..	..	114	29	84	33	..	..

Serial number.	District or State	Patwa. Males	Patwa. Females	Qussab. Males.	Qussab. Females	Rajput. Males	Rajput. Females.	Ranghar Males.	Ranghar Females
	2	185	186	187	188	189	190	191	192
	British Territory ..	**44**	**183**	**87,425**	**79,132**	**101,259**	**92,782**	**335**	**835**
	Agra Province	**43**	**183**	**71,391**	**64,543**	**82,992**	**73,281**	**335**	**835**
	Benares Division ..	*2*	*87*	*2,273*	*2,333*	*413*	*376*	..	..
1	Benares	2	87	417	391	25	8	..	..
2	Mirzapur	..	..	235	258	7	10	..	..
	Native States	..	..	**2,663**	**2,505**	**3**	..	..	..
3	Rampur	..	..	2,604	2,430	3	..	..	..
4	Tehri-Garhwal	..	..	..	..	..	..	..	..
5	Benares Raj	..	..	59	73	..	..	..	..

nationality B.—Muhammadans—*(continued)*. APPENDIX.

Jhojha.		Julaha.		Kachhi.		Kadhera.		Kahar.		Kalwar.		Serial number.
Males.	Females.	Males.	Females.	Males.	Females.	Males.	Females.	Males.	Females.	Males.	Females.	
111	112	113	114	115	116	117	118	119	120	121	122	1
16,877	**13,848**	**470,412**	**448,701**	**35**	**16**	**18**	**18**	**3,159**	**3,159**	**432**	**332**	
16,877	**13,848**	**365,126**	**346,761**	**12**	**10**	**18**	**18**	**2,587**	**2,655**	**388**	**283**	
..	..	*48,590*	*51,468*	*1*	..	..	..	*15*	*8*	*9*	*1*	
..	..	15,230	14,874	..	..	..	..	1	..	..	..	1
..	..	5,131	5,385	..	..	..	..	1	..	..	..	2
..	..	**18,167**	**16,604**	..	..	..	..	**338**	**304**	..	..	
..	..	18,520	12,111	..	..	..	..	338	304	..	..	3
..	..	12	..	..	..	..	..	..	..	..	..	4
..	..	4,635	4,493	..	..	..	..	..	..	..	..	5

Kewat.		Khangar.		Khanzada.		Khatik.		Khattri.		Kisan.		Serial number.
131	132	133	134	135	136	137	138	139	140	141	142	
6	**11**	**7**	**10**	**9,183**	**8,621**	**97**	**54**	**2**	**18**	**10**	**3**	
4	**9**	**7**	**10**	**202**	**183**	**77**	**44**	**2**	**18**	**10**	**3**	
..	*7*	..	..	*29*	..	..	..	..	*17*	..	..	
..	..	..	..	1	..	..	..	..	..	..	..	1
..	7	..	..	..	..	..	..	..	17	..	..	2
..	..	..	..	..	..	..	..	..	..	..	..	
..	..	..	..	..	..	..	..	..	..	..	..	3
..	..	..	..	..	..	..	..	..	..	..	..	4
..	..	..	..	..	..	..	..	..	..	..	..	5

Kurmi.		Lodha.		Lohar.		Luniya.		Mali.		Mallah.		Manihar.		Serial number.
Males.	Females.	Males.	Females.	Males.	Females.	Males.	Females.	Males.	Females.	Males	Females.	Males.	Females.	
151	152	153	154	155	156	157	158	159	160	161	162	163	164	
198	**129**	**112**	**99**	**42,758**	**37,428**	**158**	**88**	**2,688**	**2,638**	**2,070**	**1,343**	**39,382**	**34,807**	
164	**91**	**79**	**80**	**42,725**	**37,404**	**149**	**84**	**1,654**	**1,545**	**2,007**	**1,283**	**23,450**	**20,717**	
6	*80*	..	..	*3*	..	..	..	*135*	*103*	..	..	*502*	*409*	
..	80	..	..	3	..	..	..	46	27	..	..	71	58	1
..	..	..	..	..	..	..	..	31	10	..	..	..	..	2
..	..	**14**	**9**	**3,127**	**2,856**	..	..	**111**	**100**	..	..	**661**	**638**	
..	..	14	9	8,127	2,856	..	..	111	100	..	..	661	638	3
..	..	..	..	..	..	..	..	..	..	..	..	..	..	4
..	..	..	..	..	..	..	..	..	..	..	..	..	..	5

Musahar.		Nai.		Nat.		Nau-Muslim.		Pasi.		Pathan.		Serial number.
Males.	Females.	Males.	Females.	Males.	Females.	Males.	Females.	Males.	Females.	Males.	Females.	
173	174	175	176	177	178	179	180	181	182	183	184	
365	**46**	**117,482**	**111,179**	**12,306**	**12,184**	**17,559**	**17,503**	**122**	**73**	**474,848**	**437,728**	
324	**6**	**76,349**	**72,244**	**8,164**	**8,468**	**16,154**	**14,924**	**55**	**35**	**329,032**	**300,260**	
317	..	*8,530*	*8,777*	*1,328*	*1,774*	*268*	*232*	*4*	*4*	*27,227*	*28,737*	
..	..	1,951	2,019	129	156	36	50	..	..	5,482	5,153	1
317	..	892	862	..	414	3	7	4	4	2,742	2,575	2
..	..	**4,679**	**4,204**	**227**	**232**	**221**	**157**	..	..	**25,377**	**22,758**	
..	..	4,071	8,621	150	136	158	104	..	..	23,769	21,083	3
..	..	..	..	..	..	63	53	..	..	85	51	4
..	..	608	583	77	96	..	..	..	..	1,528	1,624	5

Rangrez.		Rawa.		Saini.		Saiyid.		Shaikh.		Serial number.
Males.	Females.	Males.	Females.	Males.	Females.	Males.	Females.	Males.	Females.	
193	194	195	196	197	198	199	200	201	202	
17,475	**13,087**	**251**	**34**	**1,715**	**1,206**	**125,387**	**116,518**	**673,605**	**603,418**	
15,421	**13,096**	**251**	**34**	**1,714**	**1,206**	**93,951**	**86,581**	**539,339**	**478,143**	
982	*992*	..	..	..	..	*6 208*	*6,053*	*38,617*	*38,058*	
323	352	..	..	..	..	1,799	1,629	18,860	13,161	1
33	25	..	..	..	..	750	714	4,980	4,851	2
756	**694**	..	..	..	..	**4,456**	**3,843**	**20,076**	**17,729**	
685	614	..	..	..	..	4,094	3,476	17,656	15,824	3
..	..	..	..	..	..	82	68	598	627	4
71	80	..	..	..	..	280	299	1,812	1,778	5

TABLE XIII.—Caste, tribe race or

Serial number.	District or State.	Sonar. Males.	Sonar. Females	Taga. Males.	Taga. Females.	Tamboli Males.	Tamboli Females.	Tawaif. Males.	Tawaif. Females.
1	2	203	204	205	206	207	208	209	210
	British Territory ..	**1,438**	**1,161**	**15,427**	**13,550**	**84**	**137**	**6,289**	**11,880**
	Agra Province ..	**1,431**	**1,151**	**15,369**	**13,502**	**70**	**123**	**3,115**	**6,677**
	Benares Division ..	..	*6*	..	..	*11*	*17*	*108*	*352*
1	Benares	..	6	..	..	..	..	3	26
2	Mirzapur	..	..	..	..	..	..	.	5
	Native States ..	**24**	**21**	..	..	**4**	**5**	..	**26**
3	Rampur	24	21	..	..	4	5	..	16
4	Tehri-Garhwal	..	..	..	..	..	..	.	..
5	Benares Raj	..	..	..	..	..	..	..	10

TABLE XIII.- Caste, tribe, race or

Serial number	District or State.	Population. Males.	Population. Females	Ahar. Males.	Ahar. Females.	Ahir. Males	Ahir. Females.	Bania Males.	Bania Females.
1	2	3	4	5	6	7	8	9	10
	British Territory ..	**73,178**	**57,922**	**71**	**79**	**3,880**	**2,981**	**12,492**	**8,993**
	Agra Province ..	**69,976**	**55,677**	**53**	**56**	**3,825**	**2,935**	**12,200**	**8,811**
	Benares Division ..	*1,737*	*1,475*	..	..	*17*	*13*	*80*	*62*
1	Benares	374	263	..	..	..	..	26	18
2	Mirzapur	241	227	..	..	2	2	13	8
	Native States ..	**288**	**250**	..	..	..	..	**48**	**30**
3	Rampur	262	219	..	..	..	..	43	22
4	Tehri-Garhwal	2	1	..	..	..	..	..	..
5	Benares Raj	24	30	..	..	..	..	5	8
	District or State.	Chhipi.		Darzi.		Faqir		Gadariya.	
	2	23	24	25	26	27	28	29	30
	British Territory ..	**57**	**56**	**93**	**78**	**224**	**246**	**328**	**205**
	Agra Province ..	**56**	**56**	**84**	**70**	**224**	**246**	**325**	**200**
	Benares Division ..	..	..	..	..	..	..	..	..
1	Benares	..	..	..	..	..	..	..	..
2	Mirzapur	..	..	..	..	..	..	..	..
	Native States ..	**3**	**3**	..	..	..	..	..	..
3	Rampur	3	3	..	..	..	..	..	..
4	Tehri-Garhwal	..	..	..	..	..	..	..	..
5	Benares Raj	..	..	..	..	..	..	..	..
	District or State.	Kamboh.		Kayastha.		Khatik.		Khattri	
	2	43	44	45	46	47	48	49	50
	British Territory ..	**198**	**143**	**6,526**	**5,316**	**242**	**229**	**1,054**	**590**
	Agra Province ..	**198**	**143**	**5,764**	**4,789**	**242**	**229**	**989**	**535**
	Benares Division ..	..	..	*317*	*179*	*1*	*4*	*24*	*13*
1	Benares	..	..	81	26	1	4	15	..
2	Mirzapur	..	..	62	51	..	..	6	12
	Native States ..	..	..	**85**	**65**	..	..	**1**	**2**
3	Rampur	..	..	73	53	..	..	..	..
4	Tehri-Garhwal	..	..	..	..	.	..	..	..
5	Benares Raj	..	..	12	12	..	..	1	2
	District or State.	Mali.		Nai.		Rajput		Rawa	
	2	63	64	65	66	67	68	69	70
	British Territory ..	**69**	**49**	**385**	**317**	**17,493**	**15,237**	**336**	**237**
	Agra Province ..	**66**	**48**	**359**	**303**	**17,011**	**14,987**	**336**	**237**
	Benares Division ..	*1*	*2*	*18*	*13*	*723*	*690*	..	..
1	Benares	..	..	3	2	30	57	..	..
2	Mirzapur	..	..	..	..	6	8	..	..
	Native States ..	..	..	..	..	**9**	**10**	..	..
3	Rampur	..	..	..	..	9	10	..	..
4	Tehri-Garhwal	..	..	..	..	..	..	..	..
5	Benares Raj	..	..	..	..	..	..	..	..

nationality B.—Muhammadans—*(concluded).*

Teli.		Tharu.		Thathera.		Turk.		Minor castes or others		Serial number.
Males.	Females.	Males.	Females.	Males.	Females.	Males.	Females.	Males.	Females.	
211	212	213	214	215	216	217	218	219	220	1
121,147	**105,329**	**1**	..	**184**	**134**	**21,091**	**18,739**	**81,290**	**77,331**	
100,190	**85,397**	**1**	..	**168**	**132**	**21,090**	**18,739**	**56,457**	**52,194**	
133	*105*	..	..	..	..	..	..	*3,363*	*2,711*	
6	2	..	..	..	..	..	..	1,885	755	1
84	20	..	..	..	..	..	..	869	296	2
3,753	**3,308**	..	..	..	..	**19,667**	**17,569**	**872**	**960**	
3,753	3,308	..	..	..	..	19,667	17,669	641	782	3
..	..	..	..	..	..	..	..	44	31	4
..	..	..	..	..	..	..	..	187	147	5

nationality C.—Aryas.

Barhai.		Bharbhunja		Bl at		Bhuinhar.		Brahmin		Chamar		Serial number.
Males.	Females.	Males	Females.	Males.	Females.	Males.	Females.	Males	Females	Males.	Females.	
11	12	13	14	15	16	17	18	19	20	21	22	1
1,314	**747**	**81**	**58**	**495**	**347**	**160**	**141**	**10,205**	**7,733**	**829**	**722**	
1,300	**733**	**72**	**50**	**489**	**341**	**148**	**141**	**9,272**	**7,002**	**822**	**714**	
..	..	..	..	*1*	..	*33*	*23*	*249*	*214*	*1*	*3*	
..	..	..	..	..	..	32	23	29	10	..	..	1
..	..	..	..	..	..	..	..	95	84	..	..	2
..	..	..	..	..	..	..	..	**18**	**16**	..	..	
..	..	..	..	..	..	..	..	11	7	..	..	3
..	..	..	..	.	..	..	..	2	1	..	..	4
..	..	..	..		..	..	..	5	8	..	.	5

Goshain.		Gujar		Ja..		Kachhi.		Kahar.		Kalwar.		Serial number.
31	32	33	34	35	36	37	38	39	40	41	42	
56	**73**	**1,085**	**746**	**5,174**	**4,591**	**48**	**47**	**297**	**210**	**428**	**394**	
55	**73**	**1,085**	**746**	**5,170**	**4,539**	**47**	**47**	**269**	**199**	**303**	**298**	
..	..	..	..	*3*	..	..	..	*14*	*11*	*92*	*104*	
..	..	..	..	2	..	..	..	8	..	78	90	1
..	..	..	..	..	..	..	..	3	1	14	14	2
..	..	..	..	..	..	**11**	**14**	..	..	..	..	
..	..	..	..	.	..	11	14	..	..	..	..	3
..	..	..	..	..	..	..	..	..	..	..	..	4
..	..	..	..	..	..	..	..	..	..	..	..	5

Koeri.		Kumhar		Fur i.		Lodha.		Lohar		Mahajan.		Serial number.
51	52	53	54	55	56	57	58	59	60	61	62	
784	**671**	**94**	**63**	**1,321**	**1,018**	**1,587**	**1,402**	**240**	**177**	**134**	**106**	
756	**667**	**78**	**48**	**1,275**	**961**	**1,526**	**1,355**	**235**	**177**	**134**	**106**	
33	*20*	..	*2*	*43*	*52*	..	..	*14*	*8*	..	..	
..	..	..	..	8	5	..	..	13	8	..	..	1
1	2	..	1	34	39	..	..	..	..	..	..	2
3	..	..	..	**67**	**74**	**1**	..	..	..	**1**	..	
3	..	..	..	67	74	1	..	..	..	1	..	3
..	..	..	..	..	..	..	..	..	..	..	..	4
..	..	..	..	..	..	..	..	..	..	..	..	5

Saini.		Sonar.		Taga.		Tamboli.		Teli.		Minor castes or others.		Serial number.
71	72	73	74	75	76	77	78	79	80	81	82	
64	**47**	**1,218**	**1,076**	**2,720**	**1,942**	**107**	**99**	**135**	**126**	**1,248**	**632**	
64	**47**	**1,165**	**1,008**	**2,720**	**1,942**	**100**	**96**	**127**	**117**	**1,034**	**570**	
..	..	*44*	*28*	..	..	..	..	*4*	*5*	*26*	*29*	
..	..	24	12	..	..	..	..	1	..	13	8	1
..	..	..	..	..	..	..	..	..	..	5	10	2
..	..	**23**	**28**	..	..	**4**	**3**	..	..	**14**	**5**	
..	..	23	28	..	..	4	3	..	..	13	5	3
..	..	..	..	..	..	..	..	..	..	..	..	4
..	..	..	..	..	..	..	..	..	..	1	..	5

TABLE XV.—Occupation or means

Class A.—Production

Sub-Class I.—Exploitation of

Order 1.—Pasture and agriculture.

Serial number.	District or State.	1(a) Zamindar ba asami. Total workers and dependants.	Actual workers. Total. Males.	Actual workers. Total. Females.	Dependants.	1(b) Dakhilkar asami ba shikmi. Total workers and dependants.	Actual workers. Total. Males.	Actual workers. Total. Females.	Dependants.
1	2	3	4	5	6	7	8	9	10
	British Territory ..	429,144	116,624	30,022	282,498	184,109	55,397	22,854	105,858
	Agra Province ..	314,008	84,140	24,400	205,468	182,156	54,759	22,655	104,742
	Benares Division ..	*30,646*	*9,079*	*2,827*	*18,740*	*11,695*	*3,151*	*5,011*	*9,533*
1	Benares	5,066	1,196	444	3,426	3,238	77	1,429	1,732
2	Mirzapur	4,654	1,298	447	2,909	788	276	108	404
	Native States ..	3,144	824	146	2,174	59	12	16	31
3	Rampur	2,790	738	145	1,907	7	2	..	5
4	Tehri-Garhwal ..	..	..	..	..	..	..	..	..
5	Benares Raj ..	354	86	1	267	52	10	16	26

Class A.—Production

Sub-Class I.—Exploitation of

Order 1.—Pasture and agriculture.

Serial number.	District or State.	2(a) Zamindar ba jot khud. Total workers and dependants.	Actual workers. Total. Males.	Actual workers. Total. Females.	Dependants.	2(b) Dakhilkar asami ba jot khud. Total workers and dependants.	Actual workers. Total. Males.	Actual workers. Total. Females.	Dependants.
1	2	19	20	21	22	23	24	25	26
	British Territory ..	3,475,618	1,115,514	251,968	2,108,136	10,545,881	3,731,414	1,388,197	5,426,270
	Agra Province ..	2,984,648	961,771	233,723	1,789,155	10,488,025	3,702,155	1,386,832	5,399,038
	Benares Division ..	*241,607*	*81,918*	*10,372*	*149,317*	*1,526,750*	*514,818*	*274,239*	*737,693*
1	Benares ..	27,690	8,776	858	18,056	259,844	85,576	42,655	131,613
2	Mirzapur ..	30,334	9,736	2,045	18,553	162,181	48,941	24,047	89,193
	Native States ..	4,172	1,313	200	2,659	357,786	101,699	21,420	234,667
3	Rampur ..	1,488	531	41	916	370	96	4	270
4	Tehri-Garhwal ..	747	248	20	479	251,722	68,032	4,581	179,109
5	Benares Raj ..	1,937	534	139	1,264	105,694	33,571	16,835	55,288

Class A.—Production

Sub-Class I.—Exploitation of

Order I.—Pasture and agriculture.

Serial number.	District or State	3.—Agents, managers of landed estates (not planters), clerks, rent collectors, &c. Total workers and dependants.	Actual workers. Total. Males.	Actual workers. Total. Females.	Actual workers. Partially agriculturists. Males.	Actual workers. Partially agriculturists. Females.	Dependants.	4.—Farm servants and field labourers. Total workers and dependants.	Actual workers. Total. Males.	Actual workers. Total. Females.	Actual workers. Partially agriculturists. Males.	Actual workers. Partially agriculturists. Females.	Dependants.
1	2	35	36	37	38	39	40	41	42	43	44	45	46
	British Territory ..	195,212	85,309	844	12,709	93	109,059	4,497,822	1,587,714	1,341,091	60,759	1,389	1,569,017
	Agra Province ..	106,137	44,853	513	6,350	73	60,771	3,080,527	1,103,358	818,391	38,848	851	1,158,778
	Benares Division ..	*15,568*	*6,606*	*102*	*1,038*	*10*	*8,860*	*517,954*	*162,085*	*195,933*	*3,854*	*20*	*159,936*
1	Benares ..	5,361	1,986	24	344	..	3,851	76,494	24,306	27,406	1,502	11	24,782
2	Mirzapur ..	2,223	1,105	7	131	1	1,111	175,041	53,078	66,828	..	..	55,140
	Native States ..	1,510	569	14	72	..	927	54,221	19,078	16,669	240	1	18,474
3	Rampur ..	884	329	4	29	..	551	10,409	5,005	779	232	1	4,625
4	Tehri-Garhwal ..	8	3	..	..	..	5	1,779	658	93	4	..	1,028
5	Benares Raj ..	618	237	10	43	..	371	42,033	13,415	15,797	4	..	12,821

of raw materials.

the surface of the earth.

Part (*a*). Ordinary cultivation.

1(*e*). Asami ba Shikmi. Total workers and dependants.	Actual workers. Total. Males.	Females.	Dependants.	1.—Income from rent of agricultural land. Total workers and dependants.	Actual workers. Total. Males.	Females.	Dependants.	Serial number.
11	12	13	14	15	16	17	18	1
248,293	86,268	33,807	128,218	861,546	258,289	86,683	516,574	
195,837	68,566	24,673	102,598	692,001	207,465	71,728	412,808	
41,168	*15,676*	*8,325*	*17,167*	*89,509*	*27,906*	*16,163*	*45,440*	
15,674	5,548	3,363	6,763	23,978	6,821	5,236	11,921	1
761	218	106	437	6,203	1,792	661	3,750	2
1 670	560	128	982	4,873	1,396	290	3,187	
1,468	483	104	881	4,265	1,223	249	2,798	3
..	..	..	..	..	..	..	..	4
202	77	24	101	608	173	41	394	5

of raw materials—(*continued*).

the surface of the earth—(*continued*).

Part (*a*). Ordinary cultivation—(*continued*).

2(*c*) Asami ba jot khud. Total workers and dependants.	Actual workers. Total. Males.	Females.	Dependants.	2.—Ordinary cultivators. Total workers and dependants.	Actual workers. Total. Males.	Females.	Dependants.	Serial number.
27	28	29	30	31	32	33	34	1
13,860,064	4,805,150	2,287,656	6,767,258	27,881,563	9,652,078	3,927,821	14,301,664	
6,317,015	2,140,264	1,007,897	3,168,854	19,789,689	6,804,190	2,628,452	10,357,047	
837,031	*255,881*	*216,643*	*358,507*	*2,599,388*	*852,617*	*501,254*	*1,245,517*	
128,726	43,988	30,324	54,414	416,260	138,340	73,837	204,088	1
155,880	16,384	63,624	75,872	348,395	75,061	89,716	183,618	2
463,494	158,124	31,523	273,847	830,452	261,136	53,143	516,173	
332,287	112,959	5,232	214,096	334,145	118,586	5,277	215,282	3
22,503	6,205	764	15,534	274,972	74,485	5,365	195,122	4
113,704	38,960	25,527	49,217	221,335	73,065	42,501	105,769	5

of raw materials—(*continued*).

the surface of the earth—(*continued*).

Part (*a*). Ordinary cultivation—(*concluded*). Total order 1.—Part (*a*). Ordinary cultivation. Total workers and dependants.	Actual workers. Total. Males.	Females.	Partially agriculturists. Males.	Females.	Dependants.	Order 1.—Pasture and agriculture. Part (*b*). Growers of special products and market gardening—(*continued*). 6.—Fruit, flower, vegetable, betel, vine, areca nut, &c., growers. Total workers and dependants.	Actual workers. Total. Males.	Females.	Partially agriculturists. Males.	Females.	Dependants.	Serial number.
47	48	49	50	51	52	53	54	55	56	57	58	1
33,436,143	11,583,390	5,356,439	73,458	1,482	16,496,314	52,945	19,947	11,058	2,849	360	21,940	
23,668,354	8,159,866	3,519,084	45,198	924	11,989,404	19,167	8,292	1,918	830	45	8,957	
3,222,419	*1,049,214*	*713,452*	*4,892*	*30*	*1,459,753*	*1,837*	*972*	*144*	*96*	*7*	*721*	
522,093	171,458	106,508	1,846	11	244,137	1,384	759	94	50	5	531	1
531,862	181,031	157,212	181	1	243,619	100	51	7	8	1	42	2
891,056	282,179	70,116	312	1	538,761	744	367	116	32	3	261	
349,703	120,143	6,809	261	1	228,251	638	817	91	20	..	230	3
276,759	75,146	5,458	4	..	196,155	27	..	22	..	3	5	4
264,594	86,890	58,849	47	..	119,855	79	50	3	12	..	26	5

TABLE XV.—Occupation or means of livelihood.

Class A.—Production

Sub-Class I.—Exploitation of

Serial number.	District or State.	Order I.—Pasture and agriculture. Part (*b*). Growers of special products and market gardening—(*concld.*). Total order I.—Part (*b*). Growers of special products and market gardening. Total workers and dependants.	Actual workers. Total. Males.	Females.	Partially agriculturists. Males.	Females.	Dependants.	Order I.—Pasture and agriculture. 7.—Forest officers, Rangers, guards, &c. Total workers and dependants.	Actual workers. Total. Males.	Females.	Partially agriculturists. Males.	Females.	Dependants.
1	2	59	60	61	62	63	64	65	66	67	68	69	70
	British Territory ..	**55,719**	**21,738**	**11,078**	**2,895**	**362**	**22,903**	**7,472**	**3,876**	**389**	**689**	**2**	**3,207**
	Agra Province ..	**21,935**	**10,081**	**1,938**	**876**	**47**	**9,916**	**5,856**	**2,982**	**389**	**602**	**2**	**2,485**
	Benares Division ..	*1,846*	*977*	*144*	*96*	*7*	*725*	*480*	*167*	*12*	*15*	..	*801*
1	Benares	**1,384**	759	94	50	5	531	**15**	6	..	..	..	9
2	Mirzapur	**108**	56	7	3	1	45	**140**	56	1	12	..	83
	Native States ..	**759**	**382**	**116**	**34**	**3**	**261**	**296**	**99**	**6**	**42**	..	**191**
3	Rampur	**638**	317	91	20	..	230	**1**	1	..	..	..	..
4	Tehri-Garhwal ..	**42**	15	22	2	3	5	**108**	59	..	21	..	49
5	Benares Raj ..	**79**	50	3	12	..	26	**187**	39	6	21	..	142

Class A.—Production

Sub-Class I.—Exploitation of

Order I.—Pasture and agriculture.

Serial number.	District or state.	9.—Cattle and buffalo breeders and keepers. Total workers and dependants.	Actual workers. Total. Males.	Females.	Partially Agriculturists. Males.	Females.	Dependants.	10.—Sheep, goat and pig breeders. Total workers and dependants.	Actual workers. Total. Males.	Females.	Partially agriculturists. Males.	Females.	Dependants.
1	2	83	84	85	86	87	88	89	90	91	92	93	94
	British Territory ..	**16,049**	**5,807**	**3,321**	**766**	**222**	**6,921**	**16,613**	**6,103**	**2,780**	**652**	**287**	**7,730**
	Agra Province ..	**14,844**	**5,253**	**3,222**	**670**	**211**	**6,369**	**14,282**	**5,123**	**2,206**	**456**	**212**	**6,953**
	Benares Division ..	*176*	*93*	*12*	*13*	*5*	*71*	*2,007*	*471*	*543*	*42*	*20*	*993*
1	Benares	**117**	74	..	10	..	43	**18**	..	2	..	..	16
2	Mirzapur	**55**	16	12	3	5	27	**546**	198	115	21	5	233
	Native States ..	**26**	**10**	**2**	..	**2**	**14**	**365**	**173**	**91**	**94**	**51**	**101**
3	Rampur	**10**	8	2	..	2	..	**16**	2	13	..	..	1
4	Tehri-Garhwal ..	**10**	2	..	..	..	8	..	..	..	..	..	..
5	Benares Raj ..	**6**	..	..	..	..	6	**349**	171	78	94	51	100

Class I.—Production

Sub-Class I.—Exploitation of

Serial number.	District or State.	Order I.—Pasture and agriculture. Part (*d*). Raising of farm stock—(*concluded*). Total Order I.—Pasture and agriculture Part (*d*). Raising of farm stock. Total workers and dependants.	Actual workers. Total. Males.	Females.	Partially agriculturists. Males.	Females.	Dependants.	Order I.—Pasture and agriculture. Part (*e*). Raising of small animals. 13.—Birds, bees, silk-worms, &c. Total workers and dependants.	Actual workers. Total. Males.	Females.	Partially agriculturists. Males.	Females.	Dependants.
1	2	107	108	109	110	111	112	113	114	115	116	117	118
	British Territory ..	**765,112**	**511,564**	**109,452**	**20,688**	**11,794**	**144,096**	**849**	**479**	**135**	**13**	**2**	**235**
	Agra Province ..	**584,086**	**381,162**	**79,878**	**16,304**	**10,653**	**123,046**	**468**	**239**	**13**	**11**	**2**	**216**
	Benares Division ..	*77,911*	*44,444*	*15,275*	*2,804*	*1,174*	*18,192*	*118*	*52*	*9*	*7*	*2*	*57*
1	Benares	**11,344**	5,784	2,850	611	258	2,710	**8**	2	..	..	..	6
2	Mirzapur	**26,709**	16,654	2,882	577	130	7,173	**59**	81	9	7	2	19
	Native States ..	**13,880**	**9,643**	**2,022**	**766**	**287**	**2,215**	**90**	..	**13**	..	..	**77**
3	Rampur	**5,444**	4,715	128	90	4	601	**85**	..	9	..	..	76
4	Tehri-Garhwal ..	**849**	486	28	8	..	136	..	..	..	..	..	..
5	Benares Raj ..	**7,787**	4,442	1,866	668	283	1,479	**5**	..	4	..	..	1

of raw materials—(*continued*).

the surface of the earth—(*continued*).

Part (*c*) Forestry—(*concluded*).

8. Wood cutters, firewood, lac, catechu, rubber, &c., collectors and charcoal burners.						Total Order I.—Pasture and agriculture. Part (*c*). Forestry.						
Total workers and dependants.	Actual workers: Total. Males.	Actual workers: Total. Females.	Actual workers: Partially agriculturists. Males.	Actual workers: Partially agriculturists. Females.	Dependants.	Total workers and dependants.	Actual workers: Total. Males.	Actual workers: Total. Females.	Actual workers: Partially agriculturists. Males.	Actual workers: Partially agriculturists. Females.	Dependants.	Serial number.
71	72	73	74	75	76	77	78	79	80	81	82	1
50,489	**19,126**	**12,506**	**1,310**	**638**	**18,857**	**57,961**	**23,002**	**12,895**	**1,999**	**640**	**22,064**	
36,581	**13,399**	**9,384**	**749**	**482**	**13,798**	**42,437**	**16,381**	**9,773**	**1,351**	**484**	**16,283**	
3,905	*1,028*	*1,785*	*8*	*69*	*1,092*	***4,385***	*1,195*	*1,797*	23	*69*	*1,393*	
1,709	156	1,111	..	40	442	**1,724**	162	1,117	..	40	451	1
968	350	245	..	4	378	**1,108**	406	246	12	4	456	2
452	**116**	**167**	**3**	**14**	**169**	**748**	**215**	**173**	**45**	**14**	**360**	
129	66	..	2	..	63	**130**	67	..	2	..	63	3
34	3	25	..	..	6	**142**	62	25	21	..	55	4
289	47	142	1	14	100	**476**	86	148	22	14	242	5

of raw materials—(*continued*).

the surface of the earth—(*continued*).

Part (*d*). Raising of farm stock.

11.—Breeders of other animals; (horses, mule, camels, asses, &c.)						12.—Herdsmen, shepherds, goatherds, &c.						
Total workers and dependants.	Actual workers: Total. Males.	Actual workers: Total. Females.	Actual workers: Partially agriculturists. Males.	Actual workers: Partially agriculturists. Females.	Dependants.	Total workers and dependants.	Actual workes: Total. Males.	Actual workes: Total. Females.	Actual workes: Partially agriculturists. Males.	Actual workes: Partially agriculturists. Females.	Dependants.	Serial number.
95	96	97	98	99	100	101	102	103	104	105	106	1
1,131	**385**	**45**	**14**	..	**701**	**731,319**	**499,269**	**103,306**	**19,256**	**11,285**	**128,744**	
995	**328**	**45**	**11**	..	**622**	**553,965**	**370,458**	**74,405**	**15,167**	**10,230**	**109,102**	
28	*15*	..	*5*	..	*13*	*75,700*	*43,865*	*14,720*	*2,744*	*1,149*	*17,115*	
4	2	..	..	..	2	**11,205**	5,708	2,848	601	258	2,649	1
..	..	..	..	..	..	**26,108**	16,440	2,755	553	12	6,913	2
17	**10**	**1**	**1**	..	**6**	**13,472**	**9,450**	**1,928**	**671**	**234**	**2,094**	
16	9	1	1	..	6	**5,402**	4,696	112	89	2	594	3
1	1	..	..	..	..	**638**	483	28	8	..	127	4
..	..	..	..	..	..	**7,432**	4,271	1,788	574	232	1,373	5

of raw materials—(*continued*).

the surface of the earth—(*continued*).

Total order 1.—Pasture and agriculture. Parts (*a*), (*b*), (*c*), (*d*) and (*e*).						Order 2.—Fishing and Hunting. 14.—Fishing.						
Total workers and dependants.	Actual workers: Total. Males.	Actual workers: Total. Females.	Actual workers: Partially agriculturists. Males.	Actual workers: Partially agriculturists. Females.	Dependants.	Total workers and dependants.	Actual workers: Total. Males.	Actual workers: Total. Females.	Actual workers: Partially agriculturists. Males.	Actual workers: Partially agriculturists. Females.	Dependants.	Serial number.
119	120	121	122	123	124	125	126	127	128	129	130	1
34,315,784	**12,140,173**	**5,489,999**	**99,063**	**14,280**	**16,685,612**	**36,416**	**12,826**	**6,579**	**2,186**	**377**	**17,011**	
24,317,280	**8,567,729**	**3 610,686**	**63,740**	**12,110**	**12,138,865**	**40,527**	**10,612**	**5,479**	**1,795**	**329**	**14,436**	
3,306,679	*1,095,882*	*730,677*	*7,829*	*1,282*	*1,480,120*	***3,437***	*1,019*	*1,014*	*170*	*76*	*1,404*	
536,553	178,160	110,558	2,507	314	247,835	**813**	218	227	23	20	368	1
559,846	148,178	160,356	730	138	251,312	**361**	93	90	3	..	178	2
906,533	**292,419**	**72,440**	**1,157**	**305**	**541,674**	**1,915**	**755**	**117**	**208**	**2**	**1,043**	
356,000	125,242	6,537	378	5	224,221	**1,868**	728	112	208	2	1,028	3
277,592	75,709	5,533	85	3	196,350	**20**	13	1	..	..	6	4
272,941	91,468	60,870	749	297	121,103	**27**	14	4	..	..	9	5

Class A.—Production

Sub-Class I.—Exploitation of

Order 2.—Fishing and Hunting.—(*concluded*)

Serial number.	District or State.	15.—Hunting. Total workers and dependants.	Actual workers. Total. Males.	Actual workers. Total. Females.	Partially agriculturists. Males.	Partially agriculturists. Females.	Dependants.	Total Order 2.—Fishing and Hunting. Total workers and dependants.	Actual workers. Total. Males.	Actual workers. Total. Females.	Partially agriculturists. Males.	Partially agriculturists. Females.	Dependants.
1	2	131	132	133	134	135	136	137	138	139	140	141	142
	British Territory ..	**6,688**	**2,552**	**214**	**280**	**2**	**3,922**	**43,104**	**15,378**	**6,793**	**2,466**	**379**	**20,933**
	Agra Province ..	**3,828**	**1,394**	**127**	**139**	**2**	**2,307**	**34,355**	**12,006**	**5,606**	**1,934**	**331**	**16,743**
	Benares Division ..	*286*	*109*	*68*	*17*	*2*	*109*	*3,723*	*1,128*	*1,082*	*187*	*78*	*1,513*
1	Benares	**134**	34	64	11	2	86	**947**	252	291	34	22	404
2	Mirzapur	**105**	49	4	6	..	52	**466**	142	94	9	..	230
	Native States ..	**36**	**7**	..	..	..	**29**	**1,951**	**762**	**117**	**208**	**2**	**1,072**
3	Rampur	**33**	4	..	..	..	29	**1,901**	732	112	208	2	1,057
4	Tehri-Garhwal ..	..	..	..	..	..	..	**20**	13	1	..	..	6
5	Benares Raj ..	**3**	3	..	..	..	..	**30**	17	4	..	..	9

Class A.—Production

Sub-Class II.—Extraction of mineral.

Serial number.	District or State.	Order 5.—Salt, &c. Total Order 5.—Salt, &c. Total workers and dependants.	Actual workers. Total. Males.	Actual workers. Total. Females.	Partially agriculturists. Males.	Partially agriculturists. Females.	Dependants.	Total Sub-Class II.—Extraction of minerals—(*concld.*) Total workers and dependants.	Actual workers. Total. Males.	Actual workers. Total. Females.	Partially agriculturists. Males.	Partially agriculturists. Females.	Dependants.
1	1	155	156	157	158	169	160	161	162	163	164	165	166
	British Territory ..	**5,457**	**2,041**	**972**	**416**	**110**	**2,444**	**8,514**	**3,282**	**1,118**	**570**	**118**	**4,114**
	Agra Province ..	**3,455**	**1,188**	**780**	**193**	**83**	**1,485**	**4,832**	**1,722**	**867**	**232**	**86**	**2,243**
	Benares Division ..	*1,670*	*506*	*508*	*74*	*56*	*656*	*1,738*	*535*	*508*	*74*	*56*	*695*
1	Benares	**223**	50	76	7	7	97	**261**	61	76	7	7	124
2	Mirzapur	**51**	8	6	..	..	37	**51**	8	6	..	..	37
	Native States ..	**293**	**165**	**46**	**14**	**9**	**82**	**294**	**166**	**46**	**14**	**9**	**82**
3	Rampur	..	..	..	..	..	..	..	..	..	..	..	..
4	Tehri-Garhwal ..	..	..	..	..	..	..	**1**	1	..	..	..	..
5	Benares Raj	**293**	165	46	14	9	82	**293**	165	46	14	9	82

Class B.—Preparation and supply

Sub-Class III.—

Order 6.—

Serial number.	District or State.	22.—Cotton spinning, sizing and weaving. Total workers and dependants.	Actual workers. Total. Males.	Actual workers. Total. Females.	Partially agriculturists. Males.	Partially agriculturists. Females.	Dependants.	24.—Rope, twine and string. Total workers and dependants.	Actual workers. Total. Males.	Actual workers. Total. Females.	Partially agriculturists. Males.	Partially agriculturists. Females.	Dependants.
1.	2	179	180	181	182	183	184	185	186	187	188	189	190
	British Territory ..	**833,672**	**275,681**	**157,128**	**25,639**	**5,893**	**400,863**	**41,808**	**10,306**	**19,221**	**806**	**638**	**12,281**
	Agra Province ..	**688,853**	**225,090**	**128,067**	**17,845**	**4,140**	**333,696**	**34,169**	**8,198**	**15,969**	**500**	**271**	**10,002**
	Benares Division ..	*64,437*	*19,279*	*8,278*	*2,212*	*618*	*36,879*	*2,292*	*373*	*1,358*	*24*	*19*	*561*
1	Benares	**21,470**	7,193	1,169	315	161	13,108	**564**	149	274	18	..	241
2	Mirzapur	**1,926**	714	330	36	3	882	**191**	24	112	..	3	55
	Native States ..	**19,461**	**7,594**	**3,552**	**1,202**	**153**	**8,315**	**359**	**47**	**105**	**4**	..	**207**
3	Rampur	**13,078**	4,021	2,561	1,106	131	6,496	**359**	47	105	4	..	207
4	Tehri-Garhwal ..	**759**	243	2	24	..	514	..	..	..	..	..	..
5	Bonarcs Raj ..	**5,624**	3,330	989	72	22	1,305	..	..	..	..	..	..

of raw materials—(*continued*).

the surface of the earth—(*concluded*).

Total Sub-Class I.—Exploitation of the surface of the earth.						Sub-Class II.—Extraction of minerals. Order 3.—Mines. Total Order 3.—Mines.						
Total workers and dependants.	Actual workers. Total. Males.	Actual workers. Total. Females.	Partially agriculturists. Males.	Partially agriculturists. Females.	Dependants.	Total workers and dependants.	Actual workers. Total. Males.	Actual workers. Total. Females.	Partially agriculturists. Males.	Partially agriculturists. Females.	Dependants.	Serial number.
143	144	145	146	147	148	149	150	151	152	153	154	1
34,358,860	**12,155,551**	**5,496,792**	**1,01,529**	**14,659**	**16,706,545**	**154**	**43**	**15**	**7**	**1**	**96**	
24,351,635	**8,579,735**	**3,616,292**	**65,674**	**12,441**	**12,155,608**	**101**	**24**	**14**	..	..	**63**	
3,310,402	*1,097,010*	*731,759*	*8,009*	*1,360*	*1,481,633*	*73*	*3*	..	..	..	*10*	
537,500	178,412	110,849	2,541	336	248,239	..	..	..	..	..	..	1
560,312	148,320	160,450	739	188	251,542	..	..	..	..	..	..	2
908,484	**293,181**	**72,557**	**1,365**	**307**	**542,746**	..	..	..	..	..	..	
357,901	125 974	6,649	581	7	225,278	..	..	..	..	..	..	3
277,612	75,722	5,534	85	3	196,356	..	..	..	..	..	..	4
272,971	91,485	60,374	749	297	121,112	..	..	..	..	..	..	5

of raw materials—(*concluded*).

Total Class A.—Production of raw materials.						Class B.—Preparation and supply of material substances. Sub-Class III.—Industry. Order 6.—Textile. 21.—Cotton ginning, cleaning and pressing.						
Total workers and dependants.	Actual workers. Total. Males.	Actual workers. Total. Females.	Partially agriculturists. Males.	Partially agriculturists. Females.	Dependants.	Total workers and dependants.	Actual workers. Total. Males.	Actual workers. Total. Females.	Partially agriculturists. Males.	Partially agriculturists. Females.	Dependants.	Serial number.
167	168	169	170	171	172	173	174	175	176	177	178	1
34,367,402	**12,158,833**	**5,497,910**	**102,099**	**14,777**	**16,710,559**	**113,194**	**31,933**	**26,066**	**3,572**	**1,174**	**55,195**	
24,356,467	**8,581,457**	**3,617,159**	**65,906**	**12,527**	**12,157,851**	**104,689**	**29,608**	**23,961**	**3,085**	**1,000**	**51,120**	
3,312,140	*1,097,545*	*782,267*	*8,083*	*1,416*	*1,482,328*	*2,916*	*791*	*647*	*140*	*46*	*1,478*	
537,761	178,478	110,925	2,548	348	248,363	**335**	111	45	17	6	179	1
560,363	148,328	160,455	739	188	251,579	**228**	78	45	5	4	105	2
908,778	**293,347**	**72,603**	**1,379**	**316**	**542,828**	**2,671**	**823**	**418**	**260**	**1**	**1,430**	
357,901	125 974	6,649	581	7	225,278	**2,377**	799	252	257	1	1,326	3
277,613	75,723	5,534	85	3	196,356	..	..	..	..	..	..	4
273,264	91,650	60,420	763	306	121,194	**294**	24	166	3	...	104	5

of material substances—(*continued*).

Industry—(*continued*).

Textile—(*continued*).

25.—Other fibres (cocoanut, aloes, flax, hemp, straw, &c.)						26.—Wool carders and spinners, weavers of woollen blankets, carpets, &c.						
Total workers and dependants.	Actual workers. Total. Males.	Actual workers. Total. Females.	Partially agriculturists. Males.	Partially agriculturists. Females.	Dependants.	Total workers and dependants.	Actual workers. Total. Males.	Actual workers. Total. Females.	Partially agriculturists. Males.	Partially agriculturists. Females.	Dependants.	Serial number.
191	192	193	194	195	196	197	198	199	200	201	202	1
8,282	**2,602**	**2,131**	**150**	**51**	**3,469**	**31,878**	**9,148**	**8,919**	**1,158**	**561**	**13,811**	
7,156	**2,186**	**1,894**	**115**	**16**	**3,076**	**27,357**	**7,706**	**7,395**	**740**	**348**	**12,256**	
277	*109*	*40*	*3*	..	*128*	*3,266*	*1,260*	*617*	*143*	*20*	*1,389*	
..	..	..	..	..	..	**309**	101	48	1	..	160	1
133	26	21	1	..	86	**864**	351	108	72	..	405	2
43	..	11	..	..	32	**8,460**	**3,360**	**2,047**	**173**	**5**	**3,053**	
43	..	11	..	..	32	**192**	64	18	29	..	110	3
..	..	..	..	..	..	**39**	16	1	1	..	22	4
..	..	..	..	..	..	**8,229**	8,280	2,028	143	5	2,921	5

TABLE XV.—Occupation or means of livelihood.

Class B.—Preparation and supply

Sub-Class III.—

Serial number.	District or State.	Order 6.—Textile—(concluded). Total Order 6.—Textile. Total workers and dependants.	Actual workers. Total. Males.	Actual workers. Total. Females.	Partially agriculturists. Males.	Partially agriculturists. Females.	Dependants.	Order 7.—Hides, skins and hard materials. 32.—Tanners, curriers, leather dressers and dyers, &c. Total workers and dependants.	Actual workers. Total. Males.	Actual workers. Total. Females.	Partially agriculturists. Males.	Partially agriculturists. Females.	Dependants.
1	2	203	204	205	206	207	208	209	210	211	212	213	214
	British Territory ..	**1,133,986**	**364,176**	**231,279**	**32,985**	**8,726**	**538,531**	**121,291**	**45,383**	**8,383**	**6,729**	**943**	**67,525**
	Agra Province ..	**942,236**	**299,756**	**189,105**	**23,442**	**6,020**	**453,375**	**101,784**	**37,792**	**6,373**	**3,991**	**402**	**57,619**
	Benares Division ..	*96,357*	*29,839*	*14,872*	*2,575*	*715*	*52,646*	**8,247**	*8,432*	*1,045*	*289*	*58*	*8,770*
1	Benares ..	**44,440**	14,706	4,545	386	169	25,189	**900**	192	151	23	1	557
2	Mirzapur ..	**3,408**	1,209	627	111	10	1,572	**2,046**	778	186	84	13	1,082
	Native States ..	**32,373**	**12,192**	**6,360**	**1,710**	**163**	**13,821**	**1,070**	**357**	**47**	**109**	**1**	**666**
3	Rampur ..	**17,244**	5,245	3,144	1,459	134	8,855	**406**	119	6	43	1	181
4	Tehri-Garhwal ..	**802**	262	3	25	..	537	**367**	123	13	48	..	231
5	Benares Raj ..	**14,327**	6,685	3,213	226	29	4,429	**297**	115	28	38	..	154

Class B.—Preparation and supply

Sub-Class III.—

Serial number.	District or State.	Order 8.—Wood. 37.—Basket makers and other industries of woody material including leaves. Total workers and dependants.	Actual workers. Total. Males.	Actual workers. Total. Females.	Partially agriculturists. Males.	Partially agriculturists. Females.	Dependants.	Total Order 8.—Wood. Total workers and dependants.	Actual workers. Total. Males.	Actual workers. Total. Females.	Partially agriculturists. Males.	Partially agriculturists. Females.	Dependants.
1	2	227	228	229	230	231	232	233	234	235	236	237	238
	British Territory ..	**132,076**	**46,866**	**32,639**	**5,618**	**1,405**	**52,571**	**476,701**	**175,891**	**40,640**	**37,515**	**2,056**	**260,170**
	Agra Province ..	**97,450**	**33,948**	**24,239**	**3,421**	**965**	**39,263**	**377,491**	**138,257**	**30,901**	**27,071**	**1,434**	**208,333**
	Benares Division ..	*19,067*	*5,939*	*6,151*	*376*	*237*	*6,977*	*35,332*	*11,952*	*6,762*	*1,659*	*256*	*16,618*
1	Benares ..	**4,596**	1,554	1,309	41	16	1,783	**8,328**	2,953	1,327	347	16	4,048
2	Mirzapur ..	**3,799**	1,185	1,201	1	62	1,413	**6,954**	2,267	1,330	286	63	3,857
	Native States ..	**2,333**	**867**	**510**	**56**	**20**	**956**	**9,179**	**3,437**	**581**	**875**	**23**	**5,161**
3	Rampur ..	**317**	85	61	24	..	171	**5,479**	1,825	92	653	1	3,562
4	Tehri-Garhwal ..	**493**	205	31	15	7	257	**1,416**	742	48	98	7	626
5	Benares Raj ..	**1,523**	577	418	17	13	528	**2,284**	870	441	126	15	973

Class B.—Preparation and supply

Sub-Class III.—

Serial number.	District or State.	Order 9.—Metals—(concluded). 43.—Workers in other metals (tin, zinc, lead, quicksilver, &c.). Total workers and dependants.	Actual workers. Total. Males.	Actual workers. Total. Females.	Partially agriculturists. Males.	Partially agriculturists. Females.	Dependants.	Total Order 9.—Metals. Total workers and dependants.	Actual workers. Total. Males.	Actual workers. Total. Females.	Partially agriculturists. Males.	Partially agriculturists. Females.	Dependants.
1	2	251	252	253	254	255	256	257	258	259	260	261	262
	British Territory ..	**5,253**	**1,874**	**139**	**84**	**2**	**3,240**	**281,296**	**105,137**	**8,291**	**27,270**	**1,165**	**167,868**
	Agra Province ..	**3,468**	**1,309**	**91**	**51**	..	**2,068**	**219,444**	**80,357**	**6,446**	**18,954**	**880**	**132,641**
	Benares Division ..	*1,342*	*463*	*61*	*13*	..	*818*	*38,092*	*13,951*	*1,478*	*4,344*	*129*	*22,668*
1	Benares ..	**1,083**	882	54	2	..	647	**11,992**	3,840	351	1,036	23	7,801
2	Mirzapur ..	**4**	3	..	..	..	1	**5,580**	2,016	884	497	5	3,180
	Native States ..	**35**	**14**	..	..	..	**21**	**5,626**	**1,915**	**105**	**853**	**13**	**3,656**
3	Rampur ..	**29**	10	..	..	..	19	**2,578**	772	16	287	..	1,790
4	Tehri-Garhwal ..	**6**	4	..	..	..	2	**317**	74	12	14	..	281
5	Benares Raj ..	..	..	..	..	..	..	**2,731**	1,069	77	552	13	1,585

of material substances—(continued).

Industry—(continued).

from the animal kingdom.

Total Order 7.—Hides, skins and hard materials from the animal kingdom.						Order 8—Wood. 36.—Sawyers, carpenters, turners and joiners, &c.						
Total workers and dependants.	Actual workers. Total. Males.	Actual workers. Total. Females.	Actual workers. Partially agriculturists. Males.	Actual workers. Partially agriculturists. Females.	Dependants.	Total workers and dependants.	Actual workers. Total. Males.	Actual workers. Total. Females.	Actual workers. Partially agriculturists. Males.	Actual workers. Partially agriculturists. Females.	Dependants.	Serial number.
215	216	217	218	219	220	221	222	223	224	225	226	1
130,470	**48,342**	**9,047**	**7,041**	**1,030**	**73,081**	**344,625**	**129,025**	**8,001**	**31,887**	**651**	**207,599**	
108,681	**39,716**	**6,866**	**4,086**	**480**	**62,099**	**280,041**	**104,309**	**6,662**	**23,640**	**469**	**169,070**	
8,984	*3,467*	*1,292*	*289*	*103*	*4,225*	*16,265*	*6,018*	*611*	*1,273*	*19*	*9,641*	
998	206	155	23	1	637	**3,732**	1,399	18	806	..	2,815	1
2,133	778	186	84	13	1,169	**3,155**	1,082	119	275	1	1,944	2
1,172	**384**	**51**	**112**	**1**	**737**	**6,846**	**2,570**	**71**	**829**	**3**	**4,205**	
460	146	10	46	1	804	**5,162**	1,740	31	632	1	3,891	3
415	128	13	28	..	279	**923**	537	17	78	..	369	4
297	115	18	38	..	164	**761**	293	23	119	2	445	5

of material substances—(continued).

Industry—(continued).

Order 9—Metals.

41.—Other workers in iron and makers of implements and tools principally or exclusively of iron.						42.—Workers in brass, copper and bell metal.						
Total workers and dependants.	Actual workers. Total. Males.	Actual workers. Total. Females.	Actual workers. Partially agriculturists. Males.	Actual workers. Partially agriculturists. Females.	Dependants.	Total workers and dependants.	Actual workers. Total. Males.	Actual workers. Total. Females.	Actual workers. Partially agriculturists. Males.	Actual workers. Partially agriculturists. Females.	Dependants.	Serial number.
239	240	241	242	243	244	245	246	247	248	249	250	1
232,080	**87,203**	**6,549**	**25,383**	**1,071**	**138,328**	**38,240**	**13,642**	**1,316**	**1,457**	**84**	**23,282**	
180,979	**66,928**	**5,064**	**17,406**	**843**	**108,987**	**31,586**	**11,156**	**1,035**	**1,318**	**29**	**19,395**	
29,117	*11,137*	*995*	*8,633*	*116*	*16,985*	*6,087*	*1,931*	*268*	*560*	*9*	*8,882*	
6,653	9,264	149	517	14	4,245	**4,234**	1,188	146	517	9	2,900	1
3,883	1,884	282	364	8	2,217	**538**	274	31	21	..	238	2
4,608	**1,630**	**80**	**790**	**13**	**2,898**	**545**	**171**	**24**	**42**	..	**350**	
2,076	688	15	283	..	1,373	**164**	15	..	3	..	149	3
127	..	1	..	..	126	**179**	69	11	13	..	99	4
2,405	942	64	507	13	1,399	**202**	87	13	26	..	101	5

of material substances—(continued).

Industry—(continued).

Order 10—Ceramics.

47.—Potters and earthen pipes and bowl makers.						48.—Brick and tile makers.						
Total workers and dependants.	Actual workers. Total. Males.	Actual workers. Total. Females.	Actual workers. Partially agriculturists. Males.	Actual workers. Partially agriculturists. Females.	Dependants.	Total workers and dependants.	Actual workers. Total. Males.	Actual workers. Total. Females.	Actual workers. Partially agriculturists. Males.	Actual workers. Partially agriculturists. Females.	Dependants.	Serial number.
263	264	265	266	267	268	269	270	271	272	273	274	1
326,594	**109,470**	**71,696**	**26,677**	**9,646**	**145,428**	**17,006**	**7,265**	**1,604**	**409**	**27**	**8,137**	
273,032	**91,447**	**56,365**	**19,435**	**6,740**	**125,220**	**11,583**	**4,728**	**910**	**154**	**14**	**5,945**	
42,144	*13,678*	*12,300*	*8,974*	*1,824*	*16,166*	*601*	*207*	*138*	*13*	..	*261*	
9,390	8,072	2,581	746	330	3,737	**278**	88	28	4	..	162	1
5,921	1,999	1,488	475	117	2,434	**99**	17	59	1	..	23	2
6,449	**2,205**	**1,429**	**828**	**345**	**2,815**	**345**	**200**	**42**	**14**	..	**103**	
2,677	934	238	284	7	1,505	**340**	200	38	14	..	102	3
167	58	8	12	..	101	**1**	..	..	..	..	1	4
3,605	1,213	1,183	532	338	1,209	**4**	..	4	..	..	..	5

TABLE XV.—Occupation or means of livelihood.

Class B.—Preparation and supply

Sub-Class III.—

Serial number.	District or State.	Order 10.—Ceramics—(concluded). Total Order 10.—Ceramics. Total workers and dependants.	Actual workers. Total. Males.	Actual workers. Total. Females.	Actual workers. Partially agriculturists. Males.	Actual workers. Partially agriculturists. Females.	Dependants.	Total Order 11.—Chemical products properly so called, and analogous. Total workers and dependants.	Actual workers. Total. Males.	Actual workers. Total. Females.	Actual workers. Partially agriculturists. Males.	Actual workers. Partially agriculturists. Females.	Dependants.
1	2	275	276	277	278	279	280	281	282	283	284	285	286
	British Territory ..	**359,160**	**121,713**	**76,331**	**27,771**	**9,865**	**161,116**	**421,005**	**129,585**	**115,560**	**29,701**	**8,735**	**177,860**
	Agra Province ..	**295,384**	**99,773**	**58,944**	**19,979**	**6,861**	**136,667**	**326,181**	**102,473**	**78,366**	**19,972**	**5,753**	**145,342**
	Benares Division ..	*45,688*	*14,796*	*13,001*	*4,104*	*1,830*	*17,891*	*61,381*	*18,459*	*18,258*	*3,272*	*945*	*24,664*
1	Benares	**10,472**	3,834	2,858	755	330	4,280	**11,248**	3,292	2,954	471	82	5,002
2	Mirzapur	**6,140**	2,016	1,615	476	117	2,509	**10,191**	3,025	2,822	542	111	4,344
	Native States ..	**7,052**	**2,519**	**1,492**	**854**	**345**	**3,041**	**7,536**	**2,383**	**1,965**	**812**	**160**	**3,188**
3	Rampur	**3,274**	1,248	297	310	7	1,729	**3,580**	1,150	662	474	27	1,768
4	Tehri-Garhwal ..	**169**	58	8	12	..	103	**141**	27	14	..	..	100
5	Benares Raj ..	**3,609**	1,213	1,187	532	338	1 209	**3,815**	1,206	1,289	338	133	1,320

Class B.—Preparation and supply

Sub-Class III —

Order 12.—Food

Serial number.	District or State.	59.—Butchers. Total workers and dependants.	Actual workers. Total. Males.	Actual workers. Total. Females.	Actual workers. Partially agriculturists. Males.	Actual workers. Partially agriculturists. Females.	Dependants.	61.—Butter, cheese and ghee makers. Total workers and dependants.	Actual workers. Total. Males.	Actual workers. Total. Females.	Actual workers. Partially agriculturists. Males.	Actual workers. Partially agriculturists. Females.	Dependants.
1	2	299	300	301	302	303	304	305	306	307	308	309	310
	British Territory ..	**111,114**	**34,980**	**5,879**	**2,573**	**293**	**70,255**	**460**	**144**	**24**	**6**	..	**292**
	Agra Province ..	**85,042**	**26,792**	**4,477**	**1,399**	**219**	**53,773**	**374**	**121**	**18**	**4**	..	**235**
	Benares Division ..	*4,677*	*1,812*	*465*	*75*	*28*	*2,900*	*57*	*21*	*7*	..	..	*29*
1	Benares	**1,407**	377	62	2	2	968	**27**	12	2	..	..	13
2	Mirzapur	**296**	108	85	3	..	153	**26**	9	5	..	..	12
	Native States ..	**2,635**	**885**	**34**	**115**	..	**1,716**	**1**	..	..	..	..	**1**
3	Rampur	**2,291**	688	20	115	..	1,583	**1**	..	..	..	..	1
4	Tehri-Garhwal ..	**7**	1	..	..	..	6	..	..	..	..	..	..
5	Benares Raj ..	**337**	196	14	..	..	127	..	..	..	..	..	..

Class B.—Preparation and supply

Sub-Class III.—

Serial number.	District or State.	Order 12.—Food industries—(concluded). Total order 12.—Food industries. Total workers and dependants.	Actual workers. Total. Males.	Actual workers. Total. Females.	Actual workers. Partially agriculturists. Males.	Actual workers. Partially agriculturists. Females.	Dependants.	Order 13.—Industries. 67.—Hat, cap and turban makers. Total workers and dependants.	Actual workers. Total. Males.	Actual workers. Total. Females.	Actual workers. Partially agriculturists. Males.	Actual workers. Partially agriculturists. Females.	Dependants.
1	2	323	324	325	326	327	328	329	330	331	332	333	334
	British Territory ..	**775,536**	**157,626**	**325,685**	**15,604**	**7,564**	**292,225**	**5,481**	**963**	**1,421**	**4**	**51**	**3,097**
	Agra Province ..	**571,401**	**115,474**	**233,742**	**10,003**	**4,731**	**222,185**	**2,658**	**900**	**272**	**4**	..	**1,486**
	Benares Division ..	**81,675**	*20,543*	*30,020*	*2,181*	*915*	*31,112*	*150*	*34*	*5*	*1*	..	*111*
1	Benares	**18,014**	4,003	6,182	321	123	7,829	**58**	16	..	..	..	42
2	Mirzapur	**5,795**	1,525	2,132	101	26	2,138	..	..	..	..	..	..
	Native States ..	**14,636**	**3,174**	**5,696**	**484**	**119**	**5,766**	**3**	**2**	..	..	..	**1**
3	Rampur	**10,149**	1,948	3,889	336	24	4,312	3	2	..	..	..	1
4	Tehri-Garhwal ..	**22**	7	..	..	..	15	..	..	..	..	..	..
5	Benares Raj ..	**4,465**	1,219	1,807	148	95	1,489	..	..	..	..	..	..

of material substances—(*continued*).

Industry—(*continued*).

Order 12.—Food industries.

56.—Rice pounders and huskers and flour grinders.						58.—Grain parchers, &c.						
Total workers and dependants.	Actual workers. Total. Males.	Actual workers. Total. Females.	Actual workers. Partially agriculturists. Males.	Actual workers. Partially agriculturists. Females.	Dependants.	Total workers and dependants.	Actual workers. Total. Males.	Actual workers. Total. Females.	Actual workers. Partially agriculturists. Males.	Actual workers. Partially agriculturists. Females.	Dependants.	Serial number.
287	288	289	290	291	292	293	294	295	296	297	298	1
314,554	**11,106**	**223,491**	**491**	**3,058**	**79,957**	**245,749**	**71,147**	**89,152**	**9,099**	**4,036**	**85,450**	
239,025	**8,659**	**166,374**	**371**	**1,530**	**63,992**	**171,790**	**50,068**	**58,328**	**5,979**	**2,876**	**63,394**	
72,716	*600*	*8,218*	*12*	*115*	*3,898*	*51,278*	*14,320*	*19,943*	*1,685*	*734*	*17,015*	
3,788	84	2,707	2	19	997	**7,465**	1,882	2,803	181	98	2,771	1
1,727	157	967	1	3	603	**3,659**	1,208	1,119	91	23	1,832	2
5,829	**303**	**4,077**	**3**	**26**	**1,449**	**5,380**	**1,604**	**1,547**	**338**	**92**	**2,229**	
5,225	283	3,657	2	17	1,282	**1,921**	636	184	193	7	1,101	3
15	6	..	..	..	9	..	..	..	..	..	..	4
589	11	420	1	9	158	**3,459**	938	1,333	145	85	1,128	5

of material substances—(*continued*).

industry—(*continued*).

Industries—(*continued*).

62.—Makers of sugar, molasses and gur.						63.—Sweetmeat makers, preparers of jam and condiments, &c.						
Total workers and dependants.	Actual workers. Total. Males.	Actual workers. Total. Females.	Actual workers. Partially agriculturists. Males.	Actual workers. Partially agriculturists. Females.	Dependants.	Total workers and dependants.	Actual workers. Total. Males.	Actual workers. Total. Females.	Actual workers. Partially agriculturists. Males.	Actual workers. Partially agriculturists. Females.	Dependants.	Serial number.
311	312	313	314	315	316	317	318	319	320	321	322	1
30,839	**14,002**	**597**	**1,429**	**18**	**16,240**	**61,981**	**22,508**	**5,556**	**1,804**	**132**	**34,117**	
30,195	**13,694**	**594**	**1,390**	**18**	**15,907**	**35,870**	**13,033**	**2,887**	**700**	**68**	**19,950**	
3,255	*1,053*	*157*	*95*	*3*	*2,045*	*7,800*	*3,634*	*990*	*261*	*29*	*4,176*	
66	3	7	1	..	56	**4,627**	1,550	437	135	1	2,640	1
..	..	..	..	..	..	**72**	38	6	6	..	28	2
197	**105**	..	**18**	..	**92**	**75**	**39**	**10**	**2**	**1**	**26**	
197	105	..	18	..	92	..	..	..	..	..	..	3
..	..	..	..	..	..	..	..	..	..	..	..	4
..	..	..	..	..	..	**75**	39	10	2	1	26	5

of material substances—(*continued*).

industries—(*continued*).

of dress and toilet.

68.—Tailors, milliners, dress makers and darners, embroiderers on linen.						69.—Shoe, boot and sandal makers.						
Total workers and dependants.	Actual workers. Total. Males.	Actual workers. Total. Females.	Actual workers. Partially agriculturists. Males.	Actual workers. Partially agriculturists. Females.	Dependants.	Total workers and dependants.	Actual workers. Total. Males.	Actual workers. Total. Females.	Actual workers. Partially agriculturists. Males.	Actual workers. Partially agriculturists. Females.	Dependants.	Serial number.
335	336	337	338	339	340	341	342	343	344	345	346	1
294,843	**98,758**	**59,827**	**13,518**	**2,011**	**136,258**	**163,943**	**60,864**	**8,908**	**5,711**	**431**	**94,171**	
227,040	**75,504**	**45,927**	**8,618**	**1,435**	**105,609**	**140,444**	**51,250**	**8,030**	**3,635**	**299**	**81,164**	
22,759	*6,408*	*5,183*	*918*	*169*	*11,168*	*9,938*	*4,056*	*636*	*256*	*23*	*5,296*	
5,894	1,790	1,246	163	41	2,858	**2,231**	898	63	70	..	1,270	1
2,946	1,013	446	112	8	1,487	**2,443**	791	82	54	2	1,570	2
7,547	**1,922**	**1,391**	**344**	**29**	**4,234**	**2,152**	**945**	**28**	**127**	**2**	**1,179**	
3,645	1,045	845	273	10	1,755	**1,428**	563	2	92	2	863	3
2,966	776	185	55	4	2,005	**303**	123	2	11	..	178	4
986	101	411	16	15	474	**421**	259	24	24	..	188	5

TABLE XV.—Occupation or means of livelihood.

Class B.—Preparation and supply

Sub-Class III.—

Order 13.—Industries of

Serial number.	District or State.	71.—Washing, cleaning and dyeing. Total workers and dependants.	Actual workers. Total. Males.	Actual workers. Total. Females	Actual workers. Partially agriculturists. Males.	Actual workers. Partially agriculturists. Females.	Dependants.	72.—Barbers, hair dressers and wig makers. Total workers and dependants.	Actual workers. Total. Males.	Actual workers. Total. Females.	Actual workers. Partially agriculturists. Males.	Actual workers. Partially agriculturists. Females.	Dependants.
1	2	347	348	349	350	351	352	353	354	355	356	357	358
	British Territory ...	**372,459**	**119,431**	**98,910**	**29,946**	**10,246**	**154,118**	**474,104**	**173,143**	**66,331**	**43,075**	**3,422**	**234,630**
	Agra Province ...	**279,904**	**90,335**	**69,841**	**19,899**	**6,211**	**119,728**	**354,038**	**131,408**	**36,514**	**28,518**	**2,048**	**186,116**
	Benares Division ..	*33,477*	*11,185*	*11,004*	*2,739*	*1,290*	*11,288*	*39,138*	*15,031*	*3,898*	*4,196*	*241*	*20,209*
1	Benares	**6,930**	2,199	2,174	416	155	2,557	**8,654**	3,039	734	759	48	4,881
2	Mirzapur	**4,308**	1,484	1,300	154	58	1,524	**6,174**	2,475	483	526	9	3,216
	Native States ..	**6,754**	**2,121**	**1,376**	**899**	**146**	**3,257**	**8,079**	**2,998**	**391**	**1,221**	**27**	**4,690**
3	Rampur	**4,283**	1,418	440	626	17	2,430	**4,780**	1,691	26	695	3	3,068
4	Tehri-Garhwal ..	**20**	5	..	..	..	15	**92**	28	4	..	..	60
5	Benares Raj ..	**2,451**	703	936	273	129	812	**3,207**	1,279	361	526	24	1,567

Class B.—Preparation and supply

Sub-Class III.—

Serial number.	District or state.	Order 15.—Building Industries. Total Order 15.—Building industries. Total workers and dependants.	Actual workers. Total. Males.	Actual workers. Total. Females.	Actual workers. Partially agriculturists. Males.	Actual workers. Partially agriculturists. Females.	Dependants.	Order 16.—Construction of means of transport. Total order 16.—Construction of means of transport Total workers and dependants.	Actual workers. Total. Males.	Actual workers. Total. Females.	Actual workers. Partially agriculturists. Males.	Actual workers. Partially agriculturists. Females.	Dependants.
1	2	371	372	373	374	375	376	377	378	379	380	381	382
	British Territory ..	**136,566**	**52,298**	**8,595**	**3,586**	**465**	**75,673**	**3,420**	**1,189**	**27**	**78**	..	**2,204**
	Agra Province ..	**89,870**	**32,577**	**3,726**	**2,014**	**264**	**53,567**	**2,950**	**1,023**	**16**	**65**	..	**1,911**
	Benares Division ..	*15,000*	*5,051*	*1,353*	*381*	*36*	*8,596*	**127**	*81*	*1*	*4*	..	*45*
1	Benares	**7,834**	2,555	617	79	23	4,662	**37**	25	..	..	..	12
2	Mirzapur	**4,917**	1,828	536	233	3	2,553	**28**	18	1	4	..	9
	Native States ..	**4,000**	**1,281**	**35**	**101**	**1**	**2,684**	**421**	**160**	**3**	**36**	..	**258**
3	Rampur	**2,835**	861	20	19	..	1,954	**421**	160	3	36	..	258
4	Tehri-Garhwal ..	**995**	322	5	69	1	668	..	..	..	..	..	..
5	Benares Raj ..	**170**	98	10	13	..	62	..	..	..	..	..	..

Class B.—Preparation and supply

Sub-Class III.—

Serial number.	District or state.	Order 18.—Industries of luxury and those pertaining to literature and the arts and sciences—(*concluded*). Total order 18.—Industries of luxury and those pertaining to literature and the arts and sciences. Total workers and dependants.	Actual workers. Total. Males.	Actual workers. Total. Females.	Actual workers. Partially agriculturists. Males	Actual workers. Partially agriculturists. Females.	Dependants.	Order 19.—Industries concerned with refuse matter. 93.—Sweepers, scavengers, dust and sweeping contractors. Total workers and dependants.	Actual workers. Total. Males.	Actual workers. Total. Females.	Actual workers. Partially agriculturists. Males.	Actual workers. Partially agriculturists. Females.	Dependants.
1	2	395	396	397	398	399	400	401	402	403	404	405	406
	British Territory ..	**311,000**	**110,902**	**14,981**	**13,465**	**810**	**185,117**	**362,057**	**112,020**	**121,560**	**3,033**	**1,265**	**128,477**
	Agra Province ..	**237,463**	**84,595**	**10,643**	**8,986**	**562**	**142,225**	**327,197**	**102,443**	**108,792**	**2,450**	**977**	**115,962**
	Benares Division ..	*39,789*	*13,881*	*2,361*	*1,114*	*180*	*23,547*	*7,119*	*2,206*	*2,222*	*60*	*42*	*2,691*
1	Benares	**12,753**	4,233	697	181	19	7,823	**2,389**	614	754	11	8	1,021
2	Mirzapur	**3,496**	1,305	146	130	1	2,045	**1,044**	329	272	2	1	443
	Native States ..	**6,787**	**2,593**	**359**	**384**	**35**	**3,835**	**3,349**	**872**	**1,452**	**58**	**7**	**1,025**
3	Rampur	**3,840**	1,149	140	224	..	2,551	**3,264**	830	1,435	58	7	999
4	Tehri-Garhwal ..	**178**	62	4	20	1	112	**43**	14	14	..	..	15
5	Benares Raj ..	**2,769**	1,382	215	140	84	1,172	**42**	28	3	..	..	11

of material substances—(continued).

Industry—(continued).

dress and the toilet—(concluded). | Order 14.—Furniture Industries.

Total Order 13—Industries of dress and the toilet.						Total order 14.—Furniture industries.						
Total workers and dependants.	Actual workers. Total. Males.	Actual workers. Total. Females.	Actual workers. Partially agriculturists. Males.	Actual workers. Partially agriculturists. Females.	Dependants.	Total workers and dependants.	Actual workers. Total. Males.	Actual workers. Total. Females.	Actual workers. Partially agriculturists. Males.	Actual workers. Partially agriculturists. Females.	Dependants.	Serial number.
359	360	361	362	363	364	365	366	367	368	369	370	1
1,319,412	**456,114**	**236,538**	**92,861**	**16,196**	**626,760**	**6,285**	**2,305**	**324**	**47**	**8**	**3,656**	
1,010,696	**351,515**	**161,302**	**60,746**	**10,001**	**497,879**	**5,113**	**1,773**	**276**	**34**	**7**	**3,064**	
105,774	*36,779*	*20,812*	*8,110*	*1,724*	*45,188*	*97*	*21*	*8*	*1*	..	*68*	
23,868	7,982	4,235	1,408	**244**	11,651	**41**	13	1	..	..	27	1
15,908	5,770	2,334	846	72	7,804	**22**	2	5	..	..	15	2
24,595	**7,990**	**3,211**	**2,591**	**204**	**13,394**	**39**	**11**	..	**1**	..	**28**	
14,178	4,716	1,325	1,686	32	8,187	**39**	11	..	1	..	28	3
3,331	932	141	66	4	2,258	..	..	..	..	..	..	4
7,086	2,342	1,745	839	168	2,999	..	..	..	..	..	..	5

of material substances—(continued).

Industry—(continued).

Order 17.—Production and transmission of physical forces (heat, light, electricity, motive power, &c.). 83.—Gasworks, electric light and ice factories.						Order 18.—Industries of luxury and those pertaining to literature and the arts and sciences. 89.—Workers in precious stones and metals, enamellers, imitation jewellery makers, gilders, &c.						
Total workers and dependants.	Actual workers. Total. Males.	Actual workers. Total. Females.	Actual workers. Partially agriculturists. Males.	Actual workers. Partially agriculturists. Females.	Dependants.	Total workers and dependants.	Actual workers. Total. Males.	Actual workers. Total. Females.	Actual workers. Partially agriculturists. Males.	Actual workers. Partially agriculturists. Females.	Dependants.	Serial number.
383	384	385	386	387	388	389	390	391	392	393	394	1
716	**282**	**4**	**6**	..	**430**	**231,241**	**83,084**	**3,926**	**11,283**	**294**	**144,231**	
553	**209**	**4**	**4**	..	**340**	**181,641**	**65,089**	**3,309**	**7,668**	**280**	**113,243**	
10	*8*	..	*1*	..	*2*	*33,772*	*11,682*	*940*	*1,062*	*95*	*20,550*	
8	6	..	..	..	**2**	**9,516**	3,167	103	175	15	6,246	1
..	..	..	..	..	..	**3,083**	1,106	75	130	1	1,902	2
9	**4**	..	..	..	**3**	**4,655**	**1,301**	**39**	**304**	**2**	**3,113**	
9	4	..	..	..	5	**2,970**	941	17	204	..	2,012	3
..	..	..	..	..	..	**171**	58	4	20	1	109	4
..	..	..	..	..	..	**1,512**	502	18	80	1	992	5

of material substances—(continued).

Industry—(concluded). | Sub-Class IV—Transport.

Total Sub-Class III.—Industry.						Order 20—Transport by water. Total Order 20—Transport by water.						
Total workers and dependants.	Actual workers. Total. Males.	Actual workers. Total. Females.	Actual workers. Partially agriculturists. Males.	Actual workers. Partially agriculturists. Females.	Dependants.	Total workers and dependants.	Actual workers. Total. Males.	Actual workers. Total. Females.	Actual workers. Partially agriculturists. Males.	Actual workers. Partially agriculturists. Females.	Dependants.	Serial number.
407	408	409	410	411	412	413	414	415	416	417	418	1
5,717,610	**1,837,580**	**1,186,862**	**290,963**	**57,885**	**2,693,168**	**38,495**	**14,439**	**1,629**	**1,665**	**203**	**22,427**	
4,514,660	**1,449,941**	**889,129**	**197,808**	**37,970**	**2,175,590**	**35,389**	**13,192**	**1,441**	**1,362**	**166**	**20,756**	
535,425	*170,534*	*111,940*	*28,095*	*6,825*	*252,951*	*9,878*	*8,301*	*401*	*222*	*49*	*6,176*	
152,422	47,762	24,676	5,018	1,088	79,984	**2,574**	818	76	46	29	1,685	1
65,616	22,088	12,890	3,312	422	31,138	**3,558**	922	87	54	..	2,549	2
116,774	**38,915**	**21,310**	**8,871**	**1,071**	**56,549**	**958**	**196**	**25**	**38**	**7**	**737**	
67,350	20,065	11,088	5,592	288	36,252	**167**	68	2	15	..	97	3
7,829	2,623	262	347	18	4,944	**81**	20	2	..	..	59	4
41,595	16,227	10,015	2,952	8[illegible]5	15,358	**710**	108	21	23	7	581	5

Class B.—Preparation and supply
Sub-Class IV.—
Order 21.—Transport

Serial number.	District or State.	98.—Persons employed on the construction and maintenance of roads and bridges. Total workers and dependants.	Actual workers. Total. Males.	Actual workers. Total. Females.	Partially agriculturists. Males.	Partially agriculturists. Females.	Dependants.	102.—Porters and messengers. Total workers and dependants.	Actual workers. Total. Males.	Actual workers. Total. Females.	Partially agriculturists. Males.	Partially agriculturists. Females.	Dependants.
1	2	419	420	421	422	423	424	425	426	427	428	429	430
	British Territory ..	**20,744**	**9,330**	**1,179**	**652**	**25**	**10,235**	**37,907**	**15,983**	**2,403**	**1,002**	**51**	**19,521**
	Agra Province ..	**13,258**	**5,615**	**866**	**410**	**19**	**6,777**	**32,096**	**13,744**	**2,117**	**885**	**47**	**16,235**
	Benares Division ..	*946*	*325*	*79*	*52*	..	*542*	*1,785*	*582*	*270*	*19*	*1*	*933*
1	Benares	63	12	..	1	..	51	1,150	404	168	1	1	578
2	Mirzapur	622	198	45	31	..	379	114	46	1	4	..	67
	Native States ..	**180**	**86**	**1**	**11**	**2**	**93**	**558**	**238**	**11**	**3**	..	**309**
3	Rampur	149	60	1	2	..	88	316	184	1	2	..	181
4	Tehri-Garhwal ..	4	2	..	..	2	2	202	74	10	..	..	118
5	Benares Raj ..	27	24	..	9	..	3	40	30	..	1	..	10

Class B.—Preparation and supply
Sub-class IV.—Transport—(*concluded*).

Serial number.	District or state.	Order 22.—Transport by rail. Total, Order 22—Transport by rail. Total workers and dependants.	Auctual workers. Total. Males.	Auctual workers. Total. Females.	Partially agriculturists. Males.	Partially agriculturists. Females.	Dependants.	Order 23.—Post office, telegraph and telephone services. 105.—Post office, telegraph and telephone services. Total workers and dependants.	Actual workers. Total. Males.	Actual workers. Total. Females.	Partially agriculturists. Males.	Partially agriculturists. Females.	Dependants.
1	2	443	444	445	446	447	448	449	450	451	452	453	454
	British Territory ..	**128,223**	**53,003**	**1,263**	**2,718**	**30**	**73,957**	**26,476**	**9,702**	**59**	**814**	**1**	**16,715**
	Agra Province ..	**88,290**	**35,772**	**831**	**1,411**	**11**	**51,687**	**20,802**	**7,623**	**56**	**596**	**1**	**13,123**
	Benares Division ..	*9,279*	*4,020*	*77*	*439*	*1*	*5,182*	*1,412*	*544*	*7*	*46*	..	*861*
1	Benares	5,676	2,410	22	297	..	3,244	623	168	..	13	..	460
2	Mirzapur	790	867	34	29	..	889	84	78	..	6	..	6
	Native States ..	**753**	**372**	**6**	**27**	..	**375**	**398**	**83**	..	**4**	..	**315**
3	Rampur	539	271	2	19	..	266	239	59	..	1	..	180
4	Tehri-Garhwal ..	..	..	..	..	..	..	11	5	..	2	..	6
5	Benares Raj ..	214	101	4	8	..	109	148	19	..	1	..	129

Class B.—Preparation and supply
Sub-class V.—

Serial number.	District or state	Order 25.—Brokerage commission export. 107.—Brokers, commission agents, commercial travellers, warehouse owners and employés. Total workers and dependants.	Actual workers. Total. Males.	Actual workers. Total. Females	Partially agriculturitsts. Males.	Partially agriculturitsts. Females	Dependants.	Order 26.—Trade in textiles. 108.—Trade in piece-goods, wool, cotton, silk, hair and other textiles. Total workers and dependants.	Actual workers. Total. Males.	Actual workers. Total. Females.	Partially agriculturists. Males.	Partially agriculturists. Females.	Dependants.
1	2	467	468	469	470	471	472	473	474	475	476	477	478
	British Territory ..	**29,144**	**10,054**	**404**	**760**	**52**	**18,686**	**131,011**	**44,170**	**4,645**	**3,946**	**219**	**82,196**
	Agra Province ..	**23,603**	**8,129**	**340**	**531**	**50**	**15,134**	**98,955**	**33,266**	**3,615**	**2,596**	**174**	**62,074**
	Benares Division ..	*1,584*	*536*	*18*	*13*	..	*1,030*	*12,768*	*4,019*	*620*	*476*	*29*	*8,129*
1	Benares	888	311	..	..	..	577	4,218	1,389	86	242	5	2,743
2	Mirzapur	342	122	8	2	..	212	1,635	463	107	37	..	1,062
	Native States ..	**267**	**105**	**36**	**25**	..	**126**	**2,418**	**707**	**316**	**221**	**5**	**1,395**
3	Rampur	122	42	..	19	..	80	1,828	520	301	194	5	1,007
4	Tehri-Garhwal ..	16	4	..	1	..	12	151	71	1	12	..	79
5	Benares Raj ..	129	59	36	5	..	34	439	116	14	15	..	309

of material substances—(*continued*).

Transport—(*continued*).

by road—(*concluded*) | **Order 22.—Transport by rail.**

Total, Order 21.—Transport by road. Total workers and dependants	Actual workers. Total. Males.	Females	Partially agriculturists. Males.	Females.	Dependants.	104.—Labourers employed on railway construction. Total workers and dependants.	Actual workers. Total. Males.	Females	Partially agriculturists. Males.	Females.	Dependants.	Serial number.
431	432	433	434	435	436	437	438	439	440	441	442	1
249,588	**109,693**	**6,518**	**9,128**	**185**	**133,377**	**15,908**	**8,481**	**846**	**710**	**17**	**5,581**	
202,895	**87,868**	**5,381**	**6,940**	**155**	**109,646**	**8,076**	**4,212**	**486**	**328**	**1**	**3,378**	
25,730	*11,461*	*881*	*980*	*6*	*18,438*	*1,844*	*1,254*	*52*	*189*	..	*538*	
8,185	3,268	258	179	1	4,659	**1,585**	1,114	15	184	..	456	1
6,539	2,945	189	310	2	3,405	**142**	82	34	..	..	26	2
4,719	**1,710**	**244**	**119**	**214**	**2,765**	**63**	**52**	..	..	..	**11**	
2,595	847	218	49	209	1,530	**56**	52	..	..	..	4	3
211	81	10	..	2	120	..	..	..	..	..	..	4
1,913	782	16	70	3	1,115	**7**	..	..	..	..	7	5

of material substances—(*continued*).

Sub-class V.—Trade.

Order 24.—Banks, establishments of credit, exchange and insurance.

Total Sub-class IV.—Transport. Total workers and dependants.	Actual workers. Total. Males.	Females	Partially agriculturists. Males.	Females	Dependants.	106.—Bank managers, money lenders, exchange and insurance agents, money changers and brokers and their employés. Total workers and dependants.	Actual workers. Total. Males	Females	Partially agriculturists. Males.	Females.	Dependants.	Serial number.
455	456	457	458	459	460	461	462	463	464	465	466	1
442,782	**186,837**	**9,469**	**14,325**	**419**	**246,476**	**140,609**	**42,862**	**6,492**	**7,140**	**404**	**91,255**	
347,376	**144,455**	**7,709**	**10,309**	**333**	**195,212**	**102,214**	**31,865**	**4,988**	**5,043**	**271**	**65,361**	
46,299	*19,326*	*1,316*	*1,687*	*56*	*25,657*	*16,175*	*6,003*	*1,001*	*565*	*56*	*9,171*	
17,058	6,654	856	535	80	10,048	**7,894**	2,716	842	249	7	4,836	1
10,971	4,312	810	399	2	6,349	**1,709**	733	82	54	5	894	2
6,828	**2,361**	**275**	**188**	**221**	**4,192**	**3,674**	**1,062**	**288**	**271**	**77**	**2,324**	
3,540	1,245	222	84	209	2,073	**1,619**	352	64	17	1	1,203	3
303	106	12	2	2	185	**33**	4	1	3	..	28	4
2,985	1,010	41	102	10	1,934	**2,022**	706	223	251	76	1,093	5

of material substances—(*continued*).

Trade—(*continued*).

Order 27.—Trade in skins, leather and furs. | **Order 28.—Trade in wood.**

109.—Trade in skins, leather, furs, feathers, horn, &c. Total workers and dependants.	Actual workers. Total. Males.	Females.	Partially agriculturists. Males.	Females	Dependants	110.—Trade in wood (not fire-wood) cork, bark, &c. Total workers and dependants.	Actual workers. Total. Males.	Females	Partially agriculturists. Males.	Females.	Dependants.	Serial number.
479	480	481	482	483	484	485	486	487	488	489	490	1
10,530	**3,494**	**476**	**269**	**68**	**6,560**	**6,939**	**2,387**	**1,236**	**172**	**38**	**3,316**	
8,251	**2,576**	**347**	**122**	**19**	**5,308**	**5,551**	**1,851**	**1,039**	**105**	**25**	**2,661**	
7,523	*400*	*65*	*22*	*8*	*1,058*	*1,407*	*420*	*453*	*13*	*19*	*534*	
331	103	16	2	..	212	**442**	180	100	6	1	212	1
165	28	18	7	7	119	**587**	195	204	1	14	187	2
222	**66**	..	**6**	..	**156**	**1,259**	**393**	**257**	**44**	**1**	**609**	
216	61	..	3	..	155	**1,238**	378	256	44	1	609	3
..	..	..	..	..	..	**21**	20	1	..	..	..	4
6	5	..	3	..	1	..	..	..	..	..	..	5

TABLE XV.—Occupation or means of livelihood.

Class B.—Preparation and supply,

Sub-class V.—

Serial number.	District or State.	Order 29.—Trade in metals. 111—Trade in metals, machinery, knife, tool, &c., sellers: Total workers and dependants.	Actual workers. Total. Males.	Actual workers. Total. Females.	Actual workers. Partially agriculturists. Males.	Actual workers. Partially agriculturists. Females.	Dependants.	Order 30—Trade in pottery. 112—Trade in pottery: Total workers and dependants.	Actual workers. Total. Males.	Actual workers. Total. Females.	Actual workers. Partially agriculturists. Males.	Actual workers. Partially agriculturists. Females.	Dependants.
1	2	491	492	493	494	495	496	497	498	499	500	501	502
	British Territory ..	**6,704**	**2,205**	**212**	**119**	**8**	**4,289**	**3,382**	**1,242**	**454**	**5**	**5**	**1,686**
	Agra Province ..	**5,268**	**1,604**	**175**	**70**	**8**	**3,491**	**3,307**	**1,210**	**446**	**5**	..	**1,649**
	Benares Division ..	*385*	*144*	*25*	*7*	..	*216*	**75**	*20*	*13*	..	..	*42*
1	Benares	**210**	40	19	..	..	151	**34**	7	4	..	..	23
2	Mirzapur	**49**	32	..	1	..	17	**7**	3	1	..	..	3
	Native States ..	**2,929**	**913**	**65**	**175**	**5**	**1,951**	..	..	..	..	..	..
3	Rampur	**397**	81	6	80	1	310	..	..	..	..	..	..
4	Tehri-Garhwal ..	**2,526**	826	59	145	4	1,641	..	..	..	..	..	..
5	Benares Raj ..	**6**	6	..	..	..	..	..	..	..	..	..	..

Class B.—Praparation and supply of

Sub-Class V.—

Order 33.—Other trades

Serial number.	District or State.	116—Fish dealers: Total workers and dependants.	Actual workers. Total. Males.	Actual workers. Total. Females.	Actual workers. Partially agriculturists. Males.	Actual workers. Partially agriculturists. Females.	Dependants.	118.—Sellers of milk, butter, ghee, poultry, eggs, &c.: Total workers and dependants.	Actual workers. Total. Males.	Actual workers. Total. Females.	Actual workers. Partially agriculturists. Males.	Actual workers. Partially agriculturists. Females.	Dependants.
1	2	515	516	517	518	519	520	521	522	523	524	525	526
	British Territory ..	**11,082**	**2,377**	**4,409**	**272**	**162**	**4,296**	**112,216**	**28,783**	**36,803**	**3,924**	**1,866**	**46,630**
	Agra Province ..	**8,841**	**1,982**	**3,410**	**206**	**141**	**3,449**	**89,801**	**23,745**	**27,114**	**2,837**	**1,321**	**38,942**
	Benares Division ..	**785**	*135*	*321*	*6*	*15*	*329*	*26,793*	*5,265*	*12,438*	*676*	*378*	*9,090*
1	Benares ..	**171**	45	31	..	..	95	**6,400**	1,673	1,885	291	183	2,841
2	Mirzapur ..	**25**	16	..	..	..	9	**4,130**	733	1,645	167	37	1,752
	Native States ..	**480**	**136**	**78**	**67**	..	**266**	**2,439**	**505**	**1,064**	**120**	**30**	**870**
3	Rampur ..	**463**	131	72	67	..	260	**1,658**	305	564	69	4	729
4	Tehri-Garhwal ..	..	..	..	..	..	..	..	..	..	..	..	..
5	Benares Raj ..	**17**	5	6	..	..	6	**781**	140	500	51	26	141

Class B.—Preparation

Sub-Class V —

Serial number.	District or State.	Order 33.—Other trade in food stuffs—(*concluded*). Total Order 33.—Other trade in food stuffs: Total workers and dependants.	Actual workers. Total. Males.	Actual workers. Total. Females	Actual workers. Partially agriculturists. Males.	Actual workers. Partially agriculturists. Females.	Dependants.	Order 34.—Trade in clothing and toilet articles. 125.—Trade in ready made clothing and other articles of dress and the toilet (hats, umbrellas, socks, ready made shoes, perfumes, &c.): Total workers and dependants	Actual workers. Total. Males.	Actual workers. Total. Females.	Actual workers. Partially agriculturists. Males.	Actual workers. Partially agriculturists. Females.	Dependants.
1	2	539	540	541	542	543	544	545	546	547	548	549	550
	British Territory ...	**1,390,836**	**451,767**	**247,692**	**45,527**	**9,374**	**691,377**	**58,169**	**18,160**	**3,875**	**736**	**118**	**36,134**
	Agra Province ...	**1,094,353**	**350,898**	**195,191**	**31,277**	**7,116**	**546,264**	**45,403**	**14,009**	**2,770**	**490**	**77**	**28,624**
	Benares Division ..	**159,992**	*47,318*	*39,535*	*4,426*	*1,482*	*72,889*	*3,936*	*1,800*	*626*	*103*	*2*	*2,010*
1	Benares	**41,208**	12,007	8,277	1,083	377	20,924	**1,130**	588	12	83	..	530
2	Mirzapur	**25,574**	7,600	5,665	604	183	12,309	**558**	169	138	18	..	251
	Native States ..	**35,703**	**10,856**	**6,670**	**1,600**	**203**	**18,177**	**922**	**366**	**109**	**14**	..	**447**
3	Rampur	**25,918**	7,721	4,407	1,271	96	13,790	**662**	295	25	12	..	342
4	Tehri-Garhwal ..	**272**	147	6	25		119	**25**	10	1	..	..	14
5	Benares Raj ..	**9,513**	2,988	2,257	304	107	4,268	**235**	61	83	2	..	91

of material substances—(*continued*).

Trade—(*continued*).

Order 31.—Trade in chemical products. 113.—Trade in chemical products (drugs, dyes, paints, petroleum, explosives, &c.).						Order 32.—Hotels, cafés, restaurants, &c. Total, Order 32.—Hotels, cafés, restaurants, &c.						
Total workers and dependants.	Actual workers. Total. Males.	Actual workers. Total. Females.	Partially agriculturists. Males.	Partially agriculturists. Females.	Dependants.	Total workers and dependants.	Actual workers. Total. Males.	Actual workers. Total. Females.	Partially agriculturists. Males	Partially agriculturists. Females.	Dependants.	Serial number.
503.	504	505	506	507	508	509	510	511	512	513	514	1
19,192	**6,479**	**1,430**	**705**	**86**	**11,283**	**27,859**	**10,309**	**2,230**	**993**	**114**	**15,320**	
14,905	**4,726**	**1,164**	**477**	**67**	**9,015**	**20,556**	**7,321**	**1,898**	**604**	**93**	**11,337**	
7,837	*509*	*192*	*8*	..	*1,136*	*4,759*	*1,413*	*436*	*90*	*16*	*2,810*	
569	117	21	..	..	431	916	290	61	8	..	565	1
567	149	118	6	..	300	782	286	88	22	..	458	2
1,167	**444**	**216**	**25**	**5**	**507**	**864**	**289**	**54**	**22**	..	**521**	
515	297	9	9	..	209	738	232	34	20	..	472	3
127	82	..	..	..	95	10	10	..	2	..	..	4
525	115	207	16	5	203	116	47	20	..	..	49	5

material substances—(*continued*).

Trade—(*continued*).

in food stuffs.

121.—Grain and pulse dealers.						122.—Tobacco, opium, ganja, &c., sellers.						
Total workers and dependants.	Actual workers. Total. Males.	Actual workers. Total. Females.	Partially agriculturists. Males.	Partially agriculturists. Females.	Dependants.	Total workers and dependants.	Actual workers. Total. Males.	Actual workers. Total. Females.	Partially agriculturists. Males.	Partially agriculturists. Females.	Dependants.	Serial number.
527	528	529	530	531	532	533	534	535	536	537	538	1
669,655	**238,071**	**60,255**	**24,043**	**2,626**	**371,329**	**72,632**	**24 239**	**8,918**	**2,957**	**299**	**39,475**	
545,600	**190,963**	**49,662**	**17,261**	**2,194**	**304,975**	**48,104**	**15,941**	**5,406**	**1,055**	**187**	**26,757**	
78,180	*25,001*	*12,541*	*2,178*	*386*	*40,638*	*8,986*	*3,126*	*1,968*	*165*	*22*	*4,892*	
19,741	5,907	2,708	403	39	11,131	1,678	473	197	24	3	1,008	1
12,497	4,144	1,662	209	19	6,691	1,706	490	346	19	2	870	2
17,251	**5,812**	**1,580**	**715**	**27**	**10,059**	**627**	**157**	**16**	**7**	..	**454**	
11,398	3,939	331	534	4	7,128	620	154	16	7	..	450	3
181	96	4	18	..	81	7	3	..	..	..	4	4
5,672	1,777	1,045	163	23	2,850	..	..	..	..	..	..	5

and supply of material substances—(*continued*).

Trade (*continued*).

Order 35.—Trade in furniture. Total, Order 35.—Trade in furniture.						Order 36.—Trade in building material. 128.—Trade in building materials (stones, bricks, plaster, cements, sand, tiles, thatch, &c.).						
Total workers and dependants.	Actual workers. Total Males.	Actual workers. Total Females	Partially agriculturists. Males.	Partially agriculturists. Females	Dependants.	Total workers and dependants.	Actual workers. Total. Males.	Actual workers. Total. Females	Partially agriculturists. Males.	Partially agriculturists. Females	Dependants.	Serial number.
551	652	553	554	555	556	557	558	559	560	561	562	1
15,760	**5,473**	**1,062**	**340**	**31**	**9 225**	**3,720**	**1,109**	**380**	**51**	**6**	**2,231**	
10,028	**3,496**	**737**	**188**	**22**	**5,795**	**3,288**	**956**	**362**	**41**	**6**	**1,970**	
7,740	*615*	*133*	*38*	*16*	*992*	*887*	*214*	*181*	*19*	..	*586*	
795	328	24	10	..	443	359	44	125	..	..	190	1
292	71	46	14	16	175	363	94	2	18	..	267	2
386	**156**	**43**	**24**	**5**	**207**	**206**	**21**	**1**	**1**	..	**184**	
365	136	42	24	3	185	197	18	1	1	..	178	3
..	..	..	..	..	..	..	..	..	..	..	..	4
23	..	1	..	..	22	9	3	..	..	..	6	5

Class B.—Preparation and supply

Sub-class V.—

Serial number.	District or State.	Order 37.—Trade in means of transport. 129.—Dealers and hirers of elephants, camels, horses, cattle, asses, mules, &c., sellers (not makers) of carriages, saddlery, &c. — Total workers and dependants.	Actual workers. Total. Males.	Actual workers. Total. Females	Actual workers. Partially agriculturists. Males.	Actual workers. Partially agriculturists. Females.	Dependants.	Order 38.—Trade in fuel. 130.—Dealers in fire-wood, charcoal, coal, cowdung, &c. — Total workers and dependants.	Actual workers. Total. Males.	Actual workers. Total. Females.	Actual workers. Partially agriculturists. Males.	Actual workers. Partially agriculturists. Females.	Dependants.
1	2	563	564	565	566	567	568	569	570	571	572	573	574
	British Territory ..	**45,604**	**15,290**	**1,381**	**1,264**	**37**	**28,933**	**89,924**	**22,886**	**31,332**	**1,777**	**843**	**33,786**
	Agra Province ..	**43,279**	**14,419**	**1,285**	**1,165**	**34**	**27,575**	**78,648**	**19,638**	**28,211**	**1,196**	**452**	**30,799**
	Benares Division ..	*3,863*	*1,048*	*762*	*148*	*64*	*2,053*	*13,155*	*3,372*	*5,311*	*151*	*123*	*4,472*
1	Benares ..	178	76	17	6	..	85	3,266	652	1,491	33	39	1,123
2	Mirzapur ..	273	135	7	10	..	131	3,869	1,281	1,018	63	19	1,569
	Native States ..	**838**	**256**	**5**	**33**	..	**577**	**3,120**	**1,096**	**1,119**	**53**	**14**	**905**
3	Rampur ..	829	247	5	31	..	577	355	67	258	22	..	28
4	Tehri-Garhwal ..	..	..	..	..	..	..	25	11	..	8	..	14
5	Benares Raj ..	9	9	..	2	..	..	2,742	1,018	861	28	14	868

Class B.—Preparation and supply of

Sub-class V.—Trade—(*concluded*).

Order 41.—Trade of other sorts—(*concluded*).

Serial number.	District or State.	Total, Order 41.—Trade of other sorts. Total workers and dependants.	Actual workers. Total. Males.	Actual workers. Total. Females.	Actual workers. Partially agriculturists. Males.	Actual workers. Partially agriculturists. Females.	Dependants.	Total, Sub-class V.—Trade. Total workers and dependants.	Actual workers. Total. Males.	Actual workers. Total. Females	Actual workers. Partially agriculturists. Males.	Actual workers. Partially agriculturists. Females	Dependants.
1	2	587	588	589	590	591	592	593	594	595	596	597	598
	British Territory ..	**51,717**	**18,769**	**3,278**	**1,320**	**172**	**29,670**	**2,083,485**	**673,371**	**317,842**	**66,743**	**12,248**	**1,092,272**
	Agra Province ..	**38,048**	**14,056**	**1,685**	**973**	**119**	**22,307**	**1,637,651**	**523,828**	**252,855**	**45,952**	**9,016**	**860,968**
	Benares Division ..	*7,347*	*2,515*	*578*	*77*	*23*	*4,254*	*238,576*	*72,984*	*51,571*	*6,420*	*1,830*	*114,021*
1	Benares ..	4,592	1,946	228	10	2	2,418	69,538	21,466	11,170	1,797	434	36,902
2	Mirzapur ..	240	71	63	2	1	106	38,237	11,804	7,808	877	245	18,625
	Native States ..	**1,907**	**620**	**19**	**54**	..	**1,268**	**56,910**	**17,629**	**9,375**	**2,624**	**319**	**29,906**
3	Rampur ..	1,690	521	15	47	..	1,154	37,541	11,198	5,547	1,783	110	20,796
4	Tehri-Garhwal ..	101	32	..	1	..	69	3,314	1,173	69	192	4	2,072
5	Benares Raj ..	116	67	4	6	..	45	16,055	5,258	3,759	649	205	7,038

Class C.—Public administration

Sub-class VI.—

Order 44.—

Serial number.	District or State.	140—Army (Native States). Total workers and dependants.	Actual workers. Total. Males.	Actual workers. Total. Females.	Actual workers. Partially agriculturists. Males.	Actual workers. Partially agriculturists. Females.	Dependants.	Total, Order 42.—Army. Total workers and dependants.	Actual workers. Total. Males.	Actual workers. Total. Females.	Actual workers. Partially agriculturists. Males.	Actual workers. Partially agriculturists. Females.	Dependants.
1	2	611	612	613	614	615	616	617	618	619	620	621	622
	British Territory ..	**563**	**196**	**1**	**14**	..	**366**	**55,869**	**38,244**	**315**	**9,771**	**2**	**17,310**
	Agra Province ..	**502**	**186**	**1**	**11**	..	**315**	**43,304**	**30,091**	**172**	**7,815**	**2**	**13,041**
	Benares Division ..	..	..	..	..	..	..	*1,575*	*1,080*	..	*415*	..	*495*
1	Benares ..	..	..	..	..	..	..	1,099	995	..	406	..	104
2	Mirzapur ..	..	..	..	..	..	..	38	4	..	..	..	34
	Native States ..	**5,180**	**2,566**	..	**58**	..	**2,614**	**5,311**	**2,654**	..	**66**	..	**2,657**
3	Rampur ..	5,014	2,418	..	56	..	2,596	5,059	2,462	..	56	..	2,597
4	Tehri-Garhwal ..	12	6	..	2	..	6	96	50	..	10	..	46
5	Benares Raj ..	154	142	..	..	..	12	156	142	..	..	..	14

of material substances—(*continued*).

Trade—(*continued*).

Total, Order 39.—Trade in articles of luxury and those pertaining to letters and the arts and science.						Order 40.—Trade in refuse matter. 134.—Dealers in rags, stable refuse, &c.						
Total workers and dependants.	Actual workers. Total.		Actual workers. Partially agriculturists.		Dependants.	Total workers and dependants.	Actual workers. Total.		Actual workers. Partially agriculturists.		Dependants.	Serial number.
	Males.	Females	Males.	Females.			Males.	Females.	Males.	Females.		
575	576	577	578	579	580	581	582	583	584	585	586	1
51,360	**16,411**	**11,170**	**1,577**	**621**	**23,779**	**1,025**	**306**	**93**	**42**	**5**	**626**	
41,567	**13,642**	**8,602**	**1,069**	**433**	**19,323**	**447**	**166**	..	**1**	..	**281**	
7,651	*3,100*	*1,372*	*264*	*42*	*3,179*	*98*	*88*	..	..	..	*60*	
2,412	686	347	67	3	1,379	**96**	36	..	..	..	60	1
1,225	367	293	23	..	565	..	..	..	..	..	..	2
1,023	**299**	**177**	**56**	**6**	**547**	**5**	..	..	..	..	**5**	
851	235	124	39	3	492	**5**	..	..	..	..	5	3
7	6	..	..	..	1	..	..	..	..	..	..	4
165	58	53	17	3	54	..	..	..	..	..	..	5

material substances—(*continued*).

Total Class B.—Preparation and supply of material substances.						Class C.—Public administration and liberal arts. Sub-class VI.—Public Force. Order 42.—Army. 139.—Army (Imperial).						
Total workers and dependants.	Actual workers. Total.		Actual workers. Partially agriculturists.		Dependants.	Total workers and dependants.	Actual workers. Total.		Actual workers. Partially agriculturists.		Dependants.	Serial number.
	Males.	Females.	Males.	Females.			Males.	Females.	Males.	Females.		
599	600	601	602	603	604	605	606	607	608	609	610	1
8,243,877	**2,697,788**	**1,514,173**	**372,031**	**70,552**	**4,031,916**	**55,306**	**38,048**	**314**	**9,757**	**2**	**16,944**	
6,499,687	**2,118,224**	**1,149,693**	**254,069**	**47,319**	**3,231,770**	**42,802**	**29,905**	**171**	**7,804**	**2**	**12,726**	
820,300	*262,844*	*164,827*	*36,202*	*8,711*	*392,629*	*1,575*	*1,080*	..	*415*	..	*495*	
259,018	75,882	36,202	7,350	1,502	126,934	**1,099**	995	..	406	..	104	1
114,824	38,104	20,508	4,588	669	56,112	**38**	4	..	..	..	34	2
180,512	**58,905**	**30,960**	**11,683**	**1,611**	**90,647**	**131**	**88**	..	**8**	..	**43**	
108,431	32,508	16,802	7,459	552	59,121	**45**	44	..	..	..	1	3
11,446	3,902	843	521	19	7,201	**84**	44	..	8	..	40	4
60,635	22,495	13,815	3,703	1,040	24,325	**2**	..	..	..	..	2	5

and liberal arts—(*continued*).

Public Force—(*continued*).

Police—(*continued*).

142.—Police.						143.—Village watchmen.						
Total workers and dependants.	Actual workers. Total.		Actual workers. Partially agriculturists.		Dependants.	Total workers and dependants.	Actual workers. Total.		Actual workers. Partially agriculturists.		Dependants.	Serial number.
	Males.	Females.	Males.	Females.			Males	Females.	Males.	Females.		
623	624	625	626	627	628	629	630	631	632	633	634	1
85,462	**39,864**	**321**	**4,046**	..	**45,277**	**187,509**	**77,226**	**189**	**22,909**	**8**	**110,094**	
66,300	**31,486**	**321**	**3,248**	..	**34,493**	**145,571**	**58,975**	**165**	**14,005**	**8**	**86,431**	
7,673	*4,033*	*281*	*349*	..	*3,359*	*14,606*	*6,189*	..	*1,715*	..	*8,417*	
2,214	1,176	..	62	..	1,038	**2,535**	1,155	..	379	..	1,380	1
1,463	884	281	49	..	298	**4,988**	1,769	..	378	..	3,219	2
161	**94**	..	**13**	..	**67**	**2,298**	**902**	**2**	**397**	**2**	**1,394**	
..	..	..	..	..	..	**959**	327	2	190	2	680	3
69	45	..	9	..	24	**87**	42	..	8	..	45	4
92	49	..	4	..	43	**1,252**	538	..	199	..	719	5

Class C.—Public administration

Sub-class VI.—Public Force—(*concluded*).

Serial number.	District or State.	Order 44.—Police—(*concluded*). Total, Order 44.—Police. Total workers and dependants.	Actual workers. Total. Males.	Actual workers. Total. Females.	Actual workers. Partially agriculturists. Males.	Actual workers. Partially agriculturists. Females.	Dependants.	Total, Sub-class VI—Public Force. Total workers and dependants.	Actual workers. Total. Males.	Actual workers. Total. Females.	Actual workers. Partially agriculturists. Males.	Actual workers. Partially agriculturists. Females.	Dependants.
1	2	635	636	637	638	639	640	641	642	643	644	645	646
	British Territory ..	**272,971**	**117,090**	**510**	**26,955**	**8**	**155,371**	**328,857**	**155,338**	**825**	**36,726**	**10**	**172,694**
	Agra Province ..	**211,871**	**90,461**	**486**	**17,253**	**8**	**120,924**	**255,182**	**120,552**	**658**	**25,068**	**10**	**133,972**
	Benares Division ..	*22,279*	*10,222*	*281*	*2,064*	..	*11,776*	*23,854*	*11,302*	*281*	*2,479*	..	*12,271*
1	Benares	**4,749**	2,331	..	441	..	2,418	**5,848**	3,826	..	847	..	2,522
2	Mirzapur	**6,451**	2,653	281	422	..	3,517	**6,489**	2,657	281	422	..	3,551
	Native States ..	**2,459**	**996**	**2**	**410**	**2**	**1,461**	**7,770**	**3,650**	**2**	**476**	**2**	**4,118**
3	Rampur	**959**	327	2	190	2	630	**6,018**	2,789	2	246	2	3,227
4	Tehri-Garhwal ..	**156**	87	..	17	..	69	**252**	187	..	27	..	115
5	Benares Raj ..	**1,344**	582	..	203	..	762	**1,600**	724	..	203	..	776

Class C.—Public administration

Sub-class VII.—Public

Order 45.—Public

Serial number.	District or State.	146.—Municipal and other local (not village) service. Total workers and dependants.	Actual workers. Total. Males.	Actual workers. Total. Females.	Actual workers. Partially agriculturists. Males.	Actual workers. Partially agriculturists. Females.	Dependants.	147.—Village officials and servants other than watchmen. Total workers and dependants.	Actual workers. Total. Males	Actual workers. Total. Females	Actual workers. Partially agriculturists. Males.	Actual workers. Partially agriculturists. Females.	Dependants.
1	2	659	660	661	662	663	664	665	666	667	668	669	670
	British Territory ..	**20,868**	**7,798**	**122**	**448**	..	**12,948**	**104,477**	**30,736**	**35**	**4,337**	**7**	**73,706**
	Agra Province ..	**16,999**	**6,428**	**110**	**369**	..	**10,461**	**77,049**	**22,542**	**34**	**2,473**	**7**	**54,473**
	Benares Division ..	*1,223*	*422*	*1*	*76*	..	*800*	*9,530*	*3,104*	..	*255*	..	*6,426*
1	Benares	**709**	273	1	10	..	435	**1,811**	530	..	44	..	1,281
2	Mirzapur	**98**	34	..	..	..	64	**1,640**	553	..	20	..	1,087
	Native States ..	**29**	**12**	..	**3**	..	**17**	**2,346**	**653**	..	**49**	..	**1,693**
3	Rampur	**10**	6	..	..	..	4	**1,589**	401	..	16	..	1,188
4	Tehri-Garhwal ..	**8**	5	..	8	..	8	**30**	6	..	6	..	24
5	Benares Raj ..	**11**	1	..	..	..	10	**727**	246	..	27	..	481

Class C.—Public administration

Sub-class VIII.—Profession

Order 46.—Religion.

Serial number.	District or State.	149.—Religious mendicants, inmates of monasteries, &c. Total workers and dependants.	Actual workers. Total. Males.	Actual workers. Total. Females.	Actual workers. Partially agriculturists. Males	Actual workers. Partially agriculturists. Females	Dependants.	Total order 46—Religion. Total workers and dependants.	Actual workers. Total. Males.	Actual workers. Total. Females	Actual workers. Partially agriculturists. Males.	Actual workers. Partially agriculturists. Females	Dependants.
1	2	683	684	685	686	687	688	689	690	691	692	693	694
	British Territory ..	**21,405**	**9,097**	**4,781**	**963**	**66**	**7,527**	**263,607**	**98,087**	**22,213**	**16,490**	**1,325**	**143,307**
	Agra Province ..	**5,353**	**2,315**	**1,526**	**109**	**14**	**1,512**	**209,922**	**76,180**	**16,292**	**11,873**	**1,051**	**117,450**
	Benares Division ..	*173*	*140*	*1*	..	..	*82*	*25,618*	*9,181*	*2,191*	*1,294*	*131*	*14,296*
1	Benares	**23**	8	..	..	..	15	**13,440**	4,830	702	498	21	7,908
2	Mirzapur	**126**	126	..	..	..	..	**4,442**	1,244	517	178	23	2,681
	Native States ..	**3,154**	**1,086**	**414**	**152**	**9**	**1,654**	**7,580**	**2,544**	**586**	**588**	**22**	**4,450**
3	Rampur	**2,723**	970	296	150	9	1,457	**4,110**	1,470	343	248	12	2,297
4	Tehri-Garhwal ..	**431**	116	118	2	..	197	**2,618**	730	151	263	..	1,787
5	Benares Raj ..	..	..	..	..	..	..	**852**	344	92	77	10	416

and liberal arts—(*continued*).

Sub-class VII.—Public administration—(*continued*).

Order 45.—Public administration—(*continued*).

144.—Service of the State.						145.—Service of Native and Foreign States.						
Total workers and dependants.	Actual workers.				Dependants.	Total workers and dependants.	Actual workers.				Dependants.	Serial number.
	Total.		Partially agriculturists.				Total.		Partially agriculturists.			
	Males.	Females	Males.	Females.			Males.	Females.	Males.	Females		
647	648	649	650	651	652	653	654	655	656	657	658	1
122,624	**41,623**	**172**	**3,814**	**6**	**80,829**	**3,454**	**1,015**	**11**	**102**	**7**	**2,428**	
92,935	**31,821**	**157**	**2,828**	**6**	**60,957**	**3,276**	**983**	**11**	**97**	**7**	**2,282**	
12,244	*4,646*	*11*	*441*	*1*	*7,587*	*102*	*88*	..	*4*	..	*69*	
3,635	1,318	2	78	..	2,820	**7**	..	..	..	..	7	1
1,390	581	..	29	..	809	**46**	22	..	4	..	24	2
398	**164**	..	**53**	..	**234**	**15,397**	**4,641**	**163**	**279**	..	**10,593**	
37	7	..	..	..	30	**14,628**	4,340	168	195	..	10,125	3
56	27	..	18	..	29	**225**	63	..	89	..	162	4
305	130	..	85	..	175	**544**	238	..	45	..	303	5

and liberal arts—(*continued*).

administration—(*concluded*).

administration—(*concluded*).

Sub-class VIII Professions and liberal arts.

Order 46.—Religion.

Total order 45 and sub-class VII.—Public administration.						148.—Priests, ministers, &c.						
Total workers and dependants.	Actual workers.				Dependants.	Total workers and dependants.	Actual workers.				Dependants.	Serial number.
	Total.		Partially agriculturists.				Total.		Partially agriculturists.			
	Males.	Females.	Males.	Females.			Males.	Females.	Males.	Females.		
671	672	673	674	675	676	677	678	679	680	681	682	1
251,423	**81,172**	**340**	**8,701**	**20**	**169,911**	**202,685**	**74,496**	**15,294**	**13,488**	**1,173**	**112,896**	
190,259	**61,774**	**312**	**5,767**	**20**	**128,173**	**172,388**	**62,233**	**13,027**	**10,087**	**962**	**97,128**	
23,099	*8,205*	*12*	*776*	*1*	*14,882*	*21,357*	*7,286*	*2,066*	*1,062*	*130*	*12,005*	
6,162	2,116	8	182	..	4 048	**10,744**	8,628	661	815	21	6,455	1
3,174	1,190	..	53	..	1,984	**3,333**	846	445	134	22	2,042	2
18,170	**5,470**	**165**	**384**	..	**12,537**	**1,599**	**539**	**118**	**134**	**10**	**942**	
16,264	4,754	163	211	..	11,347	**1,067**	865	86	89	2	666	3
319	101	..	66	..	218	**29**	10	..	1	..	19	4
1,587	615	..	107	..	972	**503**	164	82	**44**	8	257	5

and liberal arts—(*continued*).

and liberal arts—(*continued*).

Order 47.—Law—(*concluded*).

152.—Lawyers of all kinds, including kazis, law agents and mukhtiars.						Total order 47—Law.						
Total workers and dependants.	Actual workers.				Dependants.	Total workers and dependants.	Actual workers.				Dependants.	Serial number.
	Total.		Partially agriculturists.				Total.		Partially agriculturists.			
	Males.	Females.	Males.	Females.			Males.	Females.	Males.	Females.		
695	696	697	698	699	700	701	702	703	704	705	706	1
16,630	**4,282**	**55**	**624**	..	**12,293**	**36,941**	**9,995**	**74**	**1,192**	..	**26,872**	
13,402	**3,670**	**55**	**503**	..	**9,677**	**28,537**	**7,934**	**71**	**922**	..	**20,532**	
2,111	*432*	*4*	*71*	..	*1,675*	*3,768*	*952*	*4*	*133*	..	*2,812*	
854	151	..	10	..	708	**1,530**	381	..	25	..	1,199	1
87	20	..	1	..	67	**286**	95	..	8	..	191	2
257	**46**	..	**5**	..	**191**	**575**	**183**	**5**	**24**	..	**387**	
252	**44**	..	4	..	188	**390**	122	5	4	..	268	3
5	2	..	1	..	3	**26**	8	..	7	..	18	4
..	..	..	..	..	..	**159**	53	..	13	..	106	5

Class C.—Public administration

Sub-class VIII.—Professions

Order 48.—Medicine.

Serial number.	District or State.	154.—Medical practitioners of all kinds, including dentists, oculists and veterinary surgeons. Total workers and dependants.	Actual workers. Total. Males.	Actual workers. Total. Females.	Actual workers. Partially agriculturists. Males	Actual workers. Partially agriculturists. Females.	Dependants.	155.—Midwives, vaccinators, compounders, nurses, masseurs, &c. Total workers and dependants.	Actual workers. Total. Males.	Actual workers. Total. Females	Actual workers. Partially agriculturists. Males.	Actual workers. Partially agriculturists. Females	Dependants.
1	2	707	708	709	710	711	712	713	714	715	716	717	718
	British Territory ..	**29,559**	**8,678**	**491**	**765**	**8**	**20,390**	**31,683**	**3,214**	**18,075**	**187**	**305**	**10,394**
	Agra Province ..	**22,297**	**6,634**	**282**	**575**	**7**	**15,381**	**23,553**	**2,331**	**13,574**	**115**	**180**	**7,648**
	Benares Division ..	*2,458*	*609*	*44*	*24*	..	*1,805*	*708*	*165*	*193*	*8*	*1*	*850*
1	Benares	1,762	412	37	3	..	1,313	336	66	95	4	..	175
2	Mirzapur	107	46	3	4	..	52	134	48	36	2	..	50
	Native States ..	**491**	**128**	**5**	**16**	..	**360**	**372**	**35**	**140**	**1**	..	**197**
3	Rampur	443	108	2	18	..	333	307	30	121	..	..	156
4	Tehri-Garhwal ..	40	17	1	8	..	22	24	1	1	..	..	22
5	Benares Raj ..	8	3	..	..	..	5	41	4	18	1	..	19

Class C.—Public administration

Sub-class VIII.—Professions

Order 50.—Letters and arts and sciences.

Serial number.	District or State	Total order 50.—Letters and arts and sciences. Total workers and dependants.	Actual workers. Total. Males.	Actual workers. Total. Females.	Actual workers. Partially agriculturists. Males.	Actual workers. Partially agriculturists. Females.	Dependants.	Total sub-class VIII.—Professions and liberal arts. Total workers and dependants.	Actual workers. Total. Males.	Actual workers. Total. Females.	Actual workers. Partially agriculturists. Males.	Actual workers. Partially agriculturists. Females.	Dependants.
1	2	731	732	733	734	735	736	737	738	739	740	741	742
	British Territory ..	**90,653**	**28,292**	**16,440**	**2,431**	**724**	**45,921**	**518,297**	**173,867**	**59,131**	**23,800**	**2,388**	**285,299**
	Agra Province ..	**66,821**	**20,713**	**12,005**	**1,549**	**507**	**34,103**	**400,028**	**132,894**	**43,614**	**17,066**	**1,757**	**223,520**
	Benares Division ..	*8,966*	*1,925*	*2,534*	*205*	*33*	*4,507*	*46,756*	*14,880*	*5,126*	*1,930*	*167*	*26,750*
1	Benares	4,881	598	1,886	44	8	2,397	24,276	7,107	2,812	641	29	14,357
2	Mirzapur	460	165	50	3	..	245	5,963	1,822	621	234	23	3,520
	Native States ..	**5,660**	**1,985**	**317**	**145**	**6**	**3,358**	**15,730**	**5,259**	**1,062**	**790**	**28**	**9,409**
3	Rampur	1,407	411	188	53	6	808	7,506	2,437	667	324	18	4,402
4	Tehri-Garhwal ..	3,895	1,422	83	80	..	2,390	6,689	2,216	236	363	..	4,237
5	Benares Raj ..	358	152	46	12	..	160	1,535	606	159	103	10	770

Class D.—Miscellaneous.

Sub-class X.—Domestic service.

Order 52.—Domestic service.

Serial number.	District or State.	162.—Cooks, water carriers, door keepers, watchmen and other indoor servants. Total workers and dependants.	Actual workers. Total. Males.	Actual workers. Total. Females	Actual workers. Partially agriculturists. Males.	Actual workers. Partially agriculturists. Females.	Dependants.	163.—Private grooms, coachmen, dog boys, &c. Total workers and dependants.	Actual workers. Total. Males.	Actual workers. Total. Females.	Actual workers. Partially agriculturists. Males.	Actual workers. Partially agriculturists. Females.	Dependants.
1	2	755	756	757	758	759	760	761	762	763	764	765	766
	British Territory ..	**823,733**	**281,665**	**222,590**	**18,386**	**6,777**	**319,478**	**74,743**	**34,104**	**383**	**1,750**	**16**	**40,258**
	Agra Province ..	**686,924**	**235,841**	**176,589**	**15,195**	**5,393**	**274,494**	**53,417**	**24,162**	**302**	**1,083**	**7**	**28,955**
	Benares Division ..	*77,580*	*23,023*	*27,974*	*1,958*	*1,047*	*26,583*	*5,560*	*2,673*	*42*	*178*	*6*	*2,845*
1	Benares	24,401	7,820	7,274	673	261	9,307	2,438	1,226	7	64	5	1,205
2	Mirzapur	10,959	3,519	3,526	194	64	3,914	842	315	16	4	..	511
	Native States ..	**21,284**	**6,790**	**4,476**	**679**	**142**	**10,018**	**1,454**	**760**	**2**	**64**	..	**692**
3	Rampur	16,847	6,008	2,445	592	13	8,394	1,112	576	7	34	..	585
4	Tehri-Garhwal ..	2,365	225	1,019	2	47	1,121	111	42	..	4	..	69
5	Benares Raj ..	2,072	557	1,012	85	82	503	231	142	1	26	..	88

and liberal arts—(*continued*).

and liberal arts—(*continued*).

Total order 48.—Medicine. | Order 49.—Instruction. 156.—Professors and teachers of all kinds (except law, medicines, music, dancing and drawing), and clerks and servants connected with education.

Total workers and dependants.	Actual workers. Total. Males.	Actual workers. Total. Females.	Partially agriculturists. Males.	Partially agriculturists. Females.	Dependants.	Total workers and dependants.	Actual workers. Total. Males.	Actual workers. Total. Females.	Partially agriculturists. Males.	Partially agriculturists. Females.	Dependants.	Serial number.
719	720	721	722	723	724	725	726	727	728	729	730	1
61,242	11,892	18,566	952	313	30,784	65,854	25,601	1,838	2,735	26	38,415	
45,850	8,965	13,856	690	187	23,029	48,898	19,102	1,390	2,032	12	28,406	
3,166	*774*	*237*	*32*	*1*	*2,155*	*5,238*	*2,098*	*160*	*266*	*2*	*2,980*	
2,098	478	182	7	..	1,488	2,327	870	92	67	..	1,365	1
235	94	39	6	..	102	540	224	15	44	..	301	2
863	163	143	17	..	557	1,052	384	11	16	..	657	
750	138	123	13	..	489	849	293	8	6	..	545	3
64	18	2	3	..	44	86	38	..	10	..	48	4
49	7	18	1	..	24	117	50	3	..	..	64	5

and liberal arts—(*concluded*).

and liberal arts—(*concluded*).

Total class C.—Public administration and liberal arts. | Class D.—Miscellaneous. Sub-class IX.—Persons living on their income. Order 51—Persons living principally on their income. 161.—Proprietors (other than of agricultural land) fund and scholarship holders and pensioners.

Total workers and dependants.	Actual workers. Total. Males.	Actual workers. Total. Females.	Partially agriculturists. Males.	Partially agriculturists. Females.	Dependants.	Total workers and dependants.	Actual workers. Total. Males.	Actual workers. Total. Females.	Partially agriculturists. Males.	Partially agriculturists. Females.	Dependants.	Serial number.
743	744	745	746	747	748	749	750	751	752	753	754	1
1,098,377	410,377	60,296	69,227	2,418	627,904	68,602	19,470	7,274	3,635	213	41,858	
845,469	315,220	44,584	47,901	1,787	485,665	40,847	11,699	3,864	1,459	46	25,284	
93,709	*34,387*	*5,419*	*5,185*	*168*	*53,903*	*5,519*	*1,243*	*915*	*116*	*4*	*8,861*	
36,286	12,549	2,815	1,620	29	20,922	4,073	819	723	16	1	2,591	1
15,626	5,669	902	709	23	9,055	197	49	28	4	..	120	2
41,670	14,379	1,227	1,650	30	26,064	1,237	371	169	20	2	697	
29,788	9,980	832	781	20	18,976	1,166	329	165	16	1	672	3
7,260	2,454	236	456	..	4,570	33	23	3	1	1	7	4
4,622	1,945	159	413	10	2,518	38	19	1	3	..	18	5

Class D.—Miscellaneous.

Total Order.—52 and sub-class X.—Domestic service. | Sub-class XI.—Insufficiently described occupations. Order 53.—General terms which do not indicate a definite occuption. 164.—Manufacturers, businessmen and contractors otherwise unspecified.

Total workers and dependants.	Actual workers. Total. Males.	Actual workers. Total. Females.	Partially agriculturists. Males.	Partially agriculturists. Females.	Dependants.	Total workers and dependants.	Actual workers. Total. Males.	Actual workers. Total. Females.	Partially agriculturists. Males.	Partially agriculturists. Females.	Dependants.	Serial number.
767	768	769	770	771	772	773	774	775	776	777	778	1
898,476	315,769	222,973	20,136	6,793	359,734	15,759	5,742	330	524	31	9,687	
740,341	260,093	176,891	16,278	5,400	303,447	10,490	3,573	187	250	11	6,730	
83 140	*25,696*	*28,016*	*2,126*	*1,053*	*29,428*	*1,169*	*413*	*21*	*39*	..	*735*	
26,839	9,046	7,281	787	206	10,512	624	198	10	7	..	416	1
11,801	3,834	3,542	198	64	4,425	229	82	5	17	..	142	2
22,738	7,550	4,478	743	142	10,710	331	163	8	36	1	160	
17,959	6,584	2,443	626	13	8,929	303	144	8	34	1	151	3
2,476	267	1,019	6	47	1,190	28	19	..	2	..	9	4
2,303	699	1,013	111	82	591	..	..	..	..	..	..	5

Serial number	District or State.	Class D.—Miscellaneous— Sub-class XI.—Insufficiently described occupations—(*concluded*). Order 53.—General terms which do not indicate a definite occupation—(*concluded*).											
		167.—Labourers and workmen otherwise unspecified.						Total order 53.—General terms which do not indicate a definite occupation and sub-class XI.—Insufficiently described occupations.					
		Total workers and dependants.	Actual workers.				Dependants.	Total workers and dependants.	Actual workers.				Dependants.
			Total.		Partially agriculturists.				Total.		Partially agriculturists.		
			Males.	Females.	Males.	Females.			Males.	Females.	Males.	Females.	
1	2	779	780	781	782	783	784	785	786	787	788	789	790
	British Territory ..	**1,587,221**	**590,812**	**318,016**	**26,908**	**5,346**	**678,393**	**1,643,786**	**610,553**	**320,080**	**27,967**	**5,410**	**713,153**
	Agra Province ..	**1,360,497**	**500,714**	**269,994**	**20,675**	**4,303**	**389,789**	**1,399,846**	**514,663**	**271,318**	**21,272**	**4,331**	**613,865**
	Benares Division ..	*97,720*	*29,190*	*33,132*	*1,666*	*225*	*35,398*	*107,887*	*32,897*	*33,909*	*1,784*	*238*	*41,081*
1	Benares ..	**33,431**	11,482	10,059	572	114	11,890	**39,149**	13,854	10,265	614	115	15,030
2	Mirzapur ..	**13,766**	3,794	5,520	47	1	4,452	**14,278**	3,962	5,570	56	4	4,746
	Native States ..	**16,506**	**5,813**	**3,220**	**372**	**21**	**7,473**	**17,308**	**6,231**	**3,235**	**455**	**23**	**7,842**
3	Rampur ..	**12,408**	4,541	1,570	313	21	6,297	**13,070**	4,889	1,580	378	23	6,601
4	Tehri-Garhwal ..	**234**	111	9	51	..	114	**297**	141	9	54	..	147
5	Benares Raj ..	**3,864**	1,161	1,641	8	..	1,062	**3,941**	1,201	1,646	23	..	1,094

Serial number.	District or State.	Class D.—Miscellaneous—(*concluded*).											
		Sub-class XII.—Unproductive—(*concluded*). Total Sub-class XII.—Unproductive.						Total class D.—Miscellaneous.					
		Total workers and dependants.	Actual workers.				Dependants.	Total workers and dependants.	Actual workers				Dependants.
			Total.		Partially agriculturists.				Total.		Partially agriculturists.		
			Males.	Females	Males.	Females.			Males.	Females.	Males.	Females.	
1	2	803	804	805	806	807	808	809	810	811	812	813	814
	British Territory ..	**514,388**	**205,087**	**103,637**	**14,284**	**2,497**	**205,664**	**3,125,252**	**1,150,879**	**653,964**	**66,022**	**14,913**	**1,320,409**
	Agra Province ..	**394,447**	**160,021**	**72,252**	**9,920**	**1,527**	**162,174**	**2,575,481**	**946,386**	**524,325**	**48,929**	**11,304**	**1,104,770**
	Benares Division ..	*39,847*	*16,011*	*10,490*	*704*	*118*	*13,346*	*236,393*	*75,347*	*73,330*	*4,780*	*1,413*	*87,216*
1	Benares ..	**13,218**	6,282	2,995	95	8	3,941	**83,279**	30,001	21,264	1,462	390	32,014
2	Mirzapur ..	**7,712**	2,704	1,960	73	10	3,048	**33,988**	10,549	11,100	331	78	12,339
	Native States ..	**6,729**	**2,589**	**1,182**	**166**	**25**	**2,958**	**48,012**	**16,741**	**9,064**	**1,384**	**192**	**22,207**
3	Rampur ..	**2,902**	1,033	476	58	1	1,393	**35,097**	12,835	4,667	1,073	38	17,595
4	Tehri-Garhwal ..	**1,694**	589	330	8	..	775	**4,500**	1,020	1,361	69	48	2,119
5	Benares Raj ..	**2,133**	967	376	105	24	790	**8,415**	2,886	3,036	242	106	2,493

(*continued*).

Sub-class XII.—Unproductive.

Order 54.—Inmates of jails, asylums and hospitals. 168.—Inmates of jails, asylums and hospitals.						Order 55.—Beggars, vagrants, prostitutes. 169.—Beggars, vagrants, procurers, prostitutes, receivers of stolen goods, cattle poisoners.						
Total workers and dependants.	Actual workers. Total. Males.	Actual workers. Total. Females	Actual workers. Partially agriculturists. Males	Actual workers. Partially agriculturists. Females.	Dependants.	Total workers and dependants.	Actual workers. Total. Males.	Actual workers. Total. Females.	Actual workers. Partially agriculturists. Males.	Actual workers. Partially agriculturists. Females.	Dependants.	Serial number.
791	792	793	794	795	796	797	798	799	800	801	802	1
24,114	**21,704**	**1,189**	**122**	**9**	**1,221**	**490,274**	**165,363**	**102,448**	**14,162**	**2,488**	**204,443**	
19,129	**16,905**	**1,093**	**122**	**9**	**1,131**	**375,318**	**143,116**	**71,159**	**9,798**	**1,518**	**161,043**	
2,099	*1,859*	*178*	..	..	*62*	*37,748*	*14,152*	*10,312*	*704*	*118*	*13,284*	
1 827	1,683	108	..	..	24	**11,391**	4,647	2,827	95	8	3,917	1
100	62	..	..	..	38	**7,612**	2,642	1,960	78	10	3,010	3
485	**471**	**1**	..	..	**13**	**6,244**	**2,118**	**1,181**	**166**	**25**	**2,945**	
433	420	..	..	..	13	**2,469**	613	476	53	1	1,380	8
52	51	1	..	..	..	**1,642**	588	329	8	..	775	4
..	..	..	..	..	..	**2,133**	967	376	105	24	790	5

TABLE XVII.—Territorial Distribution of

All denominations.

Serial number.	District or State.	Total. Persons.	Total. Males.	Total. Females.	Distribution by race. Europeans and allied races. Males.	Europeans and allied races. Females.	Anglo-Indians. Males.	Anglo-Indians. Females.
1	2	3	4	5	6	7	8	9
	British Territory ..	**177,908**	**100,797**	**77,111**	**24,730**	**8,647**	**4,044**	**4,048**
	Agra Province	**163,028**	**91,290**	**71,738**	**19,107**	**7,091**	**3,283**	**3,246**
	Benares Division ..	*4,317*	*2,068*	*2,254*	*527*	*292*	*176*	*228*
1	Benares	1,930	927	1,003	382	151	111	181
2	Mirzapur	694	818	881	98	95	43	77
	Native States	**1,786**	**945**	**841**	**17**	**17**	..	**2**
3	Rampur	1,739	921	818	10	9	..	2
4	Tehri-Garhwal	6	3	3	2	2	..	..
5	Benares Raj	41	21	20	5	6	..	..

Baptist.

Serial number.	District or State.	Total. Persons.	Total. Males.	Total. Females.	Distribution by race. Europeans and allied races. Males.	Europeans and allied races. Females.	Anglo-Indians. Males.	Anglo-Indians. Females.
1	2	21	22	23	24	25	26	27
	British Territory ..	**2,587**	**1,359**	**1,228**	**161**	**96**	**58**	**63**
	Agra Province	**2,390**	**1 259**	**1,131**	**127**	**76**	**53**	**52**
	Benares Division ..	*55*	*18*	*37*	4	*8*	4	4
1	Benares	40	10	30	1	1	3	2
2	Mirzapur	7	4	3	3	1	1	2
	Native States	**15**	**2**	**13**	..	..	..	..
3	Rampur	8	2	6	..	..	..	..
4	Tehri-Garhwal	..	..	..	..	..	..	..
5	Benares Raj	7	..	7	..	..	..	..

Serial number.	District or State.	Protestants (unsectarian or sect not specified). Total. Persons.	Total. Males.	Total. Females.	Distribution by race. Europeans and allied races. Males.	Europeans and allied races. Females.	Anglo-Indians. Males.	Anglo-Indians. Females.	Indians. Males.	Indians. Females.	Roman Total. Persons.	Total. Males.	Total. Females.
1	2	39	40	41	42	43	44	45	46	47	48	49	50
	British Territory ..	**2,212**	**1,288**	**924**	**239**	**207**	**141**	**117**	**908**	**600**	**10,695**	**6,985**	**3,710**
	Agra Province	**1,712**	**1,005**	**707**	**173**	**146**	**116**	**82**	**716**	**479**	**8,729**	**5,661**	**3,068**
	Benares Division ..	*93*	*32*	*61*	*6*	*11*	*2*	*4*	*24*	*46*	*352*	*213*	*139*
1	Benares	48	16	32	3	8	1	4	12	20	274	179	95
2	Mirzapur	9	6	3	1	1	..	..	5	2	65	27	38
	Native States	**8**	**6**	**2**	..	**2**	..	..	**6**	..	**14**	**8**	**6**
3	Rampur	2	..	2	..	2	..	..	..	..	11	6	5
4	Tehri-Garhwal	..	..	..	..	..	..	..	..	..	..	..	..
5	Benares Raj	6	6	..	..	..	..	..	6	..	3	2	1

TABLE XVIII.—Christians by race and age.

Serial number.	District or State.	Total. Total.	Total. Males.	Total. Females.	Europeans and allied races. British subjects. All ages. Total.	All ages. Males.	All ages. Females.	0—12. Males.	0—12. Females.	12—15. Males.	12—15. Females.	15—30. Males.	15—30. Females.	30—50. Males.	30—50. Females	50 and over Males.	50 and over Females.
1	2	3	4	5	6	7	8	9	10	11	12	13	14	15	16	17	18
	British Territory ..	**41,469**	**28,774**	**12,695**	**32,780**	**24,445**	**8,335**	**2,273**	**2,128**	**443**	**382**	**16,220**	**2,470**	**4,591**	**2,554**	**918**	**801**
	Agra Province ..	**32,727**	**22,390**	**10,337**	**25,766**	**18,919**	**6,847**	**1,882**	**1,748**	**392**	**326**	**12,158**	**2,022**	**3,684**	**2,068**	**803**	**683**
	Benares Division ..	*1,228*	*703*	*520*	*799*	*515*	*284*	*70*	*58*	*8*	*11*	*249*	*78*	*144*	*100*	*44*	*37*
1	Benares ..	775	493	282	513	370	143	39	38	4	6	229	37	83	52	15	10
2	Mirzapur ..	318	141	172	193	98	95	26	14	3	3	14	25	85	33	20	20
	Native States ..	**36**	**17**	**19**	**31**	**16**	**15**	**6**	**1**	**1**	..	**4**	**6**	**3**	**6**	**2**	**2**
3	Rampur ..	21	10	11	17	9	8	5	..	..	..	1	3	1	4	2	1
4	Tehri-Garhwal ..	4	2	2	3	2	1	..	..	1	..	..	..	1	1	..	..
5	Benares Raj ..	11	5	6	11	5	6	1	1	..	..	3	3	1	1	..	1

Indians.		Anglican Communion. Total.			Distribution by race. Europeans and allied races.		Anglo-Indians.		Indians.		Serial number.
Males.	Females.	Persons.	Males.	Females.	Males.	Females.	Males.	Females.	Males.	Females	
10	11	12	13	14	15	16	17	18	19	20	1
72,02[illegible]	**64,416**	**30,900**	**20,320**	**10,580**	**14,828**	**5,499**	**2,149**	**2,115**	**3,343**	**2,966**	
68,900	**61,401**	**24,589**	**15,869**	**8,720**	**11,085**	**4,478**	**1,712**	**1,695**	**3,072**	**2,547**	
1,360	*1,734*	*1,264*	*530*	*734*	*271*	*182*	*107*	*146*	*152*	*406*	
434	721	861	356	505	182	93	57	66	117	346	1
172	209	263	119	144	65	65	34	62	20	17	2
928	**822**	**12**	**7**	**5**	**7**	**4**	..	..	..	**1**	
911	807	7	3	4	3	3	..	..	..	1	3
1	1	3	2	1	2	1	..	..	..	..	4
16	14	2	2	..	2	..	..	..	..	..	5

Indians.		Congregationalist. Total.			Distribution by race. Europeans and allied races.		Anglo-Indians.		Indians.		Serial number.
Males.	Females.	Persons.	Males.	Females.	Males.	Females.	Males.	Females.	Males.	Females.	
28	29	30	31	32	33	34	35	36	37	38	1
1,140	**1,069**	**975**	**445**	**530**	**63**	**38**	**14**	**7**	**368**	**485**	
1,079	**1,003**	**959**	**440**	**519**	**58**	**32**	**14**	**7**	**368**	**480**	
10	*30*	*242*	*95*	*147*	*6*	*3*	*1*	..	*88*	*144*	
6	27	50	21	29	2	1	..	..	19	28	1
..	..	190	74	116	4	1	1	..	69	115	2
..	**13**	**12**	**5**	**7**	**2**	**5**	..	..	**3**	**2**	
2	6	..	..	..	..	..	..	..	..	..	3
..	..	..	..	..	..	..	..	..	..	..	4
..	7	12	5	7	2	5	..	..	3	2	5

Catholic. Distribution by race. Europeans and allied races.		Anglo-Indians.		Indians.		Sect not returned. Total.			Distribution by race. Europeans and allied races.		Anglo-Indians.		Indians.		Serial number.
Males.	Females.	Males.	Females.	Males.	Females.	Persons.	Males.	Females.	Males.	Females.	Males.	Females.	Males.	Females.	
51	52	53	54	55	56	57	58	59	60	61	62	63	64	65	1
4,065	**1,632**	**1,336**	**887**	**1,584**	**1,191**	**10,030**	**5,164**	**4,866**	**398**	**141**	**88**	**438**	**4,678**	**4,287**	
3,230	**3,358**	**1,135**	**703**	**1,296**	**1,007**	**8,794**	**4,492**	**4,302**	**384**	**130**	**62**	**407**	**4,046**	**3,765**	
91	*58*	*54*	*64*	*68*	*17*	*648*	*317*	*331*	*3*	*2*	..	..	*314*	*329*	
68	29	47	51	64	15	1	1	..	..	..	..	..	1	..	1
19	24	5	12	8	2	89	44	45	..	..	..	..	44	45	2
7	**5**	..	..	**1**	**1**	**14**	**8**	**6**	..	..	..	..	**8**	**6**	
6	4	..	..	..	1	3	2	1	..	..	..	..	2	1	3
..	..	..	..	..	..	..	..	..	..	..	..	..	..	..	4
1	1	..	..	1	..	11	6	5	..	..	..	..	6	5	5

TABLE VII.

Name of Municipality.	Civil condition and Religion.		Population. Persons.	Population. Males.	Population. Females.	0—5. Males.	0—5. Females.
1	2		3	4	5	6	7
Cawnpore.	Total	*Total*	*167,660*	*97,489*	*70,171*	*8,273*	*8,356*
		Hindus	121,459	71,270	50,189	5,798	5,877
		Muhammadans	43,731	24,891	18,840	2,317	2,331
		Minor Religions	2,470	1,328	1,142	159	148
	Unmarried	*Total*	*56,728*	*36,701*	*20,027*	*8,272*	*8,355*
		Hindus	38,558	25,337	13,221	5,798	5,877
		Muhammadans	16,883	10,648	6,235	2,316	2,330
		Minor Religions	1,287	716	571	158	148
	Married	*Total*	*86,364*	*49,779*	*36,585*	*1*	*1*
		Hindus	63,737	37,273	26,464	..	..
		Muhammadans	21,660	11,982	9,678	1	1
		Minor Religions	967	524	443	..	..
	Widowed	*Total*	*24,568*	*11,009*	*13,559*	..	..
		Hindus	19,164	8,660	10,504	..	..
		Muhammadans	5,188	2,261	2,927	..	..
		Minor Religions	216	88	128	..	..
Jaunpur.	Total	*Total*	*32,501*	*16,863*	*15,638*	*1,775*	*1,820*
		Hindus	18,520	9,808	8,712	1,022	1,040
		Muhammadans	13,800	6,953	6,847	744	772
		Minor Religions	181	102	79	9	8
	Unmarried	*Total*	*11,134*	*6,720*	*4,414*	*1,759*	*1,798*
		Hindus	5,614	3,449	2,165	1,010	1,021
		Muhammadans	5,445	3,226	2,219	741	769
		Minor Religions	75	45	30	8	8
	Married	*Total*	*16,230*	*8,482*	*7,748*	*14*	*22*
		Hindus	9,858	5,343	4,515	11	19
		Muhammadans	6,292	3,094	3,198	2	3
		Minor Religions	80	45	35	1	..
	Widowed	*Total*	*5,137*	*1,661*	*3,476*	*2*	..
		Hindu	3,048	1,016	2,032	1	..
		Muhammadans	2,063	633	1,430	1	..
		Minor Religions	26	12	14	..	..
Mirzapur.	Total	*Total*	*54,794*	*28,672*	*26,122*	*2,976*	*3,080*
		Hindus	43,915	22,950	20,965	2,327	2,441
		Muhammadans	10,521	5,565	4,956	636	615
		Minor Religions	358	157	201	13	24
	Unmarried	*Total*	*16,245*	*9,700*	*6,545*	*2,696*	*2,981*
		Hindus	12,233	7,349	4,884	2,084	2,372
		Muhammadans	3,823	2,275	1,548	599	585
		Minor Religions	189	76	113	13	24
	Married	*Total*	*28,336*	*14,605*	*13,733*	*265*	*85*
		Hindus	22,901	11,765	11,136	235	57
		Muhammadans	5,315	2,772	2,543	30	28
		Minor Religions	122	68	54	..	..
	Widowed	*Total*	*10,211*	*4,367*	*5,844*	*15*	*14*
		Hindus	8,781	3,836	4,945	8	12
		Muhammadans	1,383	518	865	7	2
		Minor Religions	47	13	34	..	..
Fyzabad.	Total	*Total*	*54,187*	*30,125*	*24,062*	*2,529*	*2,508*
		Hindus	40,808	23,029	17,779	1,752	1,766
		Muhammadans	12,968	6,866	6,102	747	716
		Minor Religions	411	230	181	30	21
	Unmarried ..	*Total*	*17,617*	*11,471*	*6,146*	*2,489*	*2,470*
		Hindus	12,726	8,495	4,231	1,719	1,735
		Muhammadans	4,728	2,876	1,852	740	714
		Minor Religions	163	100	63	30	21
	Married	*Total*	*27,036*	*14,803*	*12,233*	*39*	*30*
		Hindus	20,364	11,328	9,036	32	28
		Muhammadans	6,464	3,360	3,104	7	2
		Minor Religions	206	115	93	..	..
	Widowed	*Total*	*9,534*	*3,851*	*5,683*	*1*	*3*
		Hindus	7,718	3,206	4,512	1	3
		Muhammadans	1,776	630	1,146	..	..
		Minor Religions	40	15	25	..	..

5—10.		10—15.		15—20.		20—40.		40—60.		60 and over.	
Males.	Females.	Males.	Females.	Males.	Females.	Males.	Females.	Males.	Females.	Males.	Females.
8	9	10	11	12	13	14	15	16	17	18	19
7,811	*7,485*	*8,561*	*5,321*	*8,466*	*5,502*	*40,788*	*26,890*	*19,015*	*12,631*	*4,575*	*3,986*
5,421	5,087	5,975	3,645	6,180	3,864	30,524	19,554	14,200	9,285	3,222	2,877
2,260	2,233	2,434	1,557	2,159	1,480	9,790	6,971	4,624	3,197	1,307	1,071
130	165	152	119	177	158	474	365	191	149	46	38
7,670	*7,170*	*7,558*	*2,956*	*5,125*	*514*	*7,068*	*786*	*849*	*197*	*159*	*49*
5,307	4,850	5,143	1,817	3,462	207	4,915	870	588	86	124	14
2,233	2,157	2,266	1,081	1,526	227	2,025	354	250	108	32	33
130	163	149	108	137	80	128	62	11	8	3	2
134	*314*	*942*	*2,309*	*3,075*	*4,778*	*29,876*	*22,781*	*13,858*	*5,834*	*2,393*	*568*
107	237	784	1,779	2,463	3,487	22,149	16,512	10,180	4,072	1,590	377
27	75	156	519	575	1,215	6,913	6,000	3,583	1,686	777	182
..	2	2	11	37	76	314	269	145	76	26	9
7	*1*	*61*	*56*	*266*	*210*	*4,344*	*3,323*	*4,308*	*6,600*	*2,023*	*3,369*
7	..	48	49	205	170	3,460	2,672	3,432	5,127	1,508	2,486
..	1	12	7	58	38	852	617	841	1,408	498	856
..	..	1	..	3	2	32	34	35	65	17	27
1,967	*1,848*	*1,840*	*1,308*	*1,288*	*1,117*	*5,575*	*5,481*	*3,260*	*3,025*	*1,158*	*1,039*
1,084	960	1,020	686	706	602	3,343	3,159	2,002	1,711	631	554
873	878	800	612	578	506	2,197	2,298	1,243	1,300	528	481
10	10	20	10	9	9	35	24	15	14	4	4
1,893	*1,672*	*1,545*	*607*	*725*	*109*	*688*	*169*	*88*	*44*	*22*	*15*
1,026	817	774	219	304	30	272	64	52	13	11	5
857	846	752	383	414	76	415	104	36	31	11	10
10	9	19	9	7	3	1	1	..	..	..	..
69	*163*	*280*	*669*	*519*	*962*	*4,372*	*4,500*	*2,559*	*1,814*	*669*	*118*
54	133	235	446	373	538	2,754	2,588	1,555	728	361	63
15	29	44	222	144	418	1,591	1,893	993	578	305	55
..	1	1	1	2	6	27	19	11	8	3	..
5	*13*	*15*	*32*	*44*	*46*	*515*	*812*	*613*	*1,667*	*467*	*906*
4	10	11	25	29	34	317	507	895	970	259	486
1	3	4	7	15	12	191	301	214	691	207	416
..	..	..	..	..	..	7	4	4	6	1	4
2,848	*2,836*	*2,661*	*2,188*	*2,189*	*1,812*	*9,631*	*9,685*	*6,199*	*5,005*	*2,168*	*1,521*
2,134	2,144	2,017	1,745	1,780	1,450	7,692	7,852	5,147	4,068	1,853	1,265
692	671	629	4,169	398	320	1,879	1,772	1,024	914	307	248
22	21	15	22	11	42	60	61	28	23	8	8
2,581	*2,401*	*1,959*	*742*	*1,025*	*118*	*1,193*	*198*	*187*	*89*	*59*	*21*
1,896	1,807	1,418	507	793	58	980	89	142	35	41	16
668	575	532	214	223	30	199	85	41	54	18	5
22	19	14	21	9	30	14	19	4	..	..	..
243	*399*	*642*	*1,387*	*1,057*	*1,612*	*7,358*	*8,049*	*4,081*	*2,021*	*960*	*180*
216	306	551	1,188	895	1,324	5,815	6,534	3,278	1,588	775	139
26	91	90	198	160	276	1,501	1,488	784	428	181	39
..	2	1	1	2	12	42	27	19	10	4	2
25	*36*	*60*	*54*	*107*	*82*	*1,080*	*1,448*	*1,931*	*2,895*	*1,149*	*1,320*
22	31	53	50	92	68	897	1,229	1,727	2,445	1,037	1,110
3	5	7	4	15	14	179	199	199	437	108	204
..	..	..	..	..	..	4	15	5	13	4	6
2,737	*2,456*	*2,473*	*1,856*	*2,302*	*1,711*	*11,111*	*8,523*	*6,778*	*5,230*	*2,195*	*1,783*
1,965	1,788	1,765	1,313	1,732	1,192	8,707	6,360	5,459	4,054	1,649	1,306
748	648	689	524	548	500	2,312	2,097	1,284	1,145	538	472
24	20	19	19	22	19	92	66	35	31	8	5
2,614	*2,236*	*1,930*	*942*	*1,180*	*166*	*2,188*	*206*	*823*	*100*	*247*	*26*
1,844	1,582	1,279	580	801	93	1,828	153	786	71	238	17
746	634	634	348	362	70	352	49	34	28	8	9
24	20	17	14	17	3	8	4	3	1	1	..
113	*201*	*500*	*885*	*1,025*	*1,472*	*7,762*	*6,982*	*4,367*	*2,387*	*997*	*276*
111	187	447	704	842	1,085	5,896	5,118	3,328	1,777	672	187
2	14	51	176	178	428	1,790	1,809	1,012	591	320	89
..	..	2	5	5	14	76	55	27	19	5	..
10	*19*	*43*	*29*	*97*	*73*	*1,161*	*1,335*	*1,588*	*2,743*	*951*	*1,481*
10	19	39	29	89	64	983	1,089	1,345	2,206	739	1,102
..	..	4	..	8	7	170	239	238	526	210	374
..	..	..	..	..	2	8	7	5	11	2	5

TABLE XV.

Occupation or means of livelihood

Class.	Sub-class.	Order.	Group number.	Occupation or means of livelihood.	Cawnpore. Total workers and dependants.	Actual workers. Total. Males.	Actual workers. Total. Females.	Actual workers. Partially agriculturists. Males.	Actual workers. Partially agriculturists. Females.	Dependants.
1	2	3	4	5	6	7	8	9	10	11
				Total all classes	167,660	70,605	10,234	373	3	86,821
				A.—Production of raw materials ..	7,112	3,057	348	23	..	3,707
				I.—Exploitation of the surface of the earth	7,098	3,056	341	23	..	3,701
				1.—Pasture and agriculture ..	6,772	2,938	328	13	..	3,506
				(a) Ordinary cultivation ..	4,640	2,165	178	9	..	2,297
A.—Production of raw materials.	I.- Exploitation of the surface of the earth.	1.—Pasture and agriculture. (a) Ordinary cultivation.	1	Income from rent of agricultural land.	1,277	463	14	..	..	800
			(a)	Zamindar ba asami	..	..	..	..	..	..
			(b)	Dakhilkar asami ba shikmi ..	..	..	..	..	..	..
			(c)	Asami ba shikmi	..	..	..	..	..	..
			2	Ordinary cultivation	2,365	1,310	87	..	..	968
			(a)	Zamindar ba jot khud ..	..	..	..	..	..	..
			(b)	Dakhilkar asami ba jot khud ..	..	..	..	..	..	..
			(c)	Asami ba jot khud	..	..	..	..	..	..
			3	Agents, manager of landed estates (not planters), clerks, rent collectors, &c.	614	219	..	7	..	395
			4	Farm servants and field labourers..	384	173	77	2	..	134
				(b) Growers of special products and market gardening.	391	171	36	2	..	184
		(b) Growers of special products and market gardening.	5	Tea, coffee, cinchona and indigo plantations.	..	..	..	..	..	..
			6	Fruit, flower, vegetable, betel, vine, arecanut, &c., growers.	391	171		2	..	184
				(c) Forestry	120	29	11	..	..	80
		(c) Forestry ..	7	Forest officers, rangers, guards, &c.	1	1	..	..	..	..
			8	Wood cutters, firewood, lac, catechu rubber, &c., collectors and charcoal burners.	119	28	11	..	..	80
				(d) Raising of farm stock ..	1,618	570	103	2	..	945
		(d) Raising of farm stock.	9	Cattle and buffalo breeders and keepers.	1,449	479	96	1	..	874
			10	Sheep, goat and pig breeders ..	1	..	..	..	..	1
			11	Breeders of other animals (horses, mules, camels, asses, &c.)	..	..	..	..	..	..
			12	Herdsmen, shepherds, goatherds, &c.	168	91	7	1	..	70
				(e) Raising of small animals ..	3	3	..	..	..	..
		(e) Raising of small animals.	13	Birds, bees, silkworms, &c. ..	3	3	..	..	..	..
				2. Fishing and hunting	326	118	13	10	..	195
		2. Fishing and hunting.	14	Fishing	298	109	11	8	..	178
			15	Hunting	28	9	2	2	..	17
				II.—Extraction of minerals	14	1	7	..	..	6
				3. Mines	..	..	..	..	..	..
	II.—Extraction of minerals.	3. Mines ..	16	Coal mines and petroleum wells ..	..	..	..	..	..	..
			17	Mines and metalic minerals (gold iron, mangenese &c.)	..	..	..	..	..	..
				4. Quarries of hard rocks ..	8	..	6	..	..	2
		4. Quarries of hard rock.	18	Other minerals (Jade, diamonds, lime stones, &c.)	8	..	6	..	..	2
				5. Salt &c.	6	1	1	..	..	4
		5. Salts, &c.	19	Rock, sea and marsh salt ..	..	..	..	..	..	..
			20	Extraction of saltpetre, alum and other substances soluble in water.	6	1	1	..	..	4
				B.—Preparation and supply of material substances.	92,506	36,906	4,637	122	..	50,963
				III.—Industry	57,354	23,351	3,264	77	..	30,739
				6. Textiles	17,453	7,667	706	41	..	9,086
B.—Production and supply of material substances.	III.—Industry.	6. Textiles ..	21	Cotton ginning, cleaning and pressing.	695	286	40	2	..	369
			22	Cotton spinning, sizing and weaving	13,903	6,105	527	32	..	7,271
			23	Jute spinning, pressing and weaving	45	15	2	..	..	28
			24	Rope, twine and string ..	146	43	39	..	..	64
			25	Other fibres (cocoanut, aloes, flax, hemp, straw, &c.)	82	24	9	..	..	49
			26	Wool carders and spinners, weavers, of woollen blankets, carpets, &c.	1,537	870	66	7	..	601
			27	Silk spinners and weavers ..	..	..	..	..	..	..
			28	Hair, camel and horse hair, bristles-work, brush makers, &c.	317	36	1	..	..	280
			29	Persons occupied with feathers ..	..	..	..	..	..	..
			30	Dyeing bleaching, printing, preparation and sponging of textiles.	509	202	9	..	..	298
			31	Other (lace, crape, embroideries, fringes, &c.) and insufficiently described textile industries.	219	80	13	..	..	126

Fyzabad.						Jaunpur.						Mirzapur.						
Total workers and dependants.	Actual works.				Dependants.	Total workers and dependants.	Actual workers.				Dependants.	Total workers and dependants.	Actual workers.				Dependants.	Group number.
	Total.		Partially agriculturists.				Total.		Partially agriculturists				Total.		Partially agriculturists.			
	Males.	Females.	Males.	Females.			Males.	Females.	Males.	Females.			Males.	Females.	Males.	Females.		
12	13	14	15	16	17	18	19	20	21	22	23	24	25	26	27	28	29	4
54,187	21,295	6,920	662	46	25,972	32,501	10,332	3,815	396	46	18,354	54,794	19,312	7,005	499	15	28,477	
9,527	3,827	1,277	49	3	4,423	8,857	2,903	1,145	44	1	4,809	7,467	2,800	764	22	..	3,903	
9,525	3,827	1,277	49	3	4,421	8,853	2,903	1,145	44	1	4,805	7,467	2,800	764	22	..	3,903	
9,342	*3,778*	*1,262*	*48*	*2*	*4,302*	*8,804*	*2,881*	*1,144*	*43*	*1*	*4,779*	*7,390*	*2,766*	*753*	*22*	..	*3,871*	
8,597	*3,337*	*1,221*	*31*	..	*4,089*	*8,402*	*2,719*	*1,066*	*25*	..	*4,617*	*6,196*	*2,050*	*662*	*6*	..	*3,484*	
985	*468*	*74*	..	..	*443*	*1,356*	*346*	*155*	..	..	*855*	*768*	*260*	*78*	..	..	*430*	1
791	401	47	..	..	343	700	170	42	..	..	488	289	96	10	..	..	183	(a)
..	..	..	..	..	..	154	36	28	..	..	95	183	4	52	..	..	127	(b)
194	67	27	..	..	100	502	140	90	..	..	272	296	160	16	..	..	120	(c)
5,095	*2,045*	*532*	..	..	*2,518*	*5,220*	*1,705*	*561*	..	..	*2,954*	*3,054*	*1,178*	*242*	..	..	*1,634*	2
1,119	518	61	..	..	540	1,040	319	53	..	..	668	717	259	36	..	..	422	(a)
82	28	..	..	..	54	2,525	761	816	..	..	1,448	920	404	50	..	..	466	(b)
3,894	1,499	471	..	..	1,924	1,655	625	192	..	..	838	1,417	515	156	..	..	746	(c)
770	288	10	22	..	472	787	276	..	22	..	511	657	95	..	6	..	562	3
1,747	536	605	9	..	606	1,039	392	350	3	..	297	1,717	517	342	..	..	858	4
248	*167*	*16*	*12*	*1*	*65*	*31*	*25*	..	*11*	..	*6*	*253*	*196*	..	*6*	..	*57*	
..	..	..	..	..	..	..	..	..	..	..	..	..	..	..	..	..	..	5
248	167	16	12	1	65	31	25	..	11	..	6	253	196	..	6	..	57	6
265	*150*	..	*2*	..	*115*	*283*	*109*	*69*	*5*	..	*105*	*98*	*15*	*31*	..	..	*52*	
..	..	..	..	..	..	..	..	..	..	..	..	..	..	..	..	..	..	7
265	150	..	2	..	115	283	109	69	5	..	105	98	15	31	..	..	52	8
232	*124*	*25*	*8*	*1*	*83*	*88*	*28*	*9*	*2*	*1*	*51*	*843*	*505*	*60*	*10*	..	*278*	
37	9	..	..	..	28	..	..	..	..	..	..	..	..	..	..	..	..	9
..	..	..	..	..	..	..	..	..	..	..	..	..	..	..	..	..	..	10
1	..	..	..	..	1	..	..	..	..	..	..	..	..	..	..	..	..	11
194	115	25	8	1	54	88	28	9	2	1	51	843	505	60	10	..	278	12
..	..	..	..	..	..	..	..	..	..	..	..	..	..	..	..	..	..	
..	..	..	..	..	..	..	..	..	..	..	..	..	..	..	..	..	..	13
183	*49*	*15*	*1*	*1*	*119*	*49*	*22*	*1*	*1*	..	*26*	77	*34*	*11*	..	..	*32*	
72	20	15	1	1	87	49	22	1	1	..	26	77	34	11	..	..	32	14
111	29	..	..	..	82	..	..	..	..	..	..	..	..	..	..	..	..	15
2	..	..	..	..	*2*	*4*	..	..	..	..	*4*	..	..	..	..	..	..	
..	..	..	..	..	..	..	..	..	..	..	..	..	..	..	..	..	..	
..	..	..	..	..	..	..	..	..	..	..	..	..	..	..	..	..	..	
..	..	..	..	..	..	..	..	..	..	..	..	..	..	..	..	..	..	16
..	..	..	..	..	..	..	..	..	..	..	..	..	..	..	..	..	..	17
..	..	..	..	..	..	*4*	..	..	..	..	*4*	..	..	..	..	..	..	
..	..	..	..	..	..	4	..	..	..	..	4	..	..	..	..	..	..	18
2	..	..	..	..	*2*	..	..	..	..	..	..	..	..	..	..	..	..	
..	..	..	..	..	..	..	..	..	..	..	..	..	..	..	..	..	..	19
2	..	..	..	..	2	..	..	..	..	..	..	..	..	..	..	..	..	20
25,161	8,615	2,998	255	22	13,548	15,894	4,775	1,659	214	40	9,460	30,231	9,952	3,851	259	12	16,428	
13,459	4,498	1,991	124	9	6,970	9,357	2,717	1,169	116	25	5,471	17,370	5,641	2,490	172	..	9,239	
891	*247*	*88*	*7*	..	*562*	*858*	*194*	*69*	*2*	..	*595*	*778*	*228*	*93*	*4*	..	*457*	
55	12	18	..	..	25	110	29	9	..	..	72	44	14	8	..	..	22	21
474	170	29	3	..	275	515	121	49	2	..	345	596	156	72	3	..	368	22
1	1	..	..	..	..	..	..	..	..	..	..	34	9	8	..	..	22	23
170	1	22	..	..	147	56	..	..	..	..	56	86	45	8	1	..	33	24
..	..	..	..	..	..	..	..	..	..	..	..	3	..	2	..	..	1	25
..	..	..	..	..	..	..	..	..	..	..	..	15	4	..	..	..	11	26
1	..	..	..	..	1	2	..	..	..	..	2	..	..	..	..	..	..	27
..	..	..	..	..	..	..	..	..	..	..	..	..	..	..	..	..	..	28
135	43	11	4	..	81	99	28	2	..	..	69	..	..	..	..	..	..	29
..	..	..	..	..	..	..	..	..	..	..	..	..	..	..	..	..	..	30
55	14	8	..	..	88	76	16	9	..	..	51	..	..	..	..	..	..	31

TABLE XV.

Class.	Sub-class.	Order.	Group number.	Occupation or means of livelihood.	Cawnpore. Total workers and dependants.	Actual workers. Total. Males.	Actual workers. Total. Females.	Actual workers. Partially agriculturists. Males.	Actual workers. Partially agriculturists. Females.	Dependants.
1	2	3	4	5	6	7	8	9	10	11
B.—Preparation and supply of material substances—(continued).	III.—Industry—(continued).			7. HIDES, SKINS AND HARD MATERIALS FROM THE ANIMAL KINGDOM.	*4,039*	*1,682*	*62*	*12*	..	*2,295*
		7. Hides, skins and hard materials from the animal kingdom.	32	Tanners, curriers, leather dressers, dyers, &c.	4,025	1,682	62	12	..	2,281
			33	Makers of leather articles, such as trunks, water bags, &c.	..	..	..	..	..	..
			34	Furriers	14	..	..	..	..	14
			35	Bone, ivory, horn, shell, &c., workers	..	..	..	..	..	..
				8. WOOD	*2,434*	*1,068*	*79*	*2*	..	*1,287*
		8. Wood ..	36	Sawyers, carpenters, turners and joiners, &c.	1,942	892	15	2	..	1,035
			37	Basket makers, and other industries of woody materials, including leaves	492	176	64	..	..	252
				9. METALS	*4,561*	*1,987*	*56*	*4*	..	*2,518*
		9. Metals ..	38	Forging and rolling of iron and other metals.	4	4	..	..	..	..
			39	Plough and agricultural implement makers.	1	..	..	..	..	1
			40	Makers of arms, guns, &c. ..	441	108	8	..	..	330
			41	Other workers in iron and makers of implements and tools, principally or exclusively of iron.	2,919	1,399	14	4	..	1,506
			42	Workers in brass, copper and bell metal.	788	322	28	..	..	438
			43	Workers in other metals (tin, zinc, lead, quick silver, &c.).	408	159	6	..	..	243
			44	Workers in mints, die-sinkers, &c	..	..	..	..	..	..
				10. CERAMICS	*936*	*334*	*124*	*2*	..	*478*
		10. Ceramics	45	Makers of glass and crystal ware ..	32	16	..	..	..	16
			46	Makers of porcelain and crockery ..	..	..	..	..	..	..
			47	Potters and earthern pipe and bowl makers.	714	239	110	1	..	365
			48	Brick and tile makers	190	79	14	1	..	97
			49	Others (mosaic, talc, mica, alabaster, &c., workers.)	..	..	..	..	..	..
				11. CHEMICAL PRODUCTS PROPERLY SO-CALLED, AND ANALOGOUS.	*1,207*	*425*	*108*	*4*	..	*674*
		11. Chemical products properly so-called and analogous.	50	Manufacture of matches and explosive materials.	22	4	..	..	..	18
			51	Manufacture of aerated and mineral waters.	9	2	..	..	..	7
			52	Manufacture of dies, paint and ink	28	8	..	..	..	20
			53	Manufacture and refining of vegetable and mineral oils.	1,091	386	108	2	..	597
			54	Manufacture of paper, cardboard and papier mache.	26	11	..	..	..	15
			55	Others (soap, candles, lac, cutch, perfumes and miscellaneous drugs).	31	14	..	2	..	17
				12. FOOD INDUSTRIES	*6,608*	*2,391*	*995*	*3*	..	*3,222*
		12. Food Industries.	56	Rice pounders and huskers and flour grinders.	2,297	556	806	2	..	935
			57	Bakers and biscuit makers ..	311	143	10	..	..	158
			58	Grain parchers, &c.	583	236	40	..	..	307
			59	Butchers	1,036	318	45	..	..	678
			60	Fish curers	..	..	..	..	..	..
			61	Butter, cheese and ghee makers ..	..	..	..	..	..	..
			62	Makers of sugar, molasses and gur ..	199	125	2	1	..	72
			63	Sweetmeat makers, preparers of jam and condiments, &c.	2,176	1,016	92	..	..	1,068
			64	Brewers and distillers ..	6	2	..	..	..	4
			65	Toddy drawers	..	..	..	..	..	..
			66	Manufacturers of tobacco, opium and ganja	..	..	..	..	..	..
			66a	Opium factory (manager, workmen, &c.).	..	..	..	..	..	..
				13. INDUSTRIES OF DRESS AND THE TOILET.	*11,660*	*4,648*	*604*	*6*	..	*6,408*
		13. Industries of dress and the toilet.	67	Hat, cap and turban makers ..	31	12	1	..	..	18
			68	Tailors, milliners, dress makers and darners, embroiderers on linen.	3,346	1,387	248	3	..	1,716
			69	Shoe, boot and sandal makers ..	4,613	1,728	60	..	..	2,825
			70	Other industries pertaining to dress; (gloves, socks, gaiters, belts, buttons, umbrellas, canes, &c.)	281	125	2	..	..	154
			71	Washing, cleaning and dyeing ..	1,425	516	256	2	..	653
			72	Barbers, hairdressers and wig makers	1,964	880	42	1	..	1,042
			73	Other industries connected with the toilet (tatooers, shampooers, bath houses, &c.).	..	..	..	..	..	..

Part A.—General table (second census)—(*continued*). TABLE XV.

Fyzabad						Jaunpur						Mirzapur.						
Total workers and dependants.	Actual workers.				Dependants.	Total workers and dependants.	Actual workers.				Dependants.	Total workers and dependants.	Actual workers.				Dependants.	Group number.
	Total.		Partially agriculturists.				Total.		Partially agriculturists				Total.		Partially agriculturists.			
	Males.	Females.	Males.	Females.			Males.	Females.	Males.	Females			Males.	Females.	Males.	Females.		
12	13	14	15	16	17	18	19	20	21	22	23	24	25	26	27	28	29	4
333	*141*	*6*	*14*	..	*186*	*194*	*51*	*13*	*6*	*4*	*130*	*289*	*69*	*13*	*1*	..	*207*	
117	51	3	..	..	63	167	45	13	6	4	109	289	69	13	1	..	207	32
57	20	..	..	..	37	27	6	..	..	..	21	..	..	..	..	..	..	33
159	70	3	14	..	86	..	..	..	..	..	..	..	..	..	..	..	..	34
..	..	..	..	..	..	..	..	..	..	..	..	..	..	..	..	..	..	35
650	*267*	*3*	*22*	..	*380*	*463*	*163*	*22*	*4*	*1*	*278*	*438*	*185*	*66*	*19*	..	*187*	
4	..	..	..	..	4	367	126	..	4	..	241	301	148	8	19	..	145	36
646	267	3	22	..	376	96	37	22	..	1	37	137	37	58	..	..	42	37
1,088	*396*	*60*	*6*	..	*632*	*297*	*101*	*16*	*2*	..	*180*	*2,834*	*959*	*20*	*7*	..	*1,855*	
206	66	47	..	..	93	..	..	..	..	..	..	..	..	..	..	..	..	38
..	..	..	..	..	..	..	..	..	..	..	..	..	..	..	..	..	..	39
..	..	..	..	..	..	..	..	..	..	..	..	..	..	..	..	..	..	40
..	..	..	..	..	..	248	82	14	2	..	152	998	328	9	4	..	661	41
360	146	2	3	..	212	29	2	2	..	..	25	1,836	631	11	3	..	1,194	42
492	170	11	3	..	311	20	17	..	..	..	3	..	..	..	..	..	..	43
30	14	..	..	..	16	..	..	..	..	..	..	..	..	..	..	..	..	44
597	*196*	*118*	*10*	..	*283*	*537*	*186*	*76*	*43*	*9*	*275*	*1,401*	*446*	*268*	*6*	..	*687*	
113	87	22	8	..	54	34	6	4	..	..	24	..	..	..	..	..	..	45
..	..	..	..	..	..	..	..	..	..	..	..	..	..	..	..	..	..	46
..	..	..	..	..	..	502	179	72	43	9	251	1,401	446	268	6	..	687	47
422	145	96	7	..	181	1	1	..	..	..	..	..	..	..	..	..	..	48
62	14	..	..	..	48	..	..	..	..	..	..	..	..	..	..	..	..	49
394	*125*	*62*	*9*	*2*	*207*	*990*	*303*	*103*	*11*	*2*	*584*	*3,300*	*1,318*	*553*	*32*	..	*1,429*	
..	..	..	..	..	..	23	5	2	..	..	16	..	..	..	..	..	..	50
9	4	1	..	..	4	2	2	..	..	..	..	..	..	..	..	..	..	51
2	1	..	..	..	1	3	..	..	..	..	3	..	..	..	..	..	..	52
..	..	..	..	..	..	934	287	92	11	2	555	1,150	401	245	18	..	504	53
383	120	61	9	2	202	..	..	..	..	..	..	..	..	..	..	..	..	54
..	..	..	..	..	..	28	9	9	..	..	10	2,150	917	808	19	..	925	55
3,071	*842*	*930*	*8*	*3*	*1,299*	*1,765*	*369*	*413*	*6*	*8*	*983*	*1,777*	*368*	*486*	*7*	..	*923*	
5	2	1	..	..	2	695	42	265	1	6	388	554	81	315	1	..	208	56
1,203	118	731	1	3	354	25	5	1	..	..	19	75	16	22	..	..	87	57
70	27	6	1	..	37	341	91	91	..	1	159	544	107	127	2	..	310	58
251	99	52	2	..	80	228	58	5	..	..	165	602	212	22	4	..	368	59
319	114	3	1	..	202	..	..	..	..	..	..	..	..	..	..	..	..	60
..	..	..	..	..	..	..	..	..	..	..	..	2	2	..	..	..	..	61
..	..	..	..	..	..	32	9	1	..	1	22	..	..	..	..	..	..	62
399	166	95	1	..	138	411	189	50	3	..	222	..	..	..	..	..	..	63
838	314	41	..	..	483	33	25	..	2	..	8	..	..	..	..	..	..	64
6	2	1	2	..	3	..	..	..	..	..	..	..	..	..	..	..	..	65
..	..	..	..	..	..	..	..	..	..	..	..	..	..	..	..	..	..	66
..	..	..	..	..	..	..	..	..	..	..	..	..	..	..	..	..	..	
2,841	*931*	*396*	*21*	*3*	*1,484*	*2,262*	*701*	*340*	*26*	*1*	*1,221*	*2,757*	*771*	*517*	*13*	..	*1,469*	
2	1	..	..	..	1	83	22	5	..	..	56	..	..	..	..	..	..	67
36	3	3	..	..	30	463	139	110	..	..	214	664	152	202	1	..	310	68
1,051	355	173	8	1	523	708	247	32	9	..	429	224	80	1	3	..	148	69
549	207	29	3	1	313	..	..	..	..	..	..	..	..	..	..	..	..	70
22	6	3	1	..	13	457	127	136	3	..	194	832	213	259	4	..	360	71
470	140	155	..	1	175	551	166	57	14	1	328	1,037	326	55	5	..	656	72
711	249	38	9	..	429	..	..	..	..	..	..	..	..	..	..	..	..	73

Class.	Sub-class.	Order.	Group number.	Occupation or means of livelihood.	Cawnpore. Total workers and dependants.	Actual workers. Total. Males.	Actual workers. Total. Females.	Actual workers. Partially agriculturists. Males.	Actual workers. Partially agriculturists. Females.	Dependants.
1	2	3	4	5	6	7	9	8	10	11
B.—Preparation and supply of material substances—(continued).	III.—Industry—(concluded).			14. FURNITURE INDUSTRIES ..	*372*	*141*	..	..	..	*171*
		14. Furniture industries.	74	Cabinet makers, carriage painters, &c	312	141	..	..	..	171
			75	Upholsters, tent makers, &c ..	..	..	..	..	..	..
				15. BUILDING INDUSTRIES ..	*1,164*	*341*	*4*	..	..	*819*
		15. Building industries.	76	Lime burners, cement workers ..	..	..	..	..	..	..
			77	Excavators, plinth builders and well sinkers.	..	..	..	..	..	..
			78	Stone and marble workers, masons and bricklayers.	1,121	820	4	..	..	797
			79	Others (thatchers, building contractors, house painters, tilers, plumbers, blacksmiths, &c.).	43	21	..	..	..	22
				16. CONSTRUCTION OF MEANS OF TRANSPORT.	*968*	*361*	..	..	..	*607*
		16. Construction of means of transport.	80	Cart, carriage, palki, &c. makers and wheelwrights.	29	12	..	..	..	17
			81	Saddlers, harness makers, whip and lash makers.	934	344	..	..	..	590
			82	Ship and boat builders ..	5	5	..	..	..	..
				17. PRODUCTION AND TRANSMISSION OF PHYSICAL FORCES (HEAT, LIGHT ELECTRICITY, MOTIVE POWER, &c.).	*26*	*13*	..	..	..	*13*
		17. Production and transmission of physical forces (heat, light, electricity, motive power, &c.).	83	Gas works, electric light and ice factories.	26	13	..	..	..	13
				18. INDUSTRIES OF LUXURY AND THOSE PERTAINING TO LITERATURE AND THE ARTS AND SCIENCES.	*3,760*	*1,598*	*69*	*1*	..	*2,093*
		18. Industries of luxury and those pertaining to literature and the arts and sciences.	84	Printers, lithographers, engravers, &c.	662	264	4	..	..	394
			85	Newspaper and magazine managers and editors, journalists, &c.	24	18	..	1	..	11
			86	Book-binders and stitchers, envelope makers, &c.	121	85	..	..	..	86
			87	Makers of musical instruments ..	58	21	..	..	..	37
			88	Makers of watches and clocks and optical, photographic and surgical instruments.	136	46	..	..	..	90
			89	Workers in precious stones and metals, enamellers, imitation jewellery makers, gilders, &c.	2,199	1,029	1	..	..	1,169
			90	Makers of bangles, rosaries, bead and other necklaces, spangles, lingams and sacred threads.	249	75	43	..	..	131
			91	Toy, kite, cage, fishing tackle, &c., makers, taxidermists, &c.	186	66	12	..	..	108
			92	Others, including managers, persons other than performers employed in theatres and other places of public entertainment, employes of public societies, race course service, huntsmen, &c.	125	49	9	..	..	67
				19. INDUSTRIES CONCERNED WITH REFUSE MATTERS.	*2,226*	*707*	*457*	*2*	..	*1,068*
		19. Industries concerned with refuse matters.	93	Sweepers, scavengers, dust and sweeping contractors.	2,226	701	457	2	..	1,068
	IV.—Transport.			IV.—Transport	8,355	3,795	160	20	..	4,402
				20. TRANSPORT BY WATER ..	*189*	*50*	*14*	..	..	*125*
		20. Transport by water.	94	Harbour works, dockyards and pilot.	..	..	..	..	..	..
			95	Ship owners and their employes, ship brokers, ships' officers, engineers, mariners and firemen.	..	..	..	..	..	..
			96	Persons employed on the maintenance of streams, rivers and canals (including construction).	146	39	1	..	..	106
			97	Boat owners, boatmen and towmen.	43	11	13	..	..	19

Part A.—General table (second census)—(*continued*).

Fyzabad.						Jaunpur						Mirzapur.						
Total workers and dependants.	Actual workers.				Dependants.	Total workers and dependants.	Actual workers.				Dependants.	Total workers and dependants.	Actual workers.				Dependants.	Group number.
	Total.		Partially agriculturists.				Total		Partially agriculturists				Total.		Partially agriculturists.			
	Males.	Females.	Males.	Females.			Males.	Females.	Males.	Females.			Males.	Females.	Males.	Females.		
12	13	14	15	16	17	18	19	20	21	22	23	24	25	26	27	28	29	4
56	25	3	..	..	28	13	4	..	1	..	9	79	75	..	..	..	4	
51	20	3	..	..	28	7	4	..	1	..	3	19	15	..	..	..	4	74
5	5	..	..	..	..	6	..	..	..	..	6	..	..	..	..	..	..	75
1,671	600	117	20	1	954	942	311	5	11	..	626	1,768	745	2	79	..	1,027	
22	10	4	..	..	8	5	5	..	..	..	..	..	..	..	..	..	..	76
11	8	..	1	..	3	..	..	..	..	..	..	..	..	..	..	..	..	77
1,099	420	42	11	..	637	890	286	5	11	..	599	1,629	678	2	78	..	949	78
559	162	71	8	1	306	47	20	..	..	..	27	139	67	..	1	..	72	79
22	10	..	..	..	12	3	3	..	..	..	..	20	..	5	..	..	15	
4	..	..	..	..	4	3	3	..	..	..	..	..	..	..	..	..	..	80
18	10	..	..	..	8	..	..	..	..	..	..	20	..	5	..	..	15	81
..	..	..	..	..	..	..	..	..	..	..	..	..	..	..	..	..	..	82
10	2	..	..	..	8	10	5	..	..	..	5	..	..	..	..	..	..	
10	2	..	..	..	8	10	5	..	..	..	5	..	..	..	..	..	..	83
1,206	497	30	7	..	679	753	259	13	4	..	481	1,193	398	25	4	..	770	
47	14	..	..	..	33	26	6	2	..	..	18	3	..	..	..	..	3	84
..	..	..	..	..	..	..	..	..	..	..	..	..	..	..	..	..	..	85
54	15	..	1	..	39	25	7	..	..	..	18	..	..	..	..	..	..	86
7	2	..	..	..	5	..	..	..	..	..	..	1	1	..	..	..	..	87
47	14	..	..	..	33	7	5	..	..	..	2	17	10	..	1	..	7	88
626	292	7	2	..	327	514	166	7	4	..	341	1,135	375	22	3	..	738	89
78	13	17	..	..	48	10	4	..	..	..	6	37	12	8	..	..	22	90
324	140	6	4	..	178	164	64	4	..	..	96	..	..	..	..	..	..	91
23	7	..	..	..	16	7	7	..	..	..	..	..	..	..	..	..	..	92
629	195	178	..	..	256	270	67	99	..	..	104	796	139	442	..	..	215	
628	195	178	..	..	256	270	67	99	..	..	104	796	139	442	..	..	215	93
2,728	1,116	81	26	1	1,531	1,208	483	3	27	..	722	1,455	711	38	26	..	706	
419	195	4	11	1	220	41	20	3	3	..	18	377	276	7	..	..	94	
13	..	..	..	..	13	..	..	..	..	..	..	..	..	..	..	..	..	94
13	3	..	..	..	10	..	..	..	..	..	..	..	..	..	..	..	..	95
4	1	..	..	..	3	..	..	..	..	..	..	..	..	..	..	..	..	96
389	191	4	11	1	194	41	20	3	3	..	18	377	276	7	..	..	94	97

TABLE XV.—Occupation or means of livelihood

Class.	Sub-class.	Order.	Group number.	Occupation or means of livelihood.	Cawnpore. Total workers and dependants.	Actual workers. Total. Males.	Actual workers. Total. Females.	Partially agriculturists. Males.	Partially agriculturists. Females.	Dependants.
1	2	3	4	5	6	7	8	9	10	11
B.—Preparation and supply of material substances—(continued).	IV.—Transport—(concluded).			21. TRANSPORT BY ROAD	6,156	2,923	138	16	..	3,095
		21. Transport by road.	98	Persons employed on the construction and maintenance of roads and bridges.	81	42	..	..	..	39
			99	Cart owners and drivers, coachmen, stable boys, tramway, mail car riage, &c , managers and employés (excluding private servants).	4,246	1,848	125	16	..	2,273
			100	Palki, &c., bearers and owners ..	277	153	..	..	..	124
			101	Pack elephant, camel, mule, ass and bullock owners and drivers.	21	17	..	..	..	4
			102	Porters and messengers ..	1,531	863	13	..	..	655
				22. TRANSPORT BY RAIL ..	1,320	601	5	4	..	714
		22. Transport by rail.	103	Railway employés of all kinds other than construction coolies.	1,292	594	1	4	..	697
			104	Labourers employed on railway construction.	28	7	4	..	..	17
				23. POST OFFICE, TELEGRAPH AND TELEPHONE SERVICE.	690	219	3	..	..	468
		23. Post office, telegraph and telephone service.	105	Post office, telegraph and telephone service.	690	219	3	..	..	468
	V.—Trade			V.—Trade	26,797	9,762	1,215	25	..	15,822
				24. BANKS ESTABLISHMENT OF CREDIT, EXCHANGE AND INSURANCE.	1,504	543	39	4	..	922
		24. Banks establishment of credit, exchange and insurance.	106	Bank managers, money lenders, exchange and insurance agents, money changers and brokers and their employés.	1,504	543	39	4	..	922
				25. BROKERAGE, COMMISSION AND EXPORT.	3,283	1,231	77	2	..	1,975
		25. Brokerage, commission and export.	107	Brokers, commission agents, commercial travellers, warehouse owners and employés.	3,283	1,231	77	2	..	1,975
				26. TRADE IN TEXTILES	2,737	1,017	44	1	..	1,676
		26. Trade in textiles.	108	Trade in piece goods, wool, cotton, silk, hair, and other textiles.	2,737	1,017	44	1	..	1,676
				27. TRADE IN SKINS, LEATHER AND FURS	562	211	19	1	..	332
		27. Trade in skins, leather and furs.	109	Trade in skins, leather, furs, feathers, horns, &c.	562	211	19	1	..	332
				28. TRADE IN WOOD	55	14	1	..	..	40
		28. Trade in wood.	110	Trade in wood (not firewood), cork, bark, &c.	55	14	1	..	..	40
				29. TRADE IN METALS	297	48	17	..	..	232
		29. Trade in metals.	111	Trade in metals, machinery, knife, tool, &c., sellers.	297	48	17	..	..	232
				30. TRADE IN POTTERY	429	11	..	..	..	418
		30. Trade in pottery.	112	Trade in pottery	429	11	..	..	..	418
				31. TRADE IN CHEMICAL PRODUCTS ..	375	129	9	..	..	237
		31. Trade in chemical products.	113	Trade in chemical products, drugs, dyes, paints, petroleum, explos.ves, &c	375	129	9	..	..	237
				32. HOTELS, CAFES, RESTAURANTS, &C.	443	202	31	..	..	210
		32. Hotels, cafes, restaurants, &c.	114	Vendors of wine, liquors, aerated waters, &c.	248	141	2	..	..	105
			115	Owners and managers of hotels, cookshops, sarais, &c., and their employés.	195	61	29	..	..	105
				33. OTHER TRADE IN FOOD STUFFS ..	12,537	4,640	791	15	..	7,106
		33. Other trade in food stuffs.	116	Fish dealers	189	17	7	..	..	165
			117	Grocers and sellers of vegetable, oil, salt and other condiments.	887	289	3	2	..	595
			118	Sellers of milk, butter, ghee, poultry, eggs, &c.	314	150	14	..	..	150
			119	Sellers of sweetmeats, sugar, gur and molasses	750	328	17	4	..	405
			120	Cardamom, betel-leaf, vegetables, fruits and areca-nut sellers.	3,538	1,268	310	2	..	1,960
			121	Grain and pulse dealers ..	5,063	1,730	353	7	..	2,980
			122	Tobacco, opium, ganja, &c , sellers	599	266	13	..	..	320
			123	Dealers in sheep, goats and pigs ..	57	23	..	..	..	33
			124	Dealers in hay, grass and fodder ..	1,140	569	73	..	..	498
				34. TRADE IN CLOTHING AND TOILET ARTICLES.	1,607	636	27	..	..	944
		34. Trade in clothing and toilet articles.	125	Trade in ready-made clothing and other articles of dress and the toilet (hats, umbrellas, socks, ready-made shoes, perfumes, &c.).	1,607	636	27	..	..	944

Part A.—General table (second census)—(*continued*).

Fyzabad.						Jaunpur.						Mirzápur.						
Total workers and dependants.	Actual workers. Total. Males.	Actual workers. Total. Females.	Partially agriculturists. Males.	Partially agriculturists. Females.	Dependants.	Total workers and dependants.	Actual workers. Total. Males.	Actual workers. Total. Females.	Partially agriculturists. Males.	Partially agriculturists. Females.	Dependants.	Total workers and dependants.	Actual workers. Total. Males.	Actual workers. Total. Females.	Partially agriculturists. Males.	Partially agriculturists. Females.	Dependants.	Group number.
12	13	14	15	16	17	18	19	20	21	22	23	24	25	26	27	28	29	4
1,712	*726*	*72*	*8*	..	*912*	*908*	*381*	..	*20*	..	*527*	*1,020*	*425*	*31*	*26*	..	*564*	
12	7	..	..	..	5	2	..	..	..	..	2	15	12	..	..	..	3	98
1,122	485	8	..	..	629	759	319	..	19	..	440	786	318	6	24	..	462	99
72	18	..	..	..	54	77	43	..	1	..	34	4	3	..	..	..	1	100
11	4	4	..	..	3	19	9	..	..	..	10	64	29	1	1	..	34	101
495	214	60	8	..	221	51	10	..	..	..	41	151	63	24	1	..	64	102
410	*127*	*5*	*4*	..	*278*	*178*	*53*	..	*4*	..	*125*	*58*	*10*	..	..	..	*48*	
406	127	5	4	..	274	153	37	..	4	..	116	46	10	..	..	..	36	103
4	..	..	..	..	4	25	16	..	..	..	9	12	..	..	..	..	12	104
187	*66*	..	*3*	..	*121*	*81*	*29*	..	..	..	*52*	..	..	..	..	..	..	
187	66	..	3	..	121	81	29	..	..	..	52	..	..	..	..	..	..	105
8,974	*3,001*	*926*	*105*	*12*	*5,047*	*5,329*	*1,575*	*487*	*71*	*15*	*3,267*	*11,406*	*3,600*	*1,323*	*61*	*12*	*6,483*	
811	*262*	*22*	*20*	..	*527*	*402*	*105*	*4*	*11*	..	*293*	*1,589*	*571*	*22*	*5*	..	*996*	
811	262	22	20	..	527	402	105	4	11	..	293	1,589	571	22	5	..	996	106
282	*76*	*4*	..	..	*202*	*111*	*36*	..	..	..	*75*	*453*	*153*	*1*	..	..	*299*	
282	76	4	..	..	202	111	36	..	..	..	75	453	153	1	..	..	299	107
493	*184*	..	*5*	..	*309*	*320*	*109*	*1*	*2*	..	*210*	*533*	*148*	*3*	*5*	..	*382*	
493	184	..	5	..	309	320	109	1	2	..	210	533	148	3	5	..	382	108
156	*37*	*3*	..	..	*116*	*79*	*19*	*1*	..	..	*59*	..	..	..	..	..	..	
156	37	3	..	..	116	79	19	1	..	..	59	..	..	..	..	..	..	109
34	*1*	*3*	..	..	*30*	..	..	..	..	..	..	*130*	*76*	..	*3*	..	*54*	
34	1	3	..	..	30	..	..	..	..	..	..	130	76	..	3	..	54	110
49	*19*	*3*	..	..	*27*	*8*	*7*	..	..	..	*1*	..	..	..	..	..	..	
49	19	3	..	..	27	8	7	..	..	..	1	..	..	..	..	..	..	111
..	..	..	..	..	..	..	..	..	..	..	..	..	..	..	..	..	..	
..	..	..	..	..	..	..	..	..	..	..	..	..	..	..	..	..	..	112
153	*26*	*6*	*1*	..	*121*	*56*	*12*	*2*	..	..	*42*	*196*	*34*	..	..	..	*162*	
153	26	6	1	..	121	56	12	2	..	..	42	196	34	..	..	..	162	113
172	*66*	*5*	*2*	..	*107*	*104*	*30*	*6*	*2*	..	*68*	*100*	*18*	*9*	..	..	*73*	
155	60	5	2	..	90	84	30	3	2	..	51	100	18	9	..	..	73	114
17	6	..	..	..	11	20	..	3	..	..	17	..	..	..	..	..	..	115
4,910	*1,671*	*655*	*62*	*10*	*2,584*	*3,132*	*941*	*390*	*46*	*13*	*1,801*	*7,024*	*2,100*	*1,206*	*41*	*11*	*3,778*	
1	1	..	..	..	..	..	..	..	..	..	..	..	..	..	..	..	..	116
212	57	8	1	..	147	170	43	10	..	..	117	192	19	11	..	..	162	117
805	256	162	26	8	387	649	172	119	28	9	358	767	142	195	5	1	430	118
4	..	1	..	..	3	..	..	..	..	..	..	919	297	108	7	..	514	119
1,539	488	279	19	1	772	862	245	107	12	4	510	1,392	433	226	14	1	733	120
1,914	725	155	14	..	1,034	1,220	423	126	3	..	671	3,100	976	498	14	6	1,626	121
268	108	9	2	1	151	191	55	6	3	..	180	452	208	24	1	..	225	122
31	17	..	..	..	14	10	..	6	..	..	4	..	..	..	..	..	..	123
136	19	41	..	..	76	30	3	16	..	..	11	202	30	144	..	3	28	124
266	*91*	..	*2*	..	*175*	*274*	*67*	*1*	*3*	..	*206*	*139*	*69*	*6*	..	..	*64*	
266	91	..	2	..	175	274	67	1	3	..	206	139	69	6	..	..	64	125

Class.	Sub-class.	Order.	Group number.	Occupation or means of livelihood.	Cawnpore. Total workers and dependants.	Actual workers. Total. Males.	Actual workers. Total. Females.	Actual workers. Partially agriculturists. Males.	Actual workers. Partially agriculturists. Females.	Dependants.
1	2	3	4	5	6	7	8	9	10	11
B.—Preparation and supply of material substances—(concluded).	V.—Trade—(concluded).			35. TRADE IN FURNITURE ..	*143*	*29*	*6*	..	..	*108*
		35. Trade in furniture.	126	Trade in furniture, carpets, curtains and bedding.	21	5	..	..	..	16
			127	Hardware, cooking utensils, porcelain crockery, glassware, bottles, articles for gardening, the cellar, &c.	122	24	6	..	..	92
				36. TRADE IN BUILDING MATERIALS ..	*89*	*47*	*5*	..	..	*37*
		36. Trade in building materials.	128	Trade in building materials (stones, bricks, plaster, cement, sand, tiles, thatch, &c.).	89	47	5	..	..	37
				37. TRADE IN MEANS OF TRANSPORT ..	*203*	*88*	*1*	..	..	*114*
		37. Trade in means of transport.	129	Dealers and hirers of elephants, camels, horses, cattle, asses, mules, &c., sellers (not makers) of carriage, saddlery, &c.	203	88	1	..	..	114
				38. TRADE IN FUEL.	*1,375*	*450*	*128*	*2*	..	*797*
		38. Trade in fuel.	130	Dealers in firewood, charcoal, coal, cowdung, &c.	1,375	450	128	2	..	797
				39. TRADE IN ARTICLES OF LUXURY AND THOSE PERTAINING TO LETTERS AND THE ARTS AND SCIENCES.	*602*	*269*	*9*	..	..	*324*
		39 Trade in articles of luxury and those pertaining to letters and the arts and sciences.	131	Dealers in precious stones, jewellery (real and imitation), clocks, optical instruments, &c.	29	11	..	..	..	18
			132	Dealers in common bangles, beads, necklaces, fans, small articles, toys, hunting and fishing tackle, flowers, &c.	285	168	4	..	..	118
			133	Publishers, book-sellers, stationers, dealers in music, pictures, musical instruments and curiosities.	288	90	5	..	..	193
				40. TRADE IN REFUSE MATTERS ..	*34*	*10*	*2*	..	..	*22*
		40. Trade in refuse matters.	134	Dealers in rags, stable refuse, &c. ..	34	10	2	..	..	22
				41. TRADE OF OTHER SORTS ..	*522*	*187*	*7*	..	..	*328*
		41. Trade of other sorts.	135	Shopkeepers otherwise unspecified ..	414	148	5	..	..	266
			136	Itinerant traders, pedlars, hawkers, &c.	6	2	..	..	..	4
			137	Conjurors, acrobats, fortunetellers, reciters, exhibitors of curiosities and wild animals.	22	8	..	..	..	14
			138	Other trades (including farmers) of pounds, tolls and markets.	80	34	2	..	..	44
C.—Public administration and liberal arts.				C.—Public administration and liberal arts.	13,100	5,306	473	137	..	7,321
	VI.—Public force.			VI. Public force	2,004	1,116	1	77	..	887
				42. ARMY	*99*	*26*	..	..	..	*73*
		42. Army ..	139	Army (Imperial)	98	25	..	..	..	73
			140	Army (Native states)	1	1	..	..	..	..
				43. NAVY	..	..	..	..	..	..
		43. Navy ..	141	Navy	..	..	..	..	..	..
				44. POLICE	*1,905*	*1,090*	*1*	*77*	..	*814*
		44. Police ..	142	Police	1,484	872	..	70	..	612
			143	Village watchmen	421	218	1	7	..	202
	VII.—Public administration.			VII.—Public administration	3,697	1,597	3	43	..	2,097
				45. PUBLIC ADMINISTRATION ..	*3,697*	*1,597*	*3*	*43*	..	*2,097*
		45. Public administration.	144	Service of the state	2,716	1,183	..	39	..	1,532
			145	Service of Native and foreign states.	23	10	..	2	..	13
			146	Municipal and other local (not village) service.	909	381	3	2	..	525
			147	Village officials and servants other than watchmen.	49	23	..	..	..	26
	VIII.—Professions and liberal arts.			VIII.—Professions and liberal arts ..	7,399	2,593	469	37	..	4,337
				46. RELIGION	*2,899*	*1,241*	*198*	*18*	..	*1,460*
		46. Religion	148	Priests, ministers, &c. ..	2,374	1,027	82	13	..	1,265
			149	Religious mendicants, inmates of monastries, &c.	181	43	108	..	..	30
			150	Catechists, readers, Church and Mission service.	60	18	7	..	..	35
			151	Temple, burial or burning ground service, pilgrim conductors, circumcisers.	294	158	1	5	..	130
				47. LAW	*1,053*	*272*	..	*12*	..	*781*
		47. Law	152	Lawyers of all kinds, including Kazis, law agents and mukhtiars.	541	92	..	5	..	449
			153	Lawyers, clerks, petition writers, &c.	512	180	..	7	..	332

Part A.—General table (second census)—(*continued*). TABLE XV.

Fyzabad						Jaunpur						Mirzapur						
Total workers and dependants.	Actual workers.				Dependants.	Total workers and dependants.	Actual workers.				Dependants.	Total workers and dependants.	Actual workers.				Dependants.	Group number.
	Total.		Partially agriculturists.				Total.		Partially agriculturists.				Total.		Partially agriculturists.			
	Males.	Females.	Males.	Females.			Males.	Females.	Males.	Females.			Males.	Females.	Males.	Females.		
12	13	14	15	16	17	18	19	20	21	22	23	24	25	26	27	28	29	4
30	*9*	..	..	..	*21*	*11*	*3*	..	..	..	*8*	*213*	..	..	..	..	*213*	
18	9	..	..	..	9	1	..	..	..	..	1	..	..	..	..	..	..	126
12	..	..	..	..	12	10	3	..	..	..	7	213	..	..	..	..	213	127
3	*2*	..	..	..	*1*	*52*	*16*	..	..	..	*36*	*105*	*15*	..	..	..	*90*	
3	2	..	..	..	1	52	16	..	..	..	36	105	15	..	..	..	90	128
28	*13*	..	..	..	*15*	..	..	..	..	..	..	..	..	..	..	..	..	
28	13	..	..	..	15	..	..	..	..	..	..	..	..	..	..	..	..	129
426	*126*	*79*	*2*	*2*	*221*	*163*	*49*	*26*	*3*	*2*	*88*	*578*	*225*	*45*	*4*	*1*	*308*	
426	126	79	2	2	221	163	49	26	3	2	88	578	225	45	4	1	308	130
416	*115*	*112*	*5*	..	*189*	*250*	*92*	*42*	*4*	..	*116*	*290*	*179*	*30*	*2*	..	*81*	
3	1	..	..	..	2	18	6	..	..	..	12	..	..	..	..	..	..	131
362	90	112	4	..	160	184	55	42	4	..	87	254	165	30	1	..	59	132
51	24	..	1	..	27	48	31	..	..	..	17	36	14	..	1	..	22	133
41	*10*	*10*	..	..	*21*	..	..	..	..	..	..	..	..	..	..	..	..	
41	10	10	..	..	21	..	..	..	..	..	..	..	..	..	..	..	..	134
704	*293*	*24*	*6*	..	*387*	*367*	*89*	*14*	..	..	*264*	*56*	*12*	*1*	*1*	..	*43*	
298	173	6	4	..	119	8	..	..	..	..	8	31	8	..	1	..	23	135
378	112	18	2	..	248	327	80	14	..	..	233	..	..	..	..	..	..	136
..	..	..	..	..	..	..	..	..	..	..	..	..	..	..	..	..	..	137
28		..	..	..	20	32	9	..	..	..	23	25	4	1	..	..	20	138
7,879	**3,774**	**294**	**215**	**10**	**3,811**	**3,965**	**1,332**	**131**	**107**	**1**	**2,502**	**5,490**	**2,589**	**72**	**182**	**1**	**2,829**	
735	**429**	..	**35**	..	**306**	**580**	**350**	**1**	**39**	..	**229**	**688**	**390**	..	**49**	..	**298**	
102	*40*	..	..	..	*62*	*2*	*1*	..	..	..	*1*	..	..	..	..	..	..	
102	40	..	..	..	62	2	1	..	..	..	1	..	..	..	..	..	..	139
..	..	..	..	..	..	..	..	..	..	..	..	..	..	..	..	..	..	140
..	..	..	..	..	..	..	..	..	..	..	..	..	..	..	..	..	..	
..	..	..	..	..	..	..	..	..	..	..	..	..	..	..	..	..	..	141
633	*389*	..	*35*	..	*244*	*578*	*349*	*1*	*39*	..	*228*	*688*	*390*	..	*49*	..	*298*	
579	349	..	31	..	230	533	315	1	30	..	217	438	264	..	46	..	174	142
54	40	..	4	..	14	45	34	..	9	..	11	250	126	..	3	..	124	143
2,228	**884**	**5**	**104**	..	**1,339**	**1,503**	**404**	**2**	**29**	..	**1,097**	**2,234**	**988**	..	**77**	..	**1,246**	
2,228	*884*	*5*	*104*	..	*1,339*	*1,503*	*404*	*2*	*29*	..	*1,097*	*2,234*	*988*	..	*77*	..	*1,246*	
1,713	665	1	80	..	1,047	1,221	310	..	19	..	911	2,058	904	..	73	..	1,154	144
9	3	..	..	..	6	..	..	..	..	..	..	1	..	..	..	..	1	145
436	188	4	22	..	244	232	68	2	6	..	162	7	2	..	..	..	5	146
70	28	..	2	..	42	50	26	..	4	..	24	168	82	..	4	..	86	147
4,916	**2,461**	**289**	**76**	**10**	**2,166**	**1,882**	**578**	**128**	**39**	**1**	**1,176**	**2,568**	**1,211**	**72**	**56**	**1**	**1,285**	
3,093	*1,928*	*169*	*48*	*6*	*996*	*526*	*190*	*25*	*12*	*1*	*311*	*1,595*	*927*	*21*	*38*	..	*647*	
661	203	101	14	5	357	400	107	19	11	1	274	651	247	15	12	..	389	148
154	140	1	..	..	13	..	..	..	..	..	..	..	..	..	..	..	..	149
59	12	..	..	..	47	118	83	..	1	..	35	9	..	..	..	..	9	150
2,219	1,573	67	84	1	579	8	..	6	..	..	2	935	680	6	26	..	249	151
545	*156*	*1*	*17*	..	*388*	*423*	*111*	..	*14*	..	*312*	*383*	*131*	..	*7*	..	*252*	
240	41	..	8	..	199	168	42	..	9	..	126	156	38	..	4	..	118	152
305	115	1	9	..	189	255	69	..	5	..	186	227	93	..	3	..	184	153

Class.	Sub-class.	Order.	Group number.	Occupation or means of livelihood.	Cawnpore. Total workers and dependants.	Actual workers. Total. Males.	Actual workers. Total. Females.	Partially agriculturists. Males.	Partially agriculturists. Females	Dependants.
1	2	3	4	5	6	7	8	9	10	11
C.—Public administration and liberal arts—(concluded).	VIII.—Professions and liberal arts—(concluded).			48. MEDICINE	*1,073*	*300*	*62*	3	..	*711*
		48. Medicine	154	Medical practitioners of all kinds including dentists, oculists and veterinary surgeons.	823	238	6	3	..	579
			155	Midwives, vaccinators, compounders, nurses, masseurs, &c.	250	62	56	..	..	132
				49. INSTRUCTION	*954*	*308*	*49*	*3*	..	*597*
		49. Instruction	156	Professors and teachers of all kinds (except law, medicine, music, dancing and drawing), and clerks and servants connected with education.	954	308	49	3	..	597
				50. LETTERS AND ARTS AND SCIENCES ..	*1,420*	*472*	*160*	*1*	..	*788*
		50. Letters and arts and sciences.	157	Public scribes, stenographers, &c. ..	181	82	4	..	..	95
			158	Architects, surveyors, engineers and their employes.	199	69	..	1	..	130
			159	Others (authors, photographers, artists, sculptors, astronomers, meteorologists, botanists, astrologers, &c.).	133	49	1	..	..	83
			160	Music composers and masters, players of all kinds of musical instruments (not military), singers, actors and dancers.	907	272	155	..	..	480
D.—Miscellaneous.				D.—Miscellaneous	**54,942**	**25,336**	**4,776**	**71**	**3**	**24,830**
				IX.—Persons living on their income ..	**2,552**	**713**	**428**	**4**	**1**	**1,411**
	IX.—Persons living on their income.			51. PERSONS LIVING PRINCIPALLY ON THEIR INCOME.	*2,552*	*713*	*428*	*4*	*1*	*1,411*
		51. Persons living principally on their income.	161	Proprietors (other than of agricultural land) fund and scholarship holders and pensioners.	2,552	713	428	4	1	1,411
				X.—Domestic service	**19,919**	**9,532**	**1,561**	**41**	..	**8,826**
	X.—Domestic service.			52. DOMESTIC SERVICE	*19,919*	*9,532*	*1,561*	*41*	..	*8,826*
		52. Domestic service.	162	Cooks, water carriers, door keepers, watchmen and other indoor servants.	18,332	8,781	1,557	40	..	7,994
			163	Private grooms, coachmen, dog boys, &c.	1,587	751	4	1	..	882
				XI.—Insufficiently described occupations ..	**29,688**	**13,734**	**2,192**	**24**	**2**	**13,762**
	XI. Insufficiently described occupations.			53. GENERAL TERMS WHICH DO NOT INDICATE A DEFINITE OCCUPATON.	*29,688*	*13,734*	*2,192*	*24*	*2*	*13,762*
		53. General terms which do not indicate a definite occupation.	164	Manufacturers, business-men and contractors otherwise unspecified.	869	292	1	1	..	576
			165	Cashiers, accountants, book keepers, clerks and other employes in unspecified offices, warehouses and shops.	4,930	2,064	45	2	..	2,821
			166	Mechanics, otherwise unspecified ..	328	165	6	1	..	157
			167	Labourers and workmen otherwise unspecified.	23,561	11,213	2,140	20	2	10,203
				XII.—Unproductive	**2,783**	**1,357**	**595**	**2**	..	**831**
	XII.—Unproductive			54. INMATES OF JAILS, ASYLUMS AND HOSPITALS.	*360*	*357*	..	..	..	*3*
		54. Inmates of jails, asylums and hospitals.	168	Inmates of jails, asylums and hospitals.	360	357	..	..	..	3
				55. BEGGARS, VAGRANTS, PROSTITUTES.	*2,423*	*1,000*	*595*	*2*	..	*828*
		55. Beggars, vagrants, prostitutes	169	Beggars, vagrants, procurers, prostitutes, receivers of stolen goods, cattle poisoners.	2,423	1,000	595	2	..	828

Fyzabad.						Jaunpur.						Mirzapur.						
Total workers and dependants.	Actual workers.				Dependants.	Total workers and dependants.	Actual workers.				Dependants.	Total workers and dependants.	Actual workers.				Dependants.	Group number.
	Total.		Partially agriculturists.				Total.		Partially agriculturists				Total.		Partially agriculturists			
	Males.	Females.	Males.	Females.			Males.	Females	Males	Females.			Males.	Females.	Males.	Females		
12	13	14	15	16	17	18	19	20	21	22	23	24	25	26	27	28	29	4
395	*107*	*37*	*3*	*2*	*251*	*164*	*53*	*4*	*3*	..	*107*	*51*	*20*	*1*	*1*	..	*30*	
200	55	13	3	2	132	124	38	..	2	..	86	51	20	1	1	..	30	154
195	52	24	..	..	119	40	15	4	1	..	21	..	..	..	..	..	..	155
402	*117*	*6*	*3*	..	*279*	*271*	*86*	*4*	*7*	..	*181*	*290*	*87*	*28*	*8*	*1*	*175*	
402	117	6	3	..	279	271	86	4	7	..	181	290	87	28	8	1	175	156
481	*153*	*76*	*5*	*2*	*252*	*498*	*138*	*95*	*3*	..	*265*	*249*	*46*	*22*	*2*	..	*181*	
38	7	..	..	..	31	..	..	..	..	..	..	..	..	..	..	..	..	157
87	31	..	2	..	56	37	12	..	2	..	25	2	2	..	..	..	..	158
6	2	..	..	..	4	9	2	..	1	..	7	1	..	..	..	..	1	159
350	113	76	3	2	161	452	124	95	..	..	233	246	44	22	2	..	180	160
11,620	5,079	2,351	145	11	4,190	3,785	1,322	880	31	4	1,583	11,606	3,971	2,318	36	2	5,317	
578	182	55	17	3	341	165	42	20	3	..	103	103	32	17	..	1	54	
578	*182*	*55*	*17*	*3*	*341*	*165*	*42*	*20*	*3*	..	*103*	*103*	*32*	*17*	..	*1*	*54*	
578	182	955	17	3	341	165	42	20	3	..	103	103	32	17	..	1	54	161
4,411	1,903	958	39	..	1,550	1,565	560	448	14	..	557	4,363	1,565	666	22	1	2,132	
4,411	*1,903*	*958*	*39*	..	*1,550*	*1,565*	*560*	*448*	*14*	..	*557*	*4,363*	*1,565*	*666*	*22*	*1*	*2,132*	
3,900	1,665	955	32	..	1,280	1,423	472	448	4	..	508	3,957	1,354	666	20	1	1,937	162
511	238	3	7	..	270	142	88	..	10	..	54	406	211	..	2	..	195	163
4,175	1,695	878	75	8	1,602	1,586	558	277	14	4	751	6 392	2,040	1,457	14	..	2 895	
4,175	*1,695*	*878*	*75*	*8*	*1,602*	*1,586*	*558*	*277*	*14*	*4*	*751*	*6,392*	*2,040*	*1,457*	*14*	..	*2,895*	
169	42	11	3	..	116	30	7	..	..	..	28	73	21	1	..	..	51	164
1,250	635	44	39	..	571	372	123	5	4	..	244	122	90	..	14	..	32	165
1	1	..	..	..	..	336	125	36	5	..	175	1	1	..	..	..	..	166
2,755	1,017	823	33	8	915	848	303	236	5	4	309	6,196	1,928	1,456	..	..	2,812	167
2,456	1,299	460	12	..	697	469	162	135	..	..	172	748	334	178	..	..	236	
347	*278*	*34*	..	..	*35*	..	..	..	..	..	..	*42*	*37*	*5*	..	..	..	
347	278	34	..	..	35	..	..	..	..	..	..	42	37	5	..	..	..	168
2,109	*1,021*	*426*	*12*	..	*662*	*469*	*162*	*135*	..	..	*172*	*706*	*297*	*173*	..	..	*236*	
2,109	1,021	426	12	..	632	469	162	135	..	..	172	706	297	173	..	..	236	169